* *

CHANGING LAND

**GLUCKSMAN
IRISH DIASPORA**

IN THE GLUCKSMAN IRISH DIASPORA SERIES

Edited by Kevin Kenny

Associate Editor Miriam Nyhan Grey

* *

Changing Land

Diaspora Activism and the Irish Land War

Niall Whelehan

* * *

NEW YORK UNIVERSITY PRESS

New York

* *

NEW YORK UNIVERSITY PRESS
New York
www.nyupress.org

References to Internet websites (URLs) were accurate at the time of writing. Neither the author nor New York University Press is responsible for URLs that may have expired or changed since the manuscript was prepared.

Library of Congress Cataloging-in-Publication Data
Names: Whelehan, Niall, author.
Title: Changing land : diaspora activism and the Irish Land War / Niall Whelehan.
Description: New York : New York University Press, [2021] |
Series: The Glucksman Irish diaspora series | Includes bibliographical references and index.
Identifiers: LCCN 2021013301 | ISBN 9781479809554 (hardback) |
ISBN 9781479809622 (ebook) | ISBN 9781479809615 (ebook other)
Subjects: LCSH: Land League (Ireland) | Irish—Foreign countries—Biography. |
Irish—Political activity—Foreign countries—History—19th century. |
Land reform—Ireland—History—19th century. | Peasant uprisings—Ireland—History. |
Transnationalism. | Ireland—Emigration and immigration—History—19th century. |
Ireland—Politics and government—19th century.
Classification: LCC DA916.8 .W44 2021 | DDC 941.7081—dc23
LC record available at https://lccn.loc.gov/2021013301

New York University Press books are printed on acid-free paper, and their binding materials are chosen for strength and durability. We strive to use environmentally responsible suppliers and materials to the greatest extent possible in publishing our books.

Manufactured in the United States of America

10 9 8 7 6 5 4 3 2 1

Also available as an ebook

CONTENTS

Introduction

"We in Ireland have been isolated," Charlotte O'Brien told a newspaper correspondent at her Limerick home in March 1882, "and it is only the reflex action of emigration that is bringing us into contact with the world outside. It is not merely the returning emigrants, but their constant communications, which are infusing new life, and spreading new ideas." O'Brien, a campaigner for improved migrant traveling conditions and a supporter of the Irish Land League, made these comments in an interview with the New York–based *Irish World and American Industrial Liberator*, then in Ireland to report on the Land War of 1879–82. Her views stood apart from the opposition to emigration typically voiced by Irish political leaders. "The emigration of so many of our people," she continued, "is bringing into Irish-life a powerful mind-expanding element, which is none the less real and powerful because the so-called upper classes are untouched by it."[1]

O'Brien's remarks reflected the unprecedented mobilization of Irish emigrants in support of the Land War, the campaign to stop evictions, lower rents, and abolish landlordism in Ireland. The Land League and the Ladies' Land League—a separate women's organization—directed the agitation in Ireland and formed branches in Britain, North America, Argentina, Australia, and New Zealand that generated massive fundraising on a scale only seen again during the Irish War of Independence (1919–21). Yet this financial support was only one side of the story. As O'Brien suggested, how the Land League's supporters understood the Land War was shaped by the circulation of people and ideas between Ireland and different locations of the Irish diaspora. Emigrants contributed to internationalizing the Land War and helped to relate questions of land rights in rural Ireland to currents of urban radicalism and oppositional politics that ranged widely from liberal reform to feminism to anarchism to socialism. The story of the Land War reveals much about wider histories of radicalism. It was part of a broader ideological challenge to property rights and the inequalities they produced that sought to fundamentally change how land was thought about and used.

In the late 1870s, Ireland experienced an economic downturn that coincided with a run of poor harvests. The drop in European agricultural prices in the years 1877–79—partly a result of American competition—greatly impacted rural Ireland and hit farmers at the same time as a series of cold winters and wet summers. This significantly reduced potato harvests in 1877, 1878, and, most severely, 1879, when the yield was the lowest since the worst years of the Great Famine of 1845–52. In some parts of the country, the rapid decrease in farm incomes, combined with potato shortages, led to famine conditions.[2] Mortality figures for 1878, 1879, and 1880 attest to the gravity of the crisis: in each of these three years the number of deaths and the excess mortality rate were higher than for any other year in the entire period between 1864, when the annual registers began, and Irish independence in 1921. The worst year was 1879, when 105,089 people died, and the annual excess mortality rate climbed to a height of 237 per 100,000, up from 48 per 100,000 in 1877. By comparison, in 1918, the year of the Spanish flu epidemic, 78,695 people died, and the excess morality rate was 139 per 100,000.[3] The causes of the high death rate in 1878–80, which was spread across the island, were complex. The Poor Law Union reports listed the unusually cold weather in the first months of 1879, rather than the very low yield in potato harvests, as the primary factor, but both were surely major contributors.[4] The high death rate underlines how Land League emerged at a time of major distress across the island, which resonated deeply with popular and official memories of the Great Famine.

Formally launched at a meeting in a Dublin hotel in October 1879, the Irish National Land League developed from the Mayo Land League that originated in rallies to oppose evictions and lower rents in some of the poorer regions in the west of Ireland. In April 1879 one large rally drew some ten thousand people at Irishtown, a village in Co. Mayo. Of the day's six speakers, three spent significant portions of their lives outside of Ireland. One had lived in England, another in Scotland, and another moved permanently to the United States in 1882. Two return emigrants—Michael Davitt and John Devoy—did not address the crowd that day but played important roles in organizing the rally and drafting resolutions.[5] Devoy had returned temporarily to Ireland from New York, where he had lived since 1871; Davitt, a Mayo native, was politicized growing up in England and, during visits to the United States, he further developed his radical views on land reform. Both men were instrumental in devising the "new departure" strategy in New York, which sought to bring together the separate strands of constitutional nationalism, separatist republicanism, and land reform in a united nationalist movement in Ireland. The Land League embodied this new alliance. Another return emigrant, Anna Parnell, came back from the United States to lead the Ladies' Land League in Ireland. Emigrants were at the center of the movement from the outset.

From 1879 the Land League organized the mass campaign known as the Land War.[6] In the face of widespread arrears caused by the economic crisis, some landlords offered temporary reductions in rent, but others gave no concessions, and evictions rose steadily from 1877 to 1882.[7] The Land League's immediate goals were to stop evictions and lower rents, but its long-term aims were to fundamentally redistribute property and to end "landlordism," a catch-all term referring to the unequal distribution of land as well as to landlords' social and political power and their central place in British colonial structures in Ireland. The campaign employed an array of tactics and evictions, which entailed considerable violence against the occupants, became a focus of protests, with large crowds preventing their enactment, fracturing landlords' traditional status in the process. In 1880 Michael Davitt could claim that the organization held over two hundred thousand members among Ireland's population of five million and "virtually rule[d] the country."[8] Aided by traveling organizers and emigrant funding, the Land League coordinated mass meetings, boycotts, rent strikes, financial and legal support for tenants, and "Land League courts" to arbitrate rent disputes, as well as encouraging everyday acts of defiance. The agitation saw relatively high levels of violence, particularly acts of intimidation against those seeking to carry out, or profit from, evictions. Yet, the numbers of fatalities remained low. In 1881 the government sought to restore order by introducing emergency powers in the Protection of Persons and Property (Coercion) Act, as well as a Land Act that recognized tenants' rights to long-term security and established a commission to determine fair rents for yearly tenancies. Along with later concessions to salve rent arrears and release political prisoners, these reforms contributed to calming the unrest.[9] Mass protests would erupt again four years later in the "Plan of Campaign," but the first phase of the land agitation came to a halt by the summer of 1882.

The 1881 Land Act was radical in its own right. It introduced ambivalence into ideas of land ownership in Ireland by increasing the level of state interference in property rights and limiting landlords' ability to decide rents and changes in tenantry. The Prime Minister, William Gladstone, succeeded in selling the legislation in Parliament through promises that it was "something peculiarly 'Irish' and unexportable to Britain."[10] Laborers and smaller tenant farmers, however, were ineligible or benefited little from the new settlement, and emigration from Ireland increased both during and after the Land War. Although radical Land Leaguers were frustrated by the failure to secure more sweeping social change, the unrest had profoundly altered the tenor of social and economic relationships in rural Ireland and demonstrated the possibilities of collective action for people with no vote and no property.

One striking aspect of the Land League was its internationalism, spurred by connections between people in Ireland and emigrants in different locations as well as an awareness of the ways that the campaign linked up with wider radical and reform causes. As Michael Davitt told a London audience in 1880, landlordism was "a huge conspiracy against humanity and labour," and they were resolved to fight it "in whatever country any member of the National Land League might stand."[11] Support from outside Ireland was crucial; Anna Parnell believed the campaign would collapse "without any external help to speak of."[12] The Land War occurred at a time when the number of Irish emigrants was just about at its peak: in 1881 over three million Irish-born people lived overseas, with 1.86 million of them living in the United States. The population of Ireland itself was just over five million, meaning about 40 percent of the people born on the island were living off of it.[13] The emigrants grouped together by the term "diaspora" by no means constituted a cohesive, homogenous group and attitudes ranged widely toward Ireland and Irish political movements. Some were indifferent, some hostile, but significant numbers of emigrants maintained social and emotional ties with their homeland, or parents' homeland, that came to the fore during periods of intense political activism. The Land War represented one such period, but this heightened collective engagement between emigrants and Ireland would not prove sustainable over long periods of time. Rather, it surged and receded, depending on the circumstances.

The activism of 1879–82 was forged in "fluid and interactive processes" of migration and drew on a diaspora sensibility that connected "widely dispersed migrant groups with one another and with the homeland."[14] Emigrant supporters of the Land League might have resembled the "long-distance nationalists" described by Benedict Anderson, but this term suggests an absence of contact and detachment that was not the case during the Land War.[15] Extensive exchange between emigrants and people in Ireland took place through organizational networks and the circulation of people, newspapers, and letters. Rather than viewing Ireland and its geographically widespread diaspora as separate fields of inquiry, an integrated perspective is necessary that accounts for the reciprocal interactions between emigrants and the homeland and between emigrants in different locations.[16] While transnational studies sometimes privilege émigrés and external developments to the neglect of domestic events, the history of the Land War requires a balanced approach that incorporates local, national, and transnational perspectives to gain a deeper understanding of the relational dynamics between Ireland and the diaspora that were so crucial to the Land League and the Ladies' Land League.

The Land War has been the subject of a very rich body of scholarship that has included detailed analyses of the relationship between land and politics and its development in the context of socioeconomic change.[17] For many British statesmen and Irish nationalists, the "land question" was the central plank of the larger "Irish question," the social issue that was the means to solve the political issue of the day.[18] Writing during the Land War, one commentator asserted that "the Irish land question is *the Irish question*."[19] In an early history of the period, Alice Stopford Green argued that the Irish Parliamentary Party "used the land agitation to strengthen the National movement."[20] The Land League joined together questions of land and nation, and Charles Stewart Parnell's role as president of the organization was crucial to how he later marshaled popular support for the Irish Party's 1885 electoral success and the securing of Liberal backing for Home Rule. Conventional nationalist readings attributed the Land War's outcomes to Parnell's shrewd political instincts and a unified mass protest to right the historic wrong of colonial dispossession. In the 1970s and 1980s new studies emerged that were inspired by methodological developments in social history, including statistical approaches and, albeit to a lesser extent, theories of collective action associated with James C. Davies and Charles Tilly, among others, which framed the Land War as a product of modernizing forces in rural Ireland. These works emphasized the way contingencies and changing socioeconomic circumstances shaped the class alliances that undergirded the Land League and its members' expectations, while also illuminating the fragility of those alliances and the sharp class divisions within rural Ireland.[21] The results of the agitation may have been positive for many tenant farmers and the Irish Parliamentary Party, but not for rural laborers. Already in 1904 Michael Davitt characterized the Land War's aftermath as a "counter revolution."[22]

In many studies of the Land War, the focus on the national context has diverted attention from the depth of the internationalism in these years, while different forms of social radicalism have been subordinated to a larger nationalist narrative. True, Michael Davitt held radical views on a range of causes, and he has received much scholarly attention, though consideration of the intersection of nationalism and social radicalism often begins and ends with him.[23] The term "radical" itself has been associated in the scholarship less with ideological affinities and more with groups that were open to the use of violence, whether agrarian redressers or nationalists who wanted more than Home Rule. Yet not all radicals were Fenians or driven primarily by nationalist concerns. Survey studies of Irish labor history seem to have considered the Land League as nationalism's terrain and have given it only fleeting reference, but Fintan Lane's study of the origins of Irish socialism stands out for its discussion of the Land War.[24] Margaret Ward has highlighted radical elements in the Ladies' Land League and links with some British feminists.[25] Ely Janis and historians of the American Land League have done much to demonstrate the simultaneous engagement of emigrants with Irish land reform and urban working-class politics in the United States, as well as their ideological crossover.[26] Affinities and cooperation between Irish and Scottish land radicals in the 1880s have been brought to light by Andrew Newby.[27] These excellent studies have focused mainly on national arenas, however, and less on the back and forth movement of ideas and people between Ireland and the diaspora, as well as between emigrants in different locations.

Changing Land aims to examine the multifaceted activism inspired by the Land War and how it connected with broader radical ideas and organizations. In doing so, it traces the lives of a number of individual emigrants to tell a larger story, people who linked different networks, who served as vehicles for ideas and strategies, and who combined campaigns to change land use and ownership with activism for other causes in Ireland, Scotland, England, the United States, and Argentina, which was home to the largest Irish community outside the English-speaking world. Approaching the topic through a set of individual lives helps to negotiate the complexity of transnational relations and recapture points of contact, alliances, and contradictions between people, places, and ideologies often considered separately.[28] Many Irish political leaders in the late nineteenth and early twentieth centuries lived highly mobile lives, as is evident, for example, in the well-documented careers of Michael Davitt and the Parnell family.[29] Their cosmopolitanism is often considered to have set them apart, adding to their leadership credentials, yet many lesser-known activists also led transnational lives. The peripatetic Davitt may not have been representative of the majority of Land Leaguers, but neither was he exceptional.[30]

This approach aims to uncover new layers of radical circuitry between Ireland and disparate international locations. Looking beyond the leadership figures brings unfamiliar voices to the surface, women and men who have been on the margins of—or entirely missing from—existing accounts. Until relatively recently, their stories could not be easily traced, but the expansion of digital archival databases helps make their recovery increasingly possible. This book is not intended as a comprehensive history of emigrant engagement with the Land War: the focus is primarily on people who were preoccupied with nationalization as the answer to the land question. The main sites of activity are Ireland, Scotland, England, Argentina, and the United States, but sustained comparisons are not made between emigrant communities in different national contexts as they could lead to homogenizing interpretations and downplaying complexities in each place. Rather, the approach examines how the people in question interlinked different locations through their movements. The principal characters did not have a similar level of connection to

Irish diaspora communities in Australia, New Zealand, and Canada, and therefore these countries do not feature prominently here. Chronologically, the 1870s and 1880s are the years of concern, but the analysis extends backward to the early nineteenth century and forward to the early twentieth century to examine the activism of key individuals.

The late nineteenth century has been identified in some studies as the beginning of an age of accelerated internationalism. This was perhaps most familiar in the class-based vision of the First International, but was by no means confined to labor radicalism and included land reform, feminism, nationalism, humanitarianism, anticolonialism, liberalism, religion, as well as economic developments and technological innovation.[31] In Ireland, the transnational reception and exchange of ideas was a long-standing feature of culture and society before the late nineteenth century. Studies of eighteenth-century Ireland, for example, have demonstrated the way the circulation of Enlightenment literature advanced new understandings of gender and education, and European and transatlantic concepts of liberty helped shape Irish republicanism and radicalism in the 1790s. These encounters were not necessarily characterized by tensions between an international progressivism and an Irish conservatism.[32] In the early nineteenth century, agrarian Ribbon societies were influenced by British radical networks and ideas—a dimension that challenges traditional views of their insularity.[33] Thomas Ainge Devyr's opposition to land monopolies, discussed in chapter 5, first developed in Donegal in the 1830s, then in England and the United States. His life illuminates how the Land League built on continuities of agrarian radicalism throughout the nineteenth century. Cross-border exchange and cultural encounters were not new in the late nineteenth century, then, but they did reach a new level of intensity. Emigrants were far more numerous and their increased contacts with Ireland were facilitated by new advances in transport and communications that shortened travel times, spread news through telegraph and a rapidly expanding newspaper industry, and made postal communications more secure.

The 1880s have been identified by Jürgen Osterhammel with the first stages of modern globalization, a decade of "especially radical change" that saw intensified human migration, depression in the North Atlantic economy, advanced cross-border capitalism, violent imperialist expansion, and new types of mass politics. These years mark the beginnings of the fin de siècle, the last chapter of the long nineteenth century.[34] More recently, the "long twentieth century" has muscled its way in, staking a claim on the 1870s and 1880s as its new starting point.[35] In Irish historiography, the period of the Union, 1800–1921, has lent the long nineteenth century some resilience.[36] At the same time, familiar periodizations have been reconsidered, and new studies have pulled the 1880s into the orbit of the twentieth century.[37] The Land War produced social changes that resonated into the twentieth century, while the Land League developed a style of mass politics that influenced later generations. Figures who emerged on the scene in the early 1880s, such as Tom Clarke and John Redmond, played vital, if differing, roles in the later revolutionary era. And yet the Land War cannot be fully loosened from its nineteenth-century moorings, given the centrality of the Great Famine and post-Famine migration to the Land League generation and their worldviews. Periodizations are, of course, always interpretive and selectively emphasize or minimize continuities; the point here is that a broad consensus exists that the Land War occurred in a decade of far-reaching change in Ireland and beyond. These wider structural forces provide an important context for understanding the conflict.

* * *

Charlotte O'Brien's observations on emigration were made in an interview with the American radical economist Henry George during his year-long stay in Ireland to investigate the Land War. George arrived in Ireland officially as the "special correspondent" of the largest selling Irish American newspaper, the *Irish World*. Edited by the Galway-born Patrick Ford, the paper was aimed primarily at working-class Irish Americans, but it also advocated a global struggle to end monopolies in order to transform the social and political order. Ford claimed the paper held a readership in Ireland of sixty thousand during the Land War, largely due to the free copies sent home by emigrants in the United States through the Spread the Light Fund, which dispatched over 455,000 copies across the Atlantic before police began to seize the packages. Davitt also circulated the paper in Ireland.[38] The *Irish World* linked Irish America not only with Ireland, but also with other diaspora locations. In Britain it was sold in Glasgow, London, Liverpool, Manchester, Sheffield, and Newcastle, among other cities, and was read and circulated by Karl Marx and Friedrich Engels.[39] The paper also had readers in Argentina and Australia.[40] It represented an important channel for the transmission of ideas about land nationalization.

Henry George's primary aim in Ireland was to radicalize the unrest and advance the doctrine of land nationalization. His pamphlet *The Irish Land Question*, written before his trip to Ireland, framed the Land War as a frontline battle in a global conflict. Land was no "mere local question," George proclaimed, "it is a universal question. It involves the great problem of the distribution of wealth, which is everywhere forcing itself upon attention."[41] In 1879 he published the book that defined his reputation, *Progress and Poverty*, which declared land monopolies the root of all social ills and land a natural resource that could not be privately owned. Vast sales brought George international attention, and the book impressed Michael Davitt and Patrick Ford, who became friendly with George when he moved to New York from San Francisco in 1880. They shared with him the view that land monopoly was the defining question of the age and embraced nationalization as the only solution to the land question that would benefit all classes. This brought them into tension with the Land League executive in Ireland, which advanced the policy of peasant proprietorship, or the turning of tenants into small landowners in a competitive liberal economy, as the best means for their achieving social mobility and, ultimately, political independence. In this view Irish tenants did not have a natural right to land, but they did have the right to it as the reward for hard work.

The advocates of peasant proprietorship were in the majority in Ireland and largely controlled the Land League, yet the supporters of nationalization were not marginal and constituted an influential group. Although dismissed as "politically fatuous" in one study, the policy of nationalization was favored by Davitt, the popular figure widely regarded as the founding father of the Land League, as well as the powerful the *Irish World* newspaper and Henry George.[42] Nationalization presented a more radical program of land reform than peasant proprietorship, but both visions of land redistribution provoked a significant debate about land ownership. Moderates and radicals alike in the Land League believed that only those who worked the land held a moral right to it, which superseded inheritance and legal titles. Michael Davitt declared that "rents for land are an immoral tax upon the industries of the people." During a tour of the United States, the Scottish land reformer John Murdoch delivered public talks on "the immorality of the existing land system." The Newcastle-based trade unionist John Bryson expressed his conviction that the lands worked by tenant farmers "were morally their own, if not legally."[43] Henry George combined ethical and economic language in his attacks on land monopolies, asserting that "economic law and moral law are essentially one."[44] There was a strong moral dimension to the challenges to existing systems of property ownership and in the doctrines of both nationalization and peasant proprietorship.

The wider George-affiliated nationalization movement emerged amid the social discontent in response to the depression of the 1870s. In the interval between the demise of the First International in 1872 and the beginnings of the Second International in 1889, the lines demarcating different strands of leftist oppositional politics were not always clearly defined.[45] When Friedrich Engels observed an upturn in radicalism in Britain in 1881 and wrote "Ireland is bringing all this about, Ireland is the driving force of the Empire," he referred to diverse groups that were only loosely aligned.[46] Historian Ilham Khuri-Makdisi has observed that late nineteenth-century radicalism "was more often than not a package of (sometimes inchoate) ideas and practices that were not codified, standardized, or homogenized." Distinctions between different leftist schools of thought could often remain in the background.[47] In the 1880s socialists and more moderate reformers found common ground under the broad banner of "nationalization," even if the term "was not always used in the same sense."[48] The figure of George provided a rallying point; having sold hundreds of thousands of books, he was arguably better known than Karl Marx. It was not until 1886-87 that George distanced himself from socialism on the back of the antiradical mood generated by the Haymarket affair in the United States, when anarchists were accused of causing an explosion at a Chicago demonstration, and he began to pursue a more middle-class, reformist agenda in the "Single Tax" movement.[49] At the time of the Land War, however, the differences between Georgists and socialists were not so clear. *Progress and Poverty* maintained that the abolition of private property would advance both the "ideal of Jeffersonian democracy" and the "dream of socialism."[50] In the early 1880s, Georgism represented a broad church, and George's arrival in Ireland helped to focus more international attention on the Land War and on the British government's attempts to suppress it. George also served as a broker and his personal networks interlinked the Land League and Ladies' Land League with wider social movements.

The emigrant activists examined here either met George in person or corresponded with him directly. Chapter 1 looks at Peter O'Leary, a London-based emigrant and trade unionist who regularly toured Ireland and the United States and sought to strengthen ties between the Irish in Britain and Irish America. He met with George and advanced nationalization as the only remedy for the impoverished conditions of rural laborers. This may have placed him in the radical camp, but O'Leary also campaigned for moderate causes including temperance, assisted emigration, and sanitation improvements. Chapter 2 focuses on Marguerite Moore, a traveling agitator for the Ladies' Land League who toured Ireland, Scotland, and England and helped integrate the organization across the Irish sea. After the Land War she moved to New York and became active in feminist, labor, and Single Tax circles. In 1888 she served as a delegate at the first meeting of the International Council of Women in Washington, DC, along with representatives from North America, Europe, and India.[51] Chapter 3 shifts to a more granular analysis of the members of the Ladies' Land League in Dundee, one of the first branches in Britain. This microstudy aims to gain a better understanding of the emigrants who collected funds and attended rallies and who are too often left out of scholarship. It examines the interplay between the transnational and local dimensions of emigrant activism in a city where women far outnumbered men among Irish immigrants. Chapter 4 turns its attention to the Irish doctor John Creaghe, who corresponded with George and sought to spread his ideas in Argentina and launch a Land League–style campaign against Argentine landlords, some of whom were second-generation Irish Catholics. Frustrated with the limitations of land reform, Creaghe turned to anarchism and became a leading figure in the Argentine movement in the 1890s. Chapter 5 looks at the veteran land reformer Thomas Ainge Devyr, whose long career linked the Irish land question, English Chartism, and American agrarian radicalism. Originally from Donegal, Devyr first moved to England and then to New York in 1840. He later wrote for the *Irish World*, corresponded with Karl Marx, and claimed credit for originating the concepts of land reform embraced by the Land League and Henry George.

All of these individuals engaged with nationalism to varying levels, yet it was not always their primary concern, and it did not define their idealism. Rather, nationalism was one part of a worldview that incorporated multifaceted dimensions, including support for radical as well as liberal causes. The people examined here variously combined land reform with Georgism, socialism, feminism, and anarchism, but they also engaged with moderate causes through temperance clubs, Catholic societies, humanitarianism, trade unionism, and assisted emigration schemes. Both Peter O'Leary and Marguerite Moore supported land nationalization while at the same time working toward incremental social reforms and supporting the Home Rule party. Their style of radicalism held significant differences with John Creaghe, who espoused revolutionary anarchism. Henry George rejected the term "radicalism," maintaining it had "very little significance" because "people called Gladstone a Radical now."[52] The term "activism" has been adopted in the title to reflect this variety. "Transnational activism" might be a term more familiar to the post-1945 era, but it has a nineteenth-century application and is relevant to the range of both radical and reformist campaigning and idealism analyzed here.[53]

Investigating individual lives helps to reveal some of the limitations of the land nationalizers' networks. Although they had considerable influence, their ability to steer the agitation in Ireland was limited when confronted with the domestic strength of the advocates of peasant proprietorship, who also held transnational allies. Examining individual lives also helps to uncover some of the contradictions in the reception of the land movement. Understandings of the "universalism" of the land question were sometimes shaped by Eurocentric perspectives that placed land monopoly before all other forms of oppression and often led to indifference toward other groups and social questions. Thomas Ainge Devyr, for example, was hostile toward American abolitionism, arguing that it distracted from the greater struggle for land reform, which would transform all aspects of society for the better and in the process end slavery. Peter O'Leary's transatlantic tours shaped his ideas about race; his calls for land redistribution did not extend to the Ojibwe communities he encountered in Canada, whom he considered inferior to the Irish emigrants he hoped would settle on the same lands. John Creaghe condemned the gruesome campaigns of removal against indigenous groups in Argentina, but he was not vocal about them. His preoccupation with land rights and class arguably blinkered his perception of the most striking injustice then happening in his adopted country.

The extent of emigrant activism in different social, cultural, and regional environments during the Land War contributes to a picture of migration as a multidimensional phenomenon. The people investigated here were defined by a range of influences, not just their sender and receiver countries. Peter O'Leary, Marguerite Moore, John Creaghe and Thomas Ainge Devyr each spent time in Ireland, Britain, and the United States. For emigrants in Argentina, their engagement with the Land League was sometimes mediated more by Irish America than Ireland, through newspapers and personal links. At the 1888–89 Special Commission, set up to investigate Irish political links with violence, one British official observed that branches of the Land League in Ireland, Britain, and North America were so closely affiliated that they formed "one connected and continuous organisation."[54] Considering the home and diaspora wings of the movement in isolation from each other certainly produces only a partial picture, but the Land League and Ladies' Land League were not singular transnational entities, supported by a unitary people. Their message took on different meanings for people in different places; ideas changed when they crossed borders and when mixed with other ideologies and social realities.

The Land War inspired polyphonic activism and stimulated a heightened sense of community between Irish people at home and overseas. This was not based on nationalism alone, but collective anger regarding issues of security of housing, rent, the value of labor, and democratic rights. Examining emigrants' activism during the Land War, their contacts with Ireland, internationalism, and interactions with radical and reformist causes helps us to understand modern Ireland's social revolution as part of a wider ideological moment in world history.

Peter O'Leary, Land Nationalization, and Visitors to Ireland during the Land War

In October 1881 the *Irish World* announced that "America's Greatest Economist" was on his way to Ireland as their special correspondent. Officially tasked with writing weekly dispatches on the state of Ireland, Henry George aimed to radicalize the campaign and advance "the side of the Land League which insists upon the nationalisation of the land."[1] Yet he was not introducing a new doctrine to Ireland. Shortly before his arrival, at the Land League convention in Dublin, Peter O'Leary had strongly called for land nationalization to replace the policy of peasant proprietorship favored by the executive. Going even further than George, O'Leary declared that all land "should be the property of the State" and "subject to the rules and regulations as the State may impose for the benefit of the entire community."[2] A London-based trade unionist, O'Leary, like George, represented part of the heavy flow of traffic to Ireland during the Land War, when a wide range of people—journalists, socialists, feminists, reformers, trade unionists, humanitarians, and some who just described themselves as tourists—came to witness events firsthand and lend support to the campaign.[3]

Among these visitors were small but significant numbers of return emigrants. Peter O'Leary emigrated to England with his parents as a child in the first year of the Great Famine, and made lengthy return visits to Ireland throughout his life. He sought to frame Irish problems in an international context and his activism was shaped by British and American influences. O'Leary's involvement in the Democratic Federation and London radical circles was part of a broader endeavor to strengthen ties across the Irish Sea between urban and rural workers, and a number of British socialists, feminists, and trade unionists traveled to Ireland during the Land War. O'Leary also sought to forge tighter links between Irish communities in North America and Britain, and traveled extensively throughout Canada and the United

States in the 1870s and 1880s. In Ireland, his relationship with the Land League was an ambiguous one. Nationalism was secondary to his campaigning for a range of social causes, including agricultural laborers' rights, assisted emigration, temperance, and urban and rural sanitation. O'Leary's support for land nationalization may have earned him a "radical" name, but he combined this with more moderate activism in the South London Temperance Society, Catholic Workingmen's clubs, the reform of Friendly Societies and urban sanitation, and campaigns against fox and stag hunting.[4] He was also always ready to meet and work with officials and members of Parliament to advance incremental reforms.

O'Leary, George, and other visitors contributed to the internationalization of the Land War. The transnational dimensions of the agitation were not just defined by external developments and the activities of emigrants in disparate locations, but were also evident within Ireland itself. Examining the activities of radical visitors serves to expand the picture painted in previous studies of interactions between the Land League and English and Scottish reformers, and to highlight both the reach and the limitations of transnational influences during the Land War.[5] Ultimately, nationalization failed to leave a serious mark on Irish land policy, but its advocates did inspire a sense that the agitation, far from being an isolated struggle, resonated with a much wider agenda for social change. And among many radicals and reformers beyond Ireland, the Land War became an important point of reference in a larger vision of changing land rights and challenging existing understandings of property ownership.

Agricultural Laborers and Emigration

For the advocates of land nationalization, a key concern about the Land League's policy of peasant proprietorship was how little it offered impoverished farm laborers. Replacing landlords with a new class of tenants turned small proprietors, Henry George argued, would leave the laborers "as badly off as now, if not in some respects worse off."[6] The Liberal government's 1881 Irish Land Act granted the vaunted "three Fs": fair rent, fixity of tenure, and free sale, and a commission was established to arbitrate rent disputes for yearly tenancies. Some tenant farmers benefited from the act, though many remained ineligible under its terms, while rural laborers were completely neglected and understandably felt they were being left behind. Peter O'Leary was one of the most vocal advocates of laborers' rights in the 1870s and 1880s. The son of a migrant farm laborer, O'Leary worked as a farm laborer himself on the outskirts of London before finding an apprenticeship as a street mason in his early twenties. In the late 1860s he became active in temperance organizations as well as the Amnesty Association for Fenian prisoners in London, which also drew the support of labor leaders in England; O'Leary addressed one Hyde Park meeting with George Odger, president of the First International. An autodidact, he grew up in a bilingual home. During his fact-finding tours of Ireland, he maintained that his ability to speak Irish gave him better insight into the realities of distress to be found there.[7]

In 1873 O'Leary returned to Cork as an envoy of the National Agricultural Labourers' Union, founded in England by Joseph Arch. Working with the Cork-based Philip Johnson, O'Leary established the Irish Agricultural Labourers' Union, which lasted until the end of the decade, when it was subsumed by the Land League. The Home Rule League leader Isaac Butt surprisingly took on the role of president of the new union, which drew praise from the Fenian-leaning *Irishman* newspaper. The Young Irelander Thomas Mooney, who later became a radical journalist for the *Irish World*, also lent support.[8] In the 1870s O'Leary traveled the west and southwest of Ireland on foot, investigating laborers' conditions. In the decades since his departure, their circumstances had improved little, and they remained the class most vulnerable to economic downturns.[9] He found them to be the "worst fed, worst clad and worst housed probably in Europe" and contended they were the "victims not only of landlordism but even of the tenant farmers." They had no vote, he wrote, and "consequently no one seems to care about them."[10]

Along with unionizing, O'Leary promoted assisted emigration to alleviate rural poverty, inspired by a scheme established by Joseph Arch to bring English laborers to Canada. On this issue he came into tension with nationalists, who generally viewed assisted emigration with hostility, and it remained a point of contention throughout his life. Assisted migration to North America had long occurred from Ireland, sometimes supported by poor law unions, and during the Land War some private schemes were initiated in response to the crisis. Father James Nugent of Liverpool and Bishop John Ireland of St. Paul, Minnesota, organized migration from Connemara to the American Midwest. In one of the larger and more generous initiatives, James Hack Tuke, an English Quaker and philanthropist, assisted nearly 9500 people to emigrate from the west of Ireland to Canada and the United States from 1882 to 1884. A failed scheme to Argentina was also attempted in 1882.[11] In 1874 O'Leary undertook an extensive tour of North America to investigate assisted emigration opportunities for laborers and published a lengthy report that carefully documented the practicalities of migration, rates of wages, and costs of living in several areas in Canada and the United States.[12] He was partly motivated by his understanding that, as a class, laborers had historically emigrated to Britain because they could not afford the transatlantic passage and so lost out on the opportunities enjoyed by better-resourced migrants in North America. New assisted emigration schemes could contribute to redressing this imbalance.[13] He found conditions for would-be emigrants more favorable in Canada than the United States and set up an emigrant fund with prominent Irish Canadians. He also contributed to efforts to erect a Famine monument in Quebec Harbour.[14] O'Leary's tour connected with initiatives by the Canadian federal government to promote and incentivize immigration, which aimed to settle farmers from Ireland and Britain in western regions. From 1869 they invited journalists and others to visit in the hope they would write favorably of their impressions when they returned.[15]

Throughout this North American tour, O'Leary wore many hats—as delegate of the Irish Labourer's Union, temperance activist, Irish nationalist and emigration agent—and met with officials, businessmen, and clergymen. In the United States he developed friendly ties with the Father Matthew Temperance Society and the Catholic Temperance Union. In St. Paul, Minnesota, he was presented with the gold medal of the Catholic Abstinence Union of America by Bishop John Ireland, who assisted Irish migrants to settle in rural colonies in Minnesota.[16] O'Leary's American experiences reinforced his view of emigration as a partial solution for laborers' problems. His positive reports on Canadian opportunities were published in the *Freeman's Journal*, but were also contested in some nationalist newspapers.[17] He established lasting contacts that facilitated several visits back to North America in 1876, 1877, 1879–80, 1881–82, and 1884, each lasting between two to six months. Clearly, he no longer worked full-time as a street mason, and his extensive travels were seemingly funded by the various bodies he represented.

In North America, O'Leary interacted mainly with Irish contacts, but his encounters with non-Europeans prompted some racist reflections on the qualities of Irish emigrants and ideas of a deserving poor in rural Ireland. In contrast to Irish arrivals, he argued, Chinese immigrants were unwilling to assimilate, brought down wages, and came with "the filthiest vices." This hostility toward the Chinese was common in the labor movement in the American West at the time, and the speeches of Irish American labor leader Denis Kearney in California against the "Chinese scourge" were reprinted in the *Irish World*, which expressed considerable anti-Asian sentiment in this period. O'Leary took a slightly more moderate tone than Kearney, arguing that Chinese immigration should be regulated, not prevented entirely.[18]

His travelogue struck a more negative tone when detailing his encounters with the Ojibwe and Métis communities. Whereas O'Leary indicated an awareness that his anti-Chinese rhetoric may have been considered "illiberal" by some contemporary readers, no similar concerns were evident in his descriptions of the Ojibwe people he met along the Canadian border with Minnesota, which were characterized by both curiosity and a clear sense of European superiority. O'Leary declared that "as a race they were stuck down deep in savage abomination," and made crude comparisons with "the Romaney or Gipsy race" in Britain. He considered himself knowledgeable in the history of indigenous Americans, but made no mention of the violent colonization and resistance in the Red River region in the nineteenth century. He was also apparently unaware that, just a few years earlier, members of the Fenian Brotherhood approached the Métis, a group with mixed indigenous-European ancestry, in the hope that they would support the abortive 1871 raid into Manitoba. O'Leary's encounters with indigenous groups reinforced his views that laborers in Ireland deserved more assistance. He expressed dismay at the "enormous sums of money" spent by officials and religious institutions on reservations and conversion

missions. This money would be better directed at "the miserable condition of the Irish peasant" or the "wretched poverty in the East-End of
London."[19]

O'Leary's descriptions of the Ojibwe and Métis people seem designed to cast Irish laborers in a more positive light, to challenge what
he described as the British view of them "as a kind of semi-civilized
aborgines, little removed from savagery [sic]."[20] A poster for the 1879
Irishtown land rally meeting in Mayo declared that the call for land reform was heard from the west of Ireland to the "isles of Polynesia to the
wigwams of North America."[21] Yet there were no signs that O'Leary's
encounters sparked consideration of a common cause with dispossesed
indigenous Americans. Rather he repeated aspects of European colonial
thinking when describing "emigration to those fertile western wilds"
as "an extension of the empire of civilisation, " and he believed Irish
migrants had a role to play in future settlements.[22]

Neither did his views change. During an 1892 talk in London
O'Leary "had no hesitation in saying that as a race the Indians were
unable to rise to the intellectual status of the whites." He attempted
to explain their plight within a critique of British imperialism, in that
"the fortunes of war and an instinctive land hunger had now given to
the British government power over what were called the weaker races."
He maintained that some parallels existed between the historic dispossession of indigenous people in North America and the Irish plantations, but argued that although native Irish culture had been resilient
enough to survive British colonial settlement, this was not the case
in America. He concluded that the advance of modernity meant that
"the inevitable result would be that sooner or later they [indigenous
communities] would become extinct."[23] Here he repeated a pervasive
nineteenth-century view of human extinction as part of some natural
change, rather than a consequence of violent European colonialism,
which was "used to explain, and even rationalize, human population
decimations" among indigenous groups in the United States and European empires.[24]

O'Leary returned to North America three times in the 1870s and
made further fact-finding missions in France, England, and Wales, trips
that shaped his views of social reform in Ireland. When he returned to
the southwest of Ireland in 1879, his speeches and reports on working

conditions in North America and Europe surely encouraged some Irish laborers to measure their own circumstances against external criteria and raised their expectations for an improved life, whether through emigration or attempts to effect changes in their own localities. Only "by comparison," he asserted, "we can form a correct estimate of any question," and "nowhere have I seen such a wretched state of things" as in Ireland.[25] Believing that laborers desperately needed more unionizing, O'Leary also began to advocate for land nationalization as a solution to their situation. At the same time, he campaigned for improvement associations to be set up in western regions to instruct locals on modern "domestic economy, simple cookery, household cleanliness and sanitation, improved cottage gardening, temperance." This "social training" would also better equip would-be emigrants for new homes in North America.[26] During this tour the consequences of the economic downturn, coupled with a poor potato harvest, were evident in the signs of famine in western regions. In response O'Leary embarked again for Canada and the United States, in part to organize new emigration opportunities, including jobs on the Manitoba railway, but primarily to raise money for a relief fund for the southwest of the island that had been started by the social reformer and humanitarian Margaret Anna Cusack, known as the "Nun of Kenmare." In an open letter in New York's *Irish American*, O'Leary spoke directly to emigrants, warning of a "repetition of the terrible scenes of the years 1847 and 1848" and stating that they had a duty to help save lives in their country of origin.[27]

In the winter of 1879–80, humanitarian relief for Ireland became highly politicized and complicated O'Leary's transatlantic relationships. That December the Duchess of Marlborough, the wife of the Irish Lord Lieutenant, launched a relief fund, which was immediately followed by another, the Mansion House Fund, organized by Edmund Dwyer Gray, the proprietor of the *Freeman's Journal* and lord mayor of Dublin. The crisis roused traditional expectations of humanitarian activity among the respectable classes, linked to official status. Both funds were successful, with the Duchess collecting £135,500 and the Mansion House Fund £182,000, but the rivalry between the two stoked lasting tensions between the Irish administration and Dublin municipal politics, as well as with the Land League.[28] That same month *New York Herald* owner James Gordon Bennett, in a burst of narcissistic altruism, started another Irish relief fund. Collections were also coordinated by Catholic bishops in the United States as well as a New York City Relief Committee, which included the city's mayor, William Grace.[29] There were imperial dimensions to Irish aid as well: an Irish Famine Relief Fund Committee established in Singapore received donations from Chinese and Indian subscribers, who were encouraged by colonial officials to contribute in the spirit of "imperial brotherhood."[30]

The Land League was averse toward these initiatives, which seemed designed to supersede its own plans for relief. A fund controlled by the Land League was soon set in motion, one of many such distress funds launched in less than a month. Charles Stewart Parnell's acrimonious relationship with Edmund Dwyer Gray brought an added element to the rivalry between the Land League and Mansion House funds. In his American tour of January 1880, Parnell cautioned that contributions to the Mansion House or Duchess of Marlborough funds would bolster the "tyrannical land system" rather than aid the people that needed it. Going a step further, Patrick Ford declared these funds, particularly the New York Herald's, were initiated in the spirit of "malignant hostility" to the Land League, and that a contributor to them should be looked upon as a "traitor."[31] The politics of relief in the winter of 1879–80 were fluid, representing another battleground of the Land War, and caused confusion among Irish Americans. O'Leary was associated primarily with the Nun of Kenmare fund, which was approved by the Land League, but in Canada his public lectures also raised $500 for the Mansion House Fund.[32] He had sailed in late November and likely did not grasp how divisive fundraising had quickly become. Nonetheless, his reported associations with the Mansion House Fund likely stymied some potential alliances, particularly with the Irish World.

Given their shared interests, O'Leary and Irish World editor Patrick Ford seemed made to be allies. During his first American tour, O'Leary had developed a promising connection with the Irish World, who found his profile as a "bona fide workingman" appealing. Its London correspondent, Thomas Mooney, knew O'Leary from his Cork unionizing in 1873 and gave his book a glowing review.[33] For a few years O'Leary contributed occasional articles and letters to the paper that emphasized unionizing and temperance and were sometimes critical of Irish America's "self-praising demonstrations on Patrick's Day, and your little societies and rings (some of them mere twaddling clubs)." Like Ford, O'Leary was convinced that alcohol abstinence and working-class improvement were inextricably linked. He remembered his own decision to give up drinking as a transformative moment, allowing him to learn how to read and write and gain an apprenticeship, and his primary aim was to teach "the dignity of having self-reliance, love of country, sobriety." His writing reflected the intermeshing of transatlantic Irish radicalism with networks of temperance, nationalism, humanitarianism, trade unionism, and assisted emigration.[34] As one study has observed, underpinning this confluence of interests "were many of the same precepts: sobriety, gaining independence from exploitative employers and landlords, respectability, and self-improvement."[35] By the end of the 1870s, however, this relationship with the *Irish World* had cooled, in part due to O'Leary's position on assisted emigration.

Following O'Leary's first transatlantic tour in the mid-1870s, several newspapers, from Dublin's *Irishman* to San Francisco's *Irish Nationalist*, questioned his rosy depiction of immigrant life and suggested he was "promoting the clearing out of the Irish people."[36] The *Irish World* published one letter asserting that anyone "who endeavours to depopulate Ireland need not flatter himself that he is a true Irishman." Besides, the letter-writer continued, hard times meant there was little work for new arrivals in America in the 1870s.[37] A Dublin-based provincial immigration agent for Ontario criticized O'Leary for being too eager to please the Canadian federal government and for failing to flag real problems faced by immigrants.[38] O'Leary made some gains for emigrant laborers in terms of official subsidies and lower passage fares, but, overall, his schemes were unsuccessful. During the Land War, the promotion of assisted emigration became more difficult for O'Leary to balance with his support for the Land League. The Boston *Pilot* saw assisted emigration from Ireland as an "evil"—curiously, more so when Canada was involved. "If they must leave home, let them come to the United States," one editorial claimed. "Canada is not the proper place."[39] In 1881 O'Leary revised his position and claimed that, while he considered some emigration healthy, he now opposed assisted emigration.[40] This turnaround did not go unnoticed by his critics, some of whom did not hold back. The *Chicago Tribune* described him as an "unmitigated humbug and fraud" who himself "should be assisted to emigrate" from

Ireland.[41] The *Brooklyn Daily Eagle*, on the other hand, continued to praise him as the "Parnell" of the laborers' movement.[42]

O'Leary cut a somewhat contradictory figure, falling between two different factions in Irish America and ultimately not openly welcomed by either. From 1881 the "official" American Land League led by Patrick Collins in Boston became increasingly distinct from a radical faction associated with Patrick Ford and the *Irish World* in New York. The doctrine of nationalization became associated with the latter, while Collins supported the policy of peasant proprietorship favored by the Land League executive in Ireland. Ford, an effective fundraiser, bypassed Collins by sending the huge sums of money collected through his paper directly to Ireland, giving his group considerable influence. When the Home Rule MP T. P. O'Connor toured America, Ford and Collins "were at daggers drawn," and he found the balancing act difficult, because, "though Collins was the head of our organization, it was through the columns of the Irish World that we got the large subscriptions that were making our movement omnipotent in Ireland, subscriptions that reached the height of four thousand pounds sometimes in a single week."[43] These divisions fractured the movement in the United States; Fanny Parnell, who first established the Ladies' Land League in New York, wrote to Collins that she would prefer the organization to "break up rather than permit any further I.W. [*Irish World*] interference and rowdyism." She removed the name of Ellen Ford, Patrick's sister, from the Ladies Land League's books. She and Collins, she said, represented the "party of common sense and honesty," and she described a state of battle with the *Irish World*, in which "one should either crush one's enemy by one's defence" or else mount no defence at all.[44] It seems O'Leary underestimated the extent of the hostility and sought to make connections with both factions. He contributed articles to the Collins-aligned *Pilot* and *Irish American*, yet his views on labor and nationalization chimed far more with the *Irish World*.[45]

The broad scope of O'Leary's activism contributed to his mixed reputation, as he combined radical land reform with more moderate demands. He consistently proved ready to engage with British officials to push for incremental change, where some Land Leaguers would have hesitated. One London newspaper observed that he was often "found in the lobby of the House of Commons interviewing M.P.s on his favourite theme."[46] During O'Leary's first tour of North America he met with Earl Dufferin, then governor-general of Canada, later viceroy of India, and also an aristocratic Irish landowner. O'Leary dedicated the published report of his trip to Dufferin, who impressed him in his performance as governor, if not in his "politics, nor his exalted rank."[47] In 1879 O'Leary wrote directly to the chancellor of the exchequer, Stafford Northcote, appealing for action to prevent famine in the west of Ireland, and he provided evidence on laborers' housing to the Richmond Commission on Agriculture.[48] In 1881 he led a delegation of laborers' representatives, including William Upton and Philip Johnson, to a meeting in London with Irish Chief Secretary William Forster and a group of MPs to discuss the lack of provision for laborers in the Land Act. Responding to questions about dwellings, wages, and sanitation, Forster maintained that laborers "must not expect too much"; the state was limited in how it could intervene, but market demand would improve wages and, in turn, dwellings.[49] In 1883 O'Leary met with the lord mayor of London to request contributions to a relief fund for tenants on estates in Ulster that were owned by the London Corporation. The mayor curtly refused, quoting statistics on significant increases in Irish bank deposits since the end of the Land War, and suggested they approach the Irish "large classes." The episode embarrassed O'Leary, who maintained that he overcame "personal scruples" to meet with the mayor in the hope of helping destitute people. Yet the meeting did raise a valid question, he wrote, about what Irish farmers who had benefited from the 1881 Land Act were doing for the laborers. He suggested the Irish diaspora was still doing more than its fair share of fundraising in 1883.[50] O'Leary's appeals to British officials indicate that he saw no tension in advocating radical land redistribution and collaborating with socialists, while at the same time working within establishment structures to push for moderate reforms.

Outside of official channels, O'Leary was an energetic unionizer who moved regularly between London and the southwest of Ireland, where, along with Philip Johnson and William Upton, he helped to launch the Munster Labour League. The Land League began to pay more attention to laborers' activism, and, more than other nationalist newspapers, the *Irishman* reported favorably on O'Leary's "zeal and energy." In London he lectured to trade unions as well as Catholic and workingmen's clubs about the need for laborers to be provided for in any Irish legislation.[51] By the summer of 1881, laborers' frustrations were intensifying with the lack of provision in the new Land Bill and the Land League's limited efforts to address this, a situation that the *Irishman* remarked "may cause the labourers to come to the conclusion that they must make a great noise, as the farmers' friends have done."[52] This would prove the case: that summer laborers in the southwest went on strike and succeeded in pushing their demands firmly up the agenda at the upcoming Land League convention.[53]

At the convention, held at Dublin's Rotunda hall in September, O'Leary addressed delegates in a talk chaired by Charles Stewart Parnell. He declared that he originally came "with some hostile intentions, as far as the executive of the Land League was concerned," because they aimed "simply to assist the farmer and do nothing for the labourer"—a view, he claimed, that was widely shared among Irish emigrants in England. Setting out a class-based view of the agitation, O'Leary contended that there was "no assimilation," just competition between the different social strata of rural Ireland. His talk drew parallels between the laborers' situation and American slavery that stood out because, rather than aiming them at landlords, he directed them at the Land League itself and the Irish middle classes, comparing their indifference to laborers' miserable conditions to the former tolerance of slavery in the United States. Although the Land League demanded that landlords "deal justly" with tenant farmers, O'Leary argued that it should also demand from "the farmer that he must deal equally justly with his labourers." Adding insult to injury, O'Leary claimed (with some oversimplification) that the Land League was sustained by funds donated "to a large extent by labourers who, years ago, left Ireland through poverty."[54] He then called for the Land League to adopt nationalization as the only policy that would benefit all classes, in language that surpassed Henry George in its explicit emphasis on state ownership, reflecting more the influence of socialist circles in London. At the convention John Ferguson, the Glasgow-based emigrant and Land Leaguer, also spoke favorably of George's theories, but avoided references to state ownership of land.[55]

Despite his initial misgivings about the Land League, however, O'Leary held discussions with Parnell at the convention, after which he decided that the "voice of conscience" was finally rising. New resolutions were agreed upon that acknowledged the neglect of laborers, recommending that they should have one representative on the Land League's executive committee. The position was offered to O'Leary, who refused, for reasons that are unclear. Recommendations were also adopted that tenant farmers contribute toward laborers' dwellings and set aside some land for their use, while, notably, the name of the Land League was to change to the Irish National Land League and Labour and Industrial Movement. Parnell expressed his satisfaction that tenants, laborers, and artisans were now "banded together in one solid organisation," and O'Leary viewed Parnell's commitments as a small victory. Patrick Ford, in contrast, bemoaned the "absurdly inefficient" resolutions.[56]

These plans for laborers' inclusion were scuttled the following month when the Land League was outlawed and several key figures were arrested, including Parnell. With the Irish organization proscribed, O'Leary appealed to Frank Byrne of the Land League of Great Britain, a more radical body than the Land League in Ireland. He asserted to Byrne that, without a new initiative for laborers, tensions between farmers and "the classes below them" would become volatile. Since the passing of the Land Act in the autumn of 1881, he explained, some tenants were "rushing into the Land Court" (to settle their rents), and that laborers, who now represented the most revolutionary element in Ireland, could sustain the momentum of the agitation. O'Leary's appeals were passed on to Patrick Egan, the Paris-based treasurer of the Land League and a more radical voice on the executive committee, and he responded that he never viewed Land League as a "tenant farmers' protection association." He invited O'Leary to Paris, where they met and agreed that more funds would be directed to laborers.[57] O'Leary then embarked on another lengthy American trip with the aim of raising more awareness of laborers' conditions and also strengthening ties between Irish emigrants in Britain and North America.

O'Leary's departure coincided with Henry George's arrival in Ireland in November 1881. The pair did not meet until the following year, when they discussed increasing the reach of the *Irish World* among Irish emigrants in England as well as among English workers. O'Leary proposed that he direct an English edition of the paper—an idea he had floated before, in 1875—and outlined the steps he would take to push its circulation, such as the inclusion of a new section on the Irish in Britain. To do the job, he asked not for a commission, but a fixed salary of fifty shillings per week (then a common wage for a skilled tradesman) for at least six months, which, he said, was the only feasible way to make it work. This arrangement would benefit the *Irish World* on both sides of the Atlantic because, as O'Leary told George, "my name is known all over that continent [North America] and in the United Kingdom." The venture, however, did not come to pass; Ford may have been cautious of O'Leary due to the reasons outlined above. Nonetheless, O'Leary continued his efforts to make London "the base from which to push the nationalization question."[58] Different versions of land nationalization circulated in British radical and labor networks long before George's *Progress and Poverty* appeared, and O'Leary's and George's links with these circles helped develop alliances with the Land League. During the Land War several British trade unionists, socialists, and feminists came to Ireland to support the agitation.

British Labor, Feminism, and the Land War

The passing of the Coercion Act in March 1881, which provided powers for detention without trial in Ireland, brought the Land League and British radicals and democrats closer together. Three months later a delegation of nine members of the newly established Democratic Federation and trade unionists from north east England and Yorkshire came to Ireland to investigate conditions firsthand. They were later followed by Helen Taylor, the prominent women's rights activist, socialist and stepdaughter of John Stuart Mill who made multiple trips to Ireland from England and joined the Ladies' Land League. The Democratic Federation was led by H. M. Hyndman, who also sat on the executive of the Land League of Great Britain, and the new organization attracted some of the leading lights of social radicalism, including Taylor, Eleanor Marx, William Morris, and Edward Aveling. From 1884 it became explicitly socialist. At its first meeting Hyndman told members that "Irish people were now fighting the battle of the English people as well as their own with reference to the land," and support for land nationalization and Home Rule was agreed upon.[59] Peter O'Leary attended these early meetings, arguing that "the real interests of the English democracy are bound up with the success of the land agitation in Ireland" and his networks reflected the significant integration between Land Leaguers and socialists in the city.[60] Events in Ireland and opposition to the 1881 Coercion Act were central to the early development of the Democratic Federation. For Frederick Engels, the organization was even too dependent on Irish support.[61]

The delegates of the Democratic Federation were first invited to Ireland by Harold Rylett, an English emigrant who moved to Co. Down in the 1870s and took up a post as a Unitarian minister and joined the Land League, becoming its chief organizer in Ulster and a member of the national executive. Similar to O'Leary, Rylett had been a part of the National Agricultural Labourers' Union and sought to develop relations between English and Irish trade unionists. He was among the few members of the Land League executive committee, along with Andrew Kettle Thomas Brennan and Davitt, to seriously engage with laborers' grievances.[62] In Ulster he understood the Land League as a nonsectarian body that "promised a common measure of justice to all, no matter what their religion may be."[63] Land League branches, which were found in every Ulster county, appealed primarily to Catholics, but also to Protestants. It apparently also attracted some members of the Orange Order; at one meeting in Armagh, according to the *Irish World*, the master of the lodge asserted that "instead of condemning the Land League they ought to applaud it for the work it did and was doing."[64] This broad appeal diminished in the autumn of 1881, when Rylett agreed to an ill-timed proposal to run as a Home Rule candidate in a Tyrone by-election (which he lost), and his candidacy gave the Land League more associations with Home Rule in Ulster.[65] Following his defeat, Rylett became a more explicit advocate of land nationalization, converting to the idea after reading a copy of *Progress and Poverty* gifted to him by Davitt. He later met with Henry George in Belfast.[66] Rylett traveled extensively throughout Ireland and also spoke at Land League rallies in Dundee, Glasgow, Liverpool, Leicester, Sheffield, Middlesbrough, and London. In his movements and contacts he represented an important link across the Irish sea.

After the Democratic Federation delegates arrived in Ireland in July 1881, the Land League facilitated their travels through Kildare, Queen's County, Wexford, Cork, Limerick, Clare, Galway, and Roscommon, giving them a platform at local demonstrations. The delegates included

Alfred Winks, W. Sabin Fredericks, Finlay Finlayson, Gavin B. Clark, and Jessie Craigen, the only woman in the group after Helen Taylor withdrew from the trip. They addressed several Land League meetings, including large demonstrations at the Rotunda and Phoenix Park in Dublin, where they were also joined by Hyndman.[67] The visibility of the Democratic Federation delegates at Land League demonstrations indicated an affinity within the organization with the idea of a common struggle. Their speeches emphasized internationalism and the communion of interest between Irish and British workers, who, they contended, held tremendous potential for change if they could work together.[68] For Gavin B. Clark, who occasionally collaborated with Peter O'Leary and was later a Crofter MP in Scotland, witnessing Irish evictions deepened his commitment to "the abolition of private property in land, and its adoption as national property."[69] All delegates condemned the Coercion Act as an assault on civil liberties and the right to collective protest that, if tolerated in Ireland, would soon come to Britain.

Jessie Craigen worked separately from the other delegates with the Ladies' Land League due to her particular admiration for the women's organization, but she also found the men's drinking off-putting. She was an unconventional suffragist, trade unionist, and temperance activist who, by many accounts, was a passionate public speaker valued for her ability to reach working-class women.[70] She accompanied Anna Parnell to Limerick to lend support to four women arrested during an eviction protest, and she later addressed a rally of over three thousand people in Clare. Her speeches in Ireland emphasized nonviolent resistance, class solidarity, and female suffrage, asserting that "Every woman ought to have a voice through the vote."[71] Upon returning to England, she told audiences that her trip attempted to build a "golden bridge" across the Irish Sea "on which love could pass."[72] Her published report of her time in Ireland detailed the evictions and episodes of police brutality she had witnessed and proposed a "Friends of Ireland Association" in England to pressurize Parliament. "Misgovernment in Ireland will sow the seeds of tyranny in England, if it not be resisted," she warned. "English as well as Irish freedom is at stake."[73] Craigen supported demands for rent strikes, and when the "No Rent Manifesto" was issued in October 1881, she wrote a pamphlet in full support of the measure, describing it as "an extreme act of self defence on the part of the Irish masses."[74] After the Land League was outlawed, she joined O'Leary and Hyndman at a large demonstration in London's Hyde Park in protest.[75]

Craigen's feminism and Irish activism were not always easily balanced. The English suffragist Lydia Becker opposed associations with the Land League, and Craigen's friend Helen Taylor was accused by the suffragist Priscilla McLaren of damaging the movement's reputation through her activism in Ireland.[76] The *Nation* reported that Craigen was boycotted at some British suffrage events, and on one occasion a Glasgow committee requested she cancel an address to the city's Land League because it was scheduled one day after her appearance at a suffrage rally where she spoke with Becker and the eminent American campaigner Elizabeth Cady Stanton.[77] Writing to Taylor, who first encouraged her to come to Ireland, Craigen maintained that her efforts for the land movement were "very extensive and very successful," and that she had made "great sacrifices for the Irish cause. I gave up my situation and threw myself on the world without a penny and without a friend." She left a paid position with the Ladies' National Association to come to Ireland, yet felt that she and the Ladies' Land League had been betrayed by the "political trickster" Charles Stewart Parnell, when he steered the agitation in a moderate direction from May 1882 and then excluded women. She had fought for the "liberty of the people," she wrote, not Parnell's political ambitions.[78] Taylor likely shared her frustration, but she continued to support the Home Rule party in the following years and distanced herself from Craigen's attacks on Parnell, leaving her a somewhat marginalized figure.

Helen Taylor was not part of the first Democratic Federation delegation, but she began traveling back and forth to Ireland in the winter of 1881–82. She came to represent a nodal point in the networks linking the Ladies' Land League, the women's rights movement, land nationalization, and the Democratic Federation. In Britain her agile campaigning intensified opposition to the Coercion Act and elevated interest in the Land War as both a radical and humanitarian cause. She corresponded with Anna Parnell from the earliest days of the Ladies' Land League and was instrumental in setting the British wing of the organization in motion.[79] Branches in Islington and Manchester were named after her, and she was a much sought-after speaker at Irish meetings across England.[80] Henry George found her to be the "most impressive speaker I had ever heard."

In her speeches in Ireland, Taylor promised that English women would "make their voices heard, and heard unanswerably, in protest against the shameless iniquities which are being perpetrated."[81]

Taylor arrived in Ireland about the same time as Henry George in November 1881. George's presence in Ireland was a coup for the *Irish World*, and Dublin's *Freeman's Journal* described *him* as "one of the most remarkable men of the age" who had "created a world-wide sensation."[82] George had long shown an interest in Ireland, evident in his section on the Great Famine in *Progress and Poverty*, and he had family links through Annie Corsina Fox, his Irish Australian wife, who accompanied him on the trip. In Ireland they and Taylor stepped into a highly charged atmosphere, with most of the Land League leadership in jail. The previous month Charles Stewart Parnell had been imprisoned in Kilmainham, which sparked two days of unrest in Dublin, and George's ally Michael Davitt had been in jail since February. From prison the Land League leaders issued the No Rent Manifesto, a declaration of a national rent strike that was designed to intensify the agitation and was the policy favored by the *Irish World*. The Land League was then outlawed, and, despite the government's attempts to pacify the country both through the 1881 Land Act and the Coercion Act, that winter episodes of agrarian violence escalated: nearly 3,500 "outrages" were recorded from October 1881 to April 1882, up from 2,600 in the same period during the previous year.[83] George's first impression was that Ireland was governed by a "reign of terror", such was the military presence there.[84] The number of soldiers in Ireland did not change dramatically during the Land War, but they were much more visible, undertaking extra duties including patroling, policing riots, and providing protection to land agents, bailiffs, sheriffs, and landlords. Famously, hundreds of troops guarded a group of fifty-seven workers who were brought to Mayo to save crops on Charles Boycott's farm in November 1880 during the effective local campaign to ostracize him, from which the term *boycott* originated.[85] From October 1881, in place of the outlawed Land League, the Ladies' Land League assumed leadership of the movement and worked closely with George and Taylor. George had been present at the first Ladies' Land League meeting in New York and admired Anna Parnell, who was deeply critical of the Land Act. In the *Irish World*, he reported in detail on the activities of Taylor and the Ladies' Land League.[86]

At George's first talk in Ireland, which Anna Parnell and Taylor helped organize, he told the Dublin audience that the Land League was leading "the van of a revolution that was destined to sweep over the civilised world" and that would unite the questions of land and labor. On the topic of peasant proprietorship, he asked, "[What] did they want with peasants of any kind"? Instead, both peasants and aristocrats should be consigned to history, and all citizens should have "an equal share in the land." The aim ought to "not be merely a political democracy, but a social democracy," a goal that he asserted was "consistent with true Christianity." George was enthusiastically received, though the chairman Alfred Webb observed that some of those present might take issue with his theories. The speech singled out several people for praise; George spoke with particular warmth for the "illustrious Englishwoman" Helen Taylor, noting that she was the new president of the Political Prisoners Association, for which his lecture was in aid.[87]

Upon her arrival in Ireland, Taylor immediately embraced an active role. She imperiously suggested she take over the running of the Ladies' Land League, and that Anna Parnell should temporarily move to Liverpool. Her argument, supported by George, was that the leading women would soon be arrested, and that it would be more damaging to the government if she were arrested in Ireland. Anna Parnell refused, believing her own presence in Ireland was critical.[88] Taylor then traveled to Co. Mayo for the inquest into the death of twenty-two-year-old Ellen McDonagh, who was killed by the Royal Irish Constabulary (RIC) during an eviction. She brought additional publicity to the case, though George believed she was more useful in Dublin.[89] Despite turning down Taylor's offer, Anna Parnell held her in high regard and later supported her attempt to run as a parliamentary candidate in 1885. In a letter, she told Taylor that she wrote that she was "the only English person, I have ever known, who looked on the Irish question entirely from the Irish point of view" and who did not shy away "from the most wearisome and disturbing drudgery in your efforts to assist the tenant farmers."[90] In New York, Patrick Ford felt that Land League radicals had found a well-positioned ally in Taylor to channel their message in Britain, and, similar to Peter O'Leary, she explored the possibility of organizing an English edition of the *Irish World*.[91] She later cofounded the English Land Nationalisation Society and campaigned for the abolition of private land ownership until the turn of the century.[92] Her *Nationalisation of the Land* pamphlet argued that the doctrine was not "a cure for all political, moral, and social evils," but that it would do more good "than any other single measure." Whereas George gradually retreated from socialism in the 1880s, Taylor increasingly called for outright state ownership of land.[93]

Both Henry and Annie George developed good friendships with Taylor and stayed at her home during trips to London, where she introduced them to her radical circles. Part of the appeal of the Irish mission for George was that it allowed him to spend time in England, where he believed the land question was also combustible. Before his departure he had also confided that he wished to visit England for "the pleasure of seeing what every intelligent American must still regard as his mother country"—a sentiment he surely kept to himself when in the company of Irish Americans.[94] George's mutually beneficial association with the Land League raised his profile in Britain, where *Progress and Poverty* sold over one hundred thousand copies between 1881 and 1883 and resonated with those already familiar with nationalization ideas through the work of John Stuart Mill, Taylor's stepfather. In London, George established connections with reformers and revolutionaries of various shades, from the Liberal MP Joseph Cowen to the renowned Russian anarchist Peter Kropotkin, then exiled in London.[95] Kropotkin, who took an interest in Ireland, commissioned the Irish anarchist Nannie Florence Dryhurst to write a series of articles on Irish conditions in the anarchist monthly *Freedom*.[96] Michael Davitt, Taylor, and Richard McGhee attempted—unsuccessfully—to bring Kropotkin to Dublin to lecture on political prisoners, but he did come to Ireland in 1888 to speak to the Cork Lecture Society. He wrote to Davitt that it would be "so great a pleasure to see you," but to his disappointment the Irish leader was in England and unable to meet.[97] Kropotkin was not the only anarchist interested in the Land War; the Boston-based Marie Le Compte, who met Kropotkin when attending the 1881 London Anarchist Congress, traveled to Ireland and was present on the platform at George's first Irish lecture at the Rotunda. Le Compte later contributed to the New Jersey–based *Labor Standard*, edited by the emigrant Irish Fenian and socialist Joseph Patrick McDonnell, who was previously active in the First International in London, was friends with Marx and Engels, and knew Peter O'Leary from the Fenian Amnesty campaign of the late 1860s.[98]

George was also hosted in London by H. M. Hyndman, whom he interviewed for the *Irish World*. Their conversation took up the front page of one edition and spelled out their affinities, but also indicated emerging differences between Georgism and socialism.[99] George felt Hyndman was too influenced by Marx, while Hyndman thought nationalization was not the panacea George believed it to be, arguing that land possessors would still exploit laborers through wages.[100] William Morris agreed, stating that George was limited by his belief that "a man wants nothing but a bit of land."[101] In E. P. Thompson's analysis, George's English converts supported his version of nationalization "for a short period only before moving forward to Socialism."[102]

George advocated a system where land could not be owned as private property. Instead, people would pay a rent or a tax to occupy it, and they would then be free to keep profits from whatever use they made of their holdings. Such would be the scale of tax on land, he argued, all other taxes would be abolished. As the 1880s progressed his followers coalesced in the single tax movement and distanced themselves from state ownership of land, insisting that land was a natural resource that could not be the property of any interest. In 1887 George himself took concerted steps to disassociate from socialism in the United States, losing much working-class support in the process. Socialists, increasingly alert to their differences with George, concluded that his brilliance lay in his descriptions of social ills, but not his cure.[103] The Democratic Federation maintained their admiration for George, but his dedicated supporters were mainly found in the English and Scottish Land Restoration Leagues from the mid-1880s. During the Land War, however, his differences with socialists were not so clear. The term "single tax" was absent from *The Irish Land Question* and appeared just three times in *Progress and Poverty*, which referred to the state as "the universal Landlord."[104] During his year in Ireland and England, George did not extend himself to clarify differences in his vision of nationalization with other leftist groups and was an effective broker between the Land League and wider radical networks.

English Miners' Delegations

Separate from the somewhat London-centric Democratic Federation, trade unionists from the northeast of England also sought to build alliances with the Land League. John Bryson and William Patterson, representatives of the Northumberland and Durham Miners' Associations, carried out two tours of Ireland. Their aim was to provide reports for working-class English readers that would serve as an alternative to official inquiries, which they believed failed to reach a popular audience. Bryson also stated that "the whole English Press had systematically misrepresented the mining people in times of disputes with their employers," and he suspected similar workings afoot in Ireland.[105] Bryson and Patterson had previously met Michael Davitt and John Ferguson at a London conference of the Land Law Reform League, an initiative of Charles Bradlaugh, the English republican and author of *The Land, The People, and the Coming Struggle*.[106] Davitt then spoke of his solidarity with trade unions and welcomed "with pleasure representatives of miners of the North."[107] Bryson took more active interest in Ireland after the passing of the Coercion Act in March 1881—a source of "sorrow and shame," he said—and addressed a Land League meeting in Jarrow that drew between seven to ten thousand people, as well as several anti-coercion meetings around Durham and Newcastle.[108] In June he and Patterson set out for Ireland.

Their trip was supported by Joseph Cowen, who himself had visited the west of Ireland when collecting evidence for the Richmond Commission on Agriculture. He then told parliament that "to say that such a state of things was an outrage upon civilization was not to condemn it sufficiently.'"[109] Cowen knew Henry George and many Irish Party MPs personally, and he was indignant at Davitt's imprisonment in February 1881, writing that it was "the meanest and most cowardly act I ever remember an English government in modern times to have been guilty of." His lengthy speeches against the Coercion Act brought the threat of suspension from parliament while also ensuring his popularity among the Irish in Britain.[110] Cowen was on the executive committee of the Land League of Great Britain, launched on his home turf in Newcastle in March 1881, and he encouraged support for Irish Home Rule and land reform among English workers. At one Newcastle demonstration he and Bryson were joined by Charles Stewart Parnell and T. P. O'Connor in front of a crowd in which "Tynesiders bred and born far outnumbered the Irishmen."[111] In this context of strong regional support for the Land League and significant anticoercion protests,

Bryson and Patterson traveled to Ireland and published their findings in Cowen's *Newcastle Chronicle*.

Their report, dotted with descriptions of poverty and their interviews with locals, told some interesting stories. The pair arrived in Dublin and made the six-hour train journey to Galway, then proceeded by jaunting car to Barna. Patterson wrote of families living in huts no more than eight square feet in size, with no chimneys, sparse furniture, and a fire fueled by horse dung gathered from the road.[112] He was not alone among visitors in emphasizing the deplorable state of rural housing, which Peter O'Leary claimed "at once strikes the eye of the stranger with horror." According to the 1881 census there were over forty thousand single-room mud cabins in Ireland, though O'Leary estimated there were over twice this number.[113] Descriptions of "wretched hovels" were a staple of travel writing during the Land War, no doubt influenced by Fanny Parnell's widely read 1880 pamphlet *The Hovels of Ireland*. Reporting for the *New York Daily Witness*, for example, Mrs. A. McDougall claimed that she "lost the power of description" when passing cabins near Ramelton, Donegal, which seemed to her unfit for human inhabitation.[114] Alongside sketches of cabins and poverty, Bryson and Patterson shared their interviews with locals about the absence of compensation for improving their holdings and the difficulties in bequeathing tenancies to children. They told of hearing how some gave fifty-two days' labor annually to landlords as part of their tenure agreements, which they were required to give upon request, meaning they lost their own crops in short-lived good weather spells. If they refused, agents took livestock that was returned when the work was done. When Bryson suggested doing this work to the principle of "ca'canny" (go slow), they told him the agents often "stood over the tenant armed with a stout cudgel, which he did not fail to lay on the back and shoulders" if he thought there was shirking. Referring to it as "slave driving," the shocked trade unionists wrote that they found the practice "so extraordinary that an official inquiry is imperative."[115] Thomas Burt, an MP and a secretary of the Northumberland Miners Association, quoted their report in Parliament, though the Irish chief secretary William Forster responded that he "could not believe there was any truth whatever in the statement."[116] After the two men returned to Galway two months later to gather further evidence, as well as traveling to Kerry and Cork, Bryson would pointedly state that, despite Forster's objections, they had not retracted their first report, and "truthfulness had stood the test."[117]

In a separate trip, representatives from the ironstone mines in Skinningrove Valley on the east coast of Yorkshire came to Ireland. Their report made a point of corroborating Bryson and Patterson. Joseph Toyn and James Chappel traveled first to Derry and Donegal and proceeded down the west coast to Limerick, stopping at various locations and interviewing locals, who seemed "wishful that the English working men should understand their grievances." Their report, which emphasized the industriousness of all the tenants they encountered in an effort to counter stereotypes,was published by the Land League and so, unsurprisingly, fully endorsed the organization's plan of action, concluding with a "call upon Englishmen to help the down-trodden people of Ireland."[118]

Bryson and Patterson spoke at a number of Land League meetings, delivering messages of support from trade unions and insisting that if miners "stood calmly by," their own freedom to take collective action would soon be threatened. They met with the Democratic Federation delegates, but avoided speaking about nationalism or nationalization at demonstrations. When Sabin Fredericks declared his sympathy with republicanism and the use of force "in defence of hearth and home," Thomas Burt was quick to point out in Parliament that he was part of the Democratic Federation, not the miners' delegation.[119] Henry George was a figure of much interest in the northeast of England; his first interview after arriving in Ireland was published in the *Newcastle Chronicle*, ahead of any Irish newspapers, and he became friends with Joseph Cowen.[120] Yet Cowen did not fully support nationalization, and Bryson and Patterson remained silent on the issue, though later in the decade some northern trade unions were more receptive.[121] Bryson and Patterson generally eschewed radical language and focused on legal reforms, the regulation of rents, an end to evictions, and measures to ensure that landlords contribute to the burden of costs for improvements and provide credit to tenants.[122]

The miners' visits strengthened ties between the Land League and English trade unionism, though the extent to which the visitors broadly represented working-class sentiment in the northeast of England is difficult to assess. Industrial workers in the region were frustrated, according to one study, by the "emphasis on Irish politics (particularly in the early 1880s) to the exclusion of their own."[123] The Land League's associations with violence were also not easily overcome, and the miners' delegates strove to challenge preconceptions and stereotypes, stating that they saw no "village tyrants clothed in rags."[124] Persuading English miners that their interests were served by an alliance with the Land League was not a straightforward task, but trade union leaders did make sustained efforts to stake out common ground, and Land League meetings around Newcastle and Durham drew significant non-Irish audiences. Following his trips to Ireland, Bryson continued to play an active role in the Land League, and a branch would be named after him in Cowpen, Northumberland.[125]

Some Irish MPs in the Land League courted working-class support in Britain, though the extent to which their appeals reflected a deep affinity or more short-term political interests is open to question. James Connolly later asserted that, once the Land War was over, Home Rule politicians "followed their class interests" and left "English and Scottish Socialists" as "the principal exponents and interpreters of Land League principles to the British masses."[126] Timothy Healy, who worked as a railway clerk in Newcastle in the 1870s, told a demonstration in Gateshead that the Land League's cause was "the cause of the Trades Unions of England, of the masters against the men, and the men against the masters. . . . It was the old question of capital against labour."[127] Yet labor radicalism, it is fair to say, was not central to Healy's subsequent political career, and his comments have the whiff of the more tokenistic appeals to British labor that seminal studies of the period by T. W. Moody and F. S. L. Lyons sensed in Parnell.[128] Both historians depicted his overtures to the British working classes and the *Irish World* constituency in the United States as due to the expediency of a leader always scheming for Home Rule. In 1881 Parnell spoke in Parliament of "the superior position of the Irish people" in the United States and his pleasure in meeting "barristers, medical men, merchants" during his tour, hinting at some disdain for manual workers.[129] The attitudes of Parnell and Healy, however, should not overshadow the fact that the Land War did represent an important chapter of solidarity between many Land Leaguers, radicals, and trade unionists. Events in Ireland shaped many

British radicals' understandings of collective action, exposed the authoritarian side of the Liberal government, and brought opportunities for new alliances to the surface.

The End of the Land War

With unrest petering out in Ireland in the summer of 1882, the Land League of Great Britain held a convention in Manchester to debate future steps. Peter O'Leary proposed a resolution to erase peasant proprietorship as the organization's policy and replace it with nationalization. He was backed by his London-based ally and fellow emigrant Thomas Kissane and H. M. Hyndman, but not by Joseph Cowen.[130] Also present were three Scotland-based emigrants, John Ferguson, Richard McGhee and Edward McHugh, who in the 1880s supported George and developed strong links between Irish and Scottish land reformers.[131] After a fractious debate, the resolution was defeated. Much had changed in the previous months, and tensions regarding nationalization were part of a simmering conflict between groups associated with Parnell and Davitt.

In the Kilmainham "treaty" of May 1882, Gladstone extended the land legislation with the Arrears Act, which benefited some smaller tenants and eased rent debts, and the government released the Land League leaders from prison. In return, Parnell promised to calm the unrest and embrace a fresh spirit of cooperation with the Liberals. A few days after the announcement of the agreement, the new chief secretary of Ireland and the under-secretary were killed in Dublin by a marginal group of militant nationalists called the Invincibles. Despite all the military protection offered to landlords and their agents during the Land War, the men had been walking alone.[132] The assassinations shocked the British political establishment as well as Irish leaders, and Anna Parnell was almost the sole voice in Ireland that questioned the Land League's rush to apologize for the killings. The government resolved to further expand emergency police powers and introduced the Prevention of Crime Act, which legalized severe powers of detention. Parnell asserted more control over the Land League, including undermining the opponents of his policy of peasant proprietorship.

Following his release from prison, Davitt publicly declared his support for nationalization at demonstrations in Liverpool, Manchester, and Cork. He then traveled to the United States, where he met with Patrick Ford and gave speeches that proclaimed the shared goals of the Land League with labor movements in the United States and Britain, and internationally. George had influenced his position, but Davitt's interest in nationalization pre-dated their meeting, and he was unhappy with the perception that he had been "converted" by George.[133] While en route to America, Davitt was thrown on the defensive by Parnell and his followers, who claimed that nationalization meant the transfer of Irish land into the ownership of the British state.[134] Interestingly, a major part of their critique of nationalization was not ideological, although they certainly considered it too idealistic and unfeasible; rather, they argued that it would divide the nationalist movement and distract from progress on Home Rule. In this view, debates about land reform were subordinate to the national question, and Davitt was accused of trying to derail the Kilmainham treaty. To prevent open conflict with Parnell, Davitt publicly downplayed nationalization over the following years, albeit remaining the target of attacks from the Home Rule party.[135] Parnell and the advocates of peasant proprietorship, backed by their own allies in Britain and the United States, consolidated their position, and the Land League was reconstituted in October 1882 as the new National League, an organization more focused on electoral politics than on land. This began what Davitt later termed the "counterrevolution," in which radical voices were marginalized, but in which he himself acquiesced when he agreed to prioritize nationalist unity.[136]

Henry George departed Ireland in October 1882, lamenting that the "Land League has been converted into a Home Rule League." He acknowledged that the Land Act and Arrears Act made "real gains" for many tenant farmers, but argued these were temporary measures that offered nothing to laborers and poorer tenants who could not afford to go to the new land courts. Parnell's strategy, he said, was not "land for the people," but land for "some of the people."[137] In a series of lengthy articles in the *Irish World*, he rebutted attacks on nationalization, arguing that he did not propose that the British state take control of Irish land; instead, he took a Spencean approach of localized collective ownership. However, his answers to the troublesome question of who would control nationalized lands in Ireland were long-winded and lacked punch. George's writings and speeches in Ireland had framed land as a resource to be exploited that people could occupy with legal protections and then sell their interest if they wished. He did not pay sufficient attention to cultural and intergenerational attachments to land, what one study has described as the "material-metaphysical dimension of 'Irish soil'": grievances rooted in popular memories of historic conquest and colonial confiscation, and the right of restitution.[138]

There were also limits to the *Irish World*'s power to remotely influence Land League policy in what was a very fluid situation. Without a strong organizational foothold in Ireland, and with their main ally Davitt in prison, Ford and George could not seriously challenge the advocates of peasant proprietorship. Large farmers were sufficiently represented in leadership roles with the Land League to stifle resolutions concerning meaningful land redistribution at meetings.[139] George's critique that peasant proprietorship would lay the basis for a conservative rural society proved accurate over the next decades. Following the 1903 Wyndham Act, peasant proprietors finally overtook landlords as the owners of rural Ireland. This process was both "a social revolution and a social counter revolution," in the interpretation of Joe Lee, in that the strong farmer had "repulsed the threat from below, from the cottier and labourer, and on the other hand he had smashed the threat from above, from the landlords."[140]

Support for nationalization did not disappear, however, but retained some popularity among rural laborers and urban workers in Ireland and the diaspora. Harold Rylett remained a Georgite in the face of accusations of stirring up dissent from Parnellites. In 1884 he cofounded the Irish Land Restoration Society in Belfast, and George returned to address one of their rallies, joined by John Ferguson, Edward McHugh and Richard McGhee from Scotland. Although the movement had some success, it struggled to survive the tensions wrought by the 1886 Home Rule crisis.[141] Rylett moved to England, where he continued to promote George's work, organizing a popular edition of *Progress and Poverty* and contributing to the *Single Tax* paper in London and the American *National Single Taxer* as their England correspondent.[142] George visited Ireland on three more occasions in the 1880s, but these were brief stops on tours mainly focused on Scotland and England. He claimed he was now "given the cold shoulder" by Irish nationalists in England, and although he was invited to speak in Dublin in 1884, Davitt vocally sought to allay concerns that it might be "an effort to create agitation in favour of land nationalisation."[143] At one National League meeting George was denounced by a Catholic priest as a "hybrid between an Englishman and a Yankee," combining familiar Anglophobia with resentments toward incoming Americans.[144] Following his 1884 tour of Britain, which was largely financed by Helen Taylor, George concluded that Scotland possessed more fertile ground for his ideas than Ireland, a conclusion that Davitt appeared to accept. Nevertheless, Davitt remained an advocate of nationalization throughout his life.[145]

After the Land War, Peter O'Leary continued to campaign for laborers' rights. The 1883 Labourers (Ireland) Act, which aimed to improve dwellings, provided some acknowledgment of his efforts and those of others, albeit one designed to give the Liberal government credit for assisting laborers without doing very much.[146] In August 1882, Parnell sought to address some of his previous commitments to laborers by agreeing to establish the Irish Labour and Industrial Union, with Davitt's involvement. Yet this body was filled with nationalists rather than laborers' representatives, and O'Leary was not involved. After only a few months it was absorbed into the National League with the agreement of Davitt, with laborers' demands again diluted in a movement driven by farmers' interests. Parnell spoke again, as he had at the 1881 convention, of mutual tolerance between social classes, while nonetheless stating, "to the labourers I would say—do not push your claims beyond the bounds of prudence and moderation."[147]

O'Leary's support for nationalization became less and less vocal, though he maintained links with the Democratic Federation and organized talks by Hyndman and William Morris at the Southwark branch of the Irish National League. Morris impressed O'Leary with his knowledge of Irish folklore, but the revolutionary ambiance disappointed Morris, who wrote to his daughter, "Dear me! such [sic] quiet respectable people!"[148] O'Leary remained active in unions among sanitation workers and in the carmen and roadmen's union, and he once spoke at a rally with the leading trade unionist and communist Tom Mann.[149] Given his London base and involvement with urban unions, it is surprising that O'Leary was never really active among urban workers in Ireland, though he was not alone among Land Leaguers on this front. It seems a missed opportunity that he did not seriously attempt to create a combined movement of rural and urban laborers in Ireland and diaspora locations. From the mid-1880s, O'Leary renewed his interest in assisted emigration and worked with an English charity that organized the placing of destitute children in Canadian institutions, and he traveled to Canada to investigate conditions and called for tighter regulation there. During this trip he also visited an Irish colony in Graceville, Minnesota, and returned to St. Paul to give a talk on temperance to the Father Matthew Society.[150] O'Leary also came to represent a type of proto–Gaelic Leaguer in later years, delivering lectures to the Southwark Irish Literary Club on Irish language, archaeology, history, and literature, and he helped to organize the 1888 Irish Exhibition in London.[151] The Southwark club provided a foundation for the Irish Literary Society, launched in 1892 by W. B. Yeats, among others. In the first history of the Irish Literary Revival, O'Leary was briefly mentioned as "a son of the people, belonging to an earlier generation, and deep in ideas upon ancient Ireland."[152]

O'Leary's transnational life offers an intriguing perspective on the Land League and illuminates how peripatetic activism was not confined to the leadership cadre. Traveling between Ireland, England, the United States, and Canada, he consciously situated the Irish laborers' cause in a transatlantic context and aimed to cultivate a diaspora sensibility through his travels. In England he spoke on the "Irish in America" and in the United States he spoke on the "Irish in England," and he gave lectures on "The Union of the Irish Race all over the World" for both audiences, reflecting his sense of himself as an agent for strengthening links between different emigrant centers and with Ireland.[153] These travels also led him to cultivate a sense of Irish ethnic superiority as a European nation. Consideration of the transnational dimensions of the Land War entails investigating external influences within Ireland as well as looking outward. Visitors to Ireland, including O'Leary, George, Taylor, and the miners, interlinked the networks of the Land League, trade unionism, socialism, women's rights, and the supporters of land nationalization. Ultimately, they met with limited success in advancing nationalization as Land League policy, but they did make important contributions to debates about reform and to the internationalization of the Land War, and they heightened the sense that it was not an isolated campaign solely concerned with national goals.

Marguerite Moore

Land Reform, Feminism, and Nationalism

In 1888 Marguerite Moore traveled to Washington, DC, for the International Council of Women conference, which brought together women's rights campaigners from several countries. The only attendee from Ireland, she was there to represent the American Woman Suffrage Association. Moore told fellow delegates that, through the Ladies' Land League, "we Irish women have already taken our place in the political van. When our brothers were imprisoned we stepped forward and carried on the work."[1] Four years earlier Moore had emigrated to New York, where she became known as a veteran of the Land War, during which her activities in Ireland and "in the cities of Great Britain advanced her into the front rank of agitators." Some journalists even linked her with the plotters behind the infamous 1882 Phoenix Park murders, but this was a fabrication: at that time she was serving a jail sentence in Tullamore for organizing resistance to evictions.[2] During the Land War, Moore traveled throughout the country and regularly crossed the Irish Sea, mobilizing support and integrating Ladies' Land League branches in England and Scotland with the organization in Ireland. She became friends with Henry and Annie George and later joined them in New York, where she was active in numerous progressive causes, including the single tax movement, labor and women's rights, and humanitarianism, while remaining engaged with Irish nationalism over the next decades. During the revolutionary years of 1912–23 she provided a direct link between the Ladies' Land League and a new generation of Cumann na mBan activists.

From the United Irishmen to the War of Independence, the figure of the wandering agitator features often in the history of Irish nationalism and has been generally considered in male terms.[3] Studies of Anna Parnell have challenged this, and the history of the Ladies' Land League, which represented a marked advance in Irish women's activism in land reform and nationalism, is most often told from her perspective, as she was its leader. Marguerite Moore's story presents an alternative view.[4] Although the Ladies' Land League came to an abrupt end in August 1882 in acrimonious division with the male Land League leadership, Moore remained active in subsequent decades and continued to advance the alliances that were forged during the Land War. By the late 1880s, feminism had moved to the center of her activities in New York, but it was combined with nationalist convictions rather than in constant tension with them. This nationalism was sometimes colorfully expressed: Moore owned a pet parrot that repeatedly squawked "God Save Ireland" and "Erin go bragh."[5] Her activism disrupted gender expectations and her trips between Ireland, Scotland, and England during the Land War illuminate the relationship between branches of the Ladies' Land League in Ireland and Britain and help to recover the geography of the organization and its members in Britain—a topic that has received little scholarly attention. After the Land War and into the twentieth century the progressive politics that Moore developed in Ireland translated into a variety of political, social, and cultural causes in the United States.

The Ladies' Land League

The Ladies' Land League emerged in a period that historian Karen Offen has characterized as one of "internationalizing feminism" in Europe.[6] It appeared in Ireland at a time of increased opportunities for women's activism in new suffrage societies in Dublin and Belfast and in the campaigns to oppose the Contagious Diseases Acts of the 1860s, which enforced compulsory medical examinations for sex workers.[7] Along with the men's Land League, the Ladies' Land League reflected an era of expanding mass politics, when new arenas of political participation emerged beyond ballot box reforms. The organization was also shaped by movement between different places, and the cosmopolitan Parnell family—sisters Anna and Fanny and their mother Delia—were central to its foundation. In the early 1870s Fanny and Delia lived in Paris, and during the Franco-Prussian War they volunteered to nurse the wounded and raise funds for the women's committee of the American

Ambulance. They later moved to the United States, and it was in New York that the Ladies' Land League was first established in October 1880, following from Fanny and Anna's management of the Irish Relief Fund. In a letter published in the *Irish World*, Fanny Parnell called for Irishwomen to "put their shoulders to the wheel" and create a women's league, which was later changed to "Ladies" to lend a more respectable air. The league held their first meeting at the Cooper Union, where the main address was delivered by Michael Davitt, who was joined on the platform by Delia Parnell, Ellen Ford and Henry George.[8]

The organization grew rapidly in the United States. The following month Fanny Parnell boasted to Davitt that branches were "springing up all over the country, and bid fair soon to outrival the men."[9] These branches coordinated massive fundraising for Ireland, similar to the men's branches in the United States. Anna Parnell returned home from New York and, following discussions with Davitt, set up the Ladies' Land League in Ireland in January 1881. According to Henry George, she was quickly recognized as the "boss" of the organization.[10] The Ladies' Land League of Great Britain soon got underway as well, and by 1882 the movement comprised thousands of members and some 800 branches worldwide, with some 500 in Ireland, 225 in the United States, at least 48 in Britain, and others scattered in Canada and Australasia.[11] The headquarters in Dublin received funds collected in Ireland, the United States, Scotland, England, Canada, Australia, New Zealand, and Argentina, as well as individual donations from France, Poland, Spain, and Switzerland.

Marguerite Moore played a pivotal role in the Ladies' Land League as a roaming agitator. She was not on the executive committee, but part of a "corps of organisers," in the words of Davitt, who also mistakenly described her as "an American."[12] Moore was born in Waterford City in July 1846, the oldest daughter of Garret Nagle, who appears to have managed the post office and rented properties in the city. He died in 1849, and her mother, Mary Jane, died in 1857. Orphaned, Moore and her sister then entered the Sacred Heart convent school in Roscrea, Co. Tipperary as boarders, under the guardianship of a priest. Both parents had named Marguerite as a beneficiary in their wills, which appears to have paid for her education and provided an inheritance of £250 when she reached adulthood. Shortly after her seventeenth birthday, she married John Henry Moore, a man from Galway who ran a hotel in

Greencastle, Donegal. Moore rarely spoke about him publicly and little more is known. Moore was young when she married; while there was some variation according to region and social class, the average marrying age for women at this time was about twenty-five years. When she came of age to receive her inheritance, her husband, legally named the secondary beneficiary, immediately pursued additional payments in court from a factor formerly employed by her father, with limited success. Moore gave birth to eight children between 1868 and 1878, six of whom survived. In 1872 the family moved from Waterford to Moville, Donegal, near her husband's hotel. Not much more is known about her early life, but Moore sometimes referred to eminent family connections. Her first cousin was the well-known nun Margaret Anna Carroll (Mother Austin), who spent most of her life in the United States and published several notable works relating to the Sisters of Mercy. Moore also claimed that her father was related to Mary Nagle, the mother of the statesman and philosopher Edmund Burke.[13]

How a married women with six surviving children, the youngest three years old and the oldest thirteen, found the time and the resources to dedicate so much of her life to the land movement is not completely clear. Certainly her inheritance helped, but £250 would not have made her independently wealthy.[14] It seems that in 1881 Moore relocated with her youngest children to Phibsborough in Dublin, while the older children remained in Donegal; presumably her husband provided support. The move would have involved leaving him, at least on a temporary basis, which was unusual for a middle-class woman in nineteenth-century Ireland. In 1884 she emigrated with four of her children to the United States. She would later describe herself as a widow and indicate that her husband died before the family emigrated.[15] Moore's continued activism in the United States suggests some degree of financial independence. She earned money from journalism and public speaking, but it does not seem that she depended on this income to survive.

The Land League had a strong presence on Donegal's Inishowen peninsula, and the Ladies' Land League took root there quickly. The Moville branch, among the first in Ireland, started in January 1881, with Moore and at least fifty other members. Moore viewed the land question in Ulster as one in which the "Catholic, Protestant, or Presbyterian tenant farmer were equally oppressed" and maintained that class-based tensions about rents and evictions allowed them to band "together for a common cause." For the Moville branch, their biggest occasion came on a wet Sunday in May 1881, when Anna Parnell visited the village and spoke with Moore and James Coll McLoughlin, president of the Derry Land League, in front of a crowd estimated in the thousands. The rally came on the back of the controversial arrests of two local Land Leaguers, Crampsey and Diver, which intensified activity in the area. Moore urged the crowd to be defiant in the face of repression and promised there were enough women to take the place of every man imprisoned. She closed with a poem about emigration, a topic that featured regularly in her speeches, which she considered a sad consequence of land inequality. Parnell told local women to prepare for the imminent suppression of the Land League and offered warm praise to the local branch and Moore.[16] It seems likely that at this meeting Parnell encouraged Moore to take on a national role, and that she was receptive. Up to that point, her skills for organization and public speaking were mainly deployed in Donegal. By the end of the year she had visited branches and organized relief in villages and towns in Armagh, Carlow, Wicklow, Leitrim, Mayo, Kilkenny, Dublin, King's County, Kerry, and southern parts of Cork, nearly three hundred and fifty miles from her home in Moville.[17] The Ladies' Land League also introduced Moore to a type of "Dublin bohemia with Parisian overtones" that included the writers Katherine Tynan and Hannah Lynch. Lynch and her sisters had previously lived in Spain, Austria, France and Italy, and for Tynan they brought a certain cosmopolitanism to the Ladies' Land League. Moore may even have shared something of this background, as she later alluded to having "spent several years" in Paris and London, but she was not precise about when she lived there.[18]

Moore quickly earned a reputation as a spirited and eloquent speaker. Her talks primarily emphasized the importance of practical relief and fundraising. In Hacketstown, Co. Carlow she told women their main duty was "to help the poor and afflicted, particularly the families of those innocent noble men who are suffering for Ireland's cause and the families of evicted tenants," who, without the Ladies' Land League, would be forced to emigrate.[19] Underscoring the charitable side of their work was a means to avoid discussing boycotting and resisting evictions, activities which could lead to arrest, though her speeches did take some bellicose turns. Policeman frequently came to take notes at meetings and were ridiculed by Moore. When a constable asked for her name in Rathdangan, Co. Wicklow, she replied, "I am not afraid to give my name: but I do hope no Irish girl will ever take a policeman's name," which apparently drew laughter from the crowd.[20] Similar to Anna Parnell, newspapers regularly commented on Moore's sense of humor.[21] Jokes by male leaders in their speeches were observed to a lesser extent, raising the question of whether the men were more humorless, but also suggesting that the Ladies' Land League used humor as a way of negotiating the newness of women public speakers for their audiences, as speaking at nationalist events had been previously confined to men.

Along with Moore, several organizers made arduous travels across Ireland, facilitated by expanding railways and communications, to establish new branches, record evictions, and document poverty and police brutality. Efficient administration was characteristic of the organization, which systematically recorded the relief grants distributed to evicted tenants and prisoners' families and required the families—or the branches representing them—to return detailed forms printed by the central branch.[22] Along with financial assistance, in late 1881 the league initiated a scheme to provide temporary wooden huts for evicted families. Stoves were imported from Glasgow, timber was prepared in Dublin, and some two hundred huts were erected that looked remarkably modern in appearance.[23] Interestingly, when the National Folklore Commission recorded local histories some fifty years later, a Leitrim woman recounted how the wooden huts, and the American dimension of the Ladies' Land League, were prominent in local memory of the Land War era.[24]

The Ladies' Land League moved well beyond the provision of relief. When the male leadership was imprisoned in October 1881, the women took control of the movement. Initially the male leaders believed that women were unlikely to be arrested and could simply hold the fort while they were incarcerated. For the same reason, the Land League invited Archbishop Croke to take on the role of president at this time, though he declined.[25] Yet the Ladies' Land League became a radical force that, according to one contemporary observer, "very soon outleagued the League."[26] They sought to implement the rent strike announced in the No Rent Manifesto, issued after the men's imprisonment, as well as organizing resistance to evictions. After the suppression of the *United Ireland* newspaper, Hannah Lynch succeeded in maintaining its weekly appearance through clandestine printing "in various centres—sometimes at Liverpool or even as far away as Paris."[27]

At the 1888–89 Special Commission on Parnellism and Crime, Moore was listed as a person "who paid for the commission of crime" during the Land War, along with Anna Parnell, Hannah Reynolds, Hannah Lynch, and Clare Stritch.[28] This claim was exaggerated and the commission was ultimately discredited, but, decades later, Jennie O'Toole's daughter revealed some of her mother's "undercover work," which involved orchestrating "the printing and circulation of lists of the names and addresses of the members of juries in agrarian trials." The lists were printed in Liverpool and sent to the Land League offices in Dublin; when staff refused to accept them, upon realizing their content, O'Toole borrowed a carriage and coachman and distributed the bundles herself.[29] At the time, Henry George believed that the women were subject to "atrocious calumnies," and that records "were falsified to prove that [Anna Parnell] and her assistants were guilty of indecencies."[30] O'Toole's account comes with the caveat that it was indirectly recounted over sixty years later, but it is suggestive of some of the clandestine aspects of the women's organization.

In December 1881, the authorities declared the Ladies' Land League an illegal organization, on the basis of an archaic law designed to control sex workers. Fearing a police sweep and hoping to ensure enough time to coordinate a response, Moore sailed to Scotland, and Anna Parnell and Nannie Lynch to England.[31] In their absence, Annie George, Henry's wife, chaired meetings and stored the printing plates for *United Ireland* under her bed until they were shipped to Liverpool.[32] In late December, Moore and Parnell returned to a confrontational atmosphere in Ireland. The manifesto to "The Women of Ireland," issued on Christmas Day, called on branches to ignore the police and to stage simultaneous protests on 1 January 1882. If arrested, members were advised to refuse bail and go to prison, which soon occurred, when Bridget McCormack was jailed in Limerick. Extra soldiers were positioned outside the prison, and protests at her arrest led to the further imprisonment of three local men.[33] In April, Anne Kirk, Mary O'Connor, and Hannah

Reynolds were imprisoned as well, with Kirk sentenced on the grounds of acting as an "emissary of an illegal society" and "creating discord". She had been investigating claims that the construction of wooden cabins was being prevented by Clifford Lloyd, a resident magistrate who arrived in Limerick via British Burma and Egypt. Compared with the more comfortable situation of the male leaders imprisoned in Kilmainham, some of these women faced twenty-two hours a day in solitary confinement, and when questioned in Parliament the chief secretary acknowledged their harsh conditions.[34] In some localities, women activists were not themselves arrested, but punished by the arrests of male relatives.[35] In all, thirteen members of the Ladies' Land League were jailed in 1882, including Marguerite Moore.

During this tense period, Henry George's letters in the *Irish World* reported "speeches of the most defiant kind from Mrs Moore," who maintained that "the law which took the men's arms could not touch the women's tongues."[36] George had met Moore when he arrived in Ireland in late 1881 and accompanied her to a number of evictions. In February, Moore was arrested for establishing a branch of an unlawful association in Ballycumber, King's County.[37] She remained free while awaiting her court hearing and traveled to speak in Ulster and then northern England in the days around St. Patrick's Day, and her new notoriety drew large audiences. Speaking in Newcastle and Birmingham, Moore said she welcomed imprisonment and declared that Irishwomen were "as willing to fill the gaols as the Irishmen were," calling on those with a vote in the audience to "avenge her at the ballot box."[38] At her hearing in April, the court heard that she had traveled to King's County to aid the families of three recently imprisoned men by forming a local branch of the Ladies' Land League with about forty members. A policeman testified that she denounced Chief Secretary Forster and spoke of the Great Famine, when "the people were left to die of starvation on the roadside," because "there was no Land League." Moore contested this report and claimed that the Ladies' Land League was a "charitable organisation" that sought "to perform the true Christian works of comforting those in prison, consoling the afflicted, feeding the hungry." The chief justice decided her aim was to "create discontent in the minds of the people" and sentenced her to six months in Tullamore jail. She was released in less than three, emerging to a cheering crowd.[39]

Across emigrant branches of the Ladies' Land League, the imprisonment of women, referred to in the *Irish World* as "proto-martyrs," stirred up more support.[40] Moore was already a familiar figure among Irish communities in Scotland and northern England; when her sentence prevented a planned trip to Scotland at Easter, she instead sent a letter that was enthusiastically applauded by a crowd of five hundred people when read by John Ferguson in Dundee.[41] Along with Anna Parnell and Kathleen Burke, a member of the Dublin executive committee, Moore's tramping back and forth between Ireland and Britain inspired new emigrant branches and spurred on existing ones. These visits established a sense of personal connection to Moore and Anna Parnell among emigrant members that helped integrate the Ladies' Land League across the Irish sea.

The Ladies' Land League in Scotland and England

The organization called the Ladies' Land League of Great Britain in reality reflected a loose association of individual branches that radiated from the Dublin headquarters rather than the first British branch in London. While this study has identified forty-eight branches in England and Scotland (there were none in Wales), there were surely more. The first was established near Clapham, south London, in February 1881, with the Louisiana-born Frances Genevieve Donovan Sullivan as president. Sullivan's husband was the journalist and Home Ruler A. M. Sullivan, and she was friends with Michael Davitt, whom she visited in Portland prison. The leading members of the branch included Helen Taylor and Hannah Lynch, who seemed to balance roles in both Dublin and London.[42] Another branch soon followed, in Newcastle, which quickly grew to about 130 members.[43] In Liverpool Mary Agnes Bligh, whose husband, Alexander, was president of the city's Land League, started another branch. The response there was at first underwhelming, though when Anna Parnell returned in November, "the hall was crowded in every part, and great numbers who could not obtain admission remained in the street till the close of the meeting." Also in attendance were RIC constables who had shadowed Parnell over from Ireland.[44] By the summer of 1881 there were more branches in Dundee, Glasgow, Manchester, and several smaller cities and towns across Britain that consistently sent money to Ireland over the next year, with branch names appearing in the fund columns of the *Nation* and *Freeman's Journal*.

Following the arrests of the Land League leaders in October 1881, Moore and Anna Parnell toured Britain extensively, particularly northern England and Scotland. In November, Parnell visited Bradford, Blackburn, Huddersfield, and Liverpool, and Moore spoke in Birmingham, Durham, Stockon-on-Tees, Darlington, and Jarrow, where she was introduced as an "organiser of the North of England Land League." Proceeds from admission went to the central fund in Dublin, via the Land League bank in Paris. Along with expanding the branches in Britain, Parnell and Moore sought recruits to come to Ireland. They approached the Liverpool branch organizer, Kate Kearney, who was unable to go, and they asked Helen Taylor to suggest a volunteer who "could come over and devote herself to following the police in order to see their brutality to the people." Parnell also wrote to her sister Fanny asking her to send volunteers from the United States, whose expenses would be covered.[45]

In the northeast of England, some branches were established under Moore's name. In all there were eighteen women's branches across this region, where Irish immigrants represented about 6 percent of the population. At a rally in Jarrow, which held a large branch of some ninety women, Moore spoke and condemned the 1881 Land Act and the Liberal government. Regarding the name of the organization, she claimed they "called it the Ladies' Land League for the sake of euphony, but it was women they wanted, not ladies." She shared the platform with John Bryson of the Northumberland Miners' Association, who had visited Ireland twice that summer and told the audience that he found "no difference" between the Land League and trade unions, and that they should view the outlawing of the Land League as a blow to workers' right to unionize anywhere. Two weeks later, in Stockton-on-Tees, Moore spoke again alongside Bryson and Joseph Cowen before an overflowing hall. Cowen declared that "the state of Ireland just now would be a disgrace to the most despotic dynasty in Europe" and urged the Ladies' Land League to "agitate fearlessly and without ceasing." Moore's talk, which closed the rally, detailed the poverty she had encountered in rural Ireland and the "cruelty and gross injustice" of the police and army. Along with Kate Scallon, head of the Newcastle branch, she urged local women to "rally around the flag of Ireland," and a considerable number were enrolled as members that evening, while Annie Kennedy was named secretary of the new Stockton-on-Tees branch.[46]

While Moore's speeches called on the women present to join in the "work of charity," these meetings were highly political. Parnell praised the "great institution of boycotting," which had become a very effective weapon in the Land War, and Moore delivered strong critiques of government policy and cheered the No Rent Manifesto. What was the difference, Moore asked a Dundee audience, between the Liberals and Conservatives, urging them to look on one as "Beelzebub, and the other as Lucifer."[47] In Glasgow's city hall, she poked fun at Forster and defied him to arrest her, declaring it "an honour and a pride to go to jail" and promising she would not "come out anything better than when I went in." She was joined that evening by John Ferguson, the leading Land League figure in Scotland, who proposed directly sending a letter to Gladstone on behalf of the city's Irish community. However, Michael Clark of the city's Land League "totally objected," and Moore's speech referred scathingly to the Prime Minister, leading Ferguson to concede there was not "perfect unanimity" and withdraw his proposal.[48]

Hostility toward the Ladies' Land League increased in the British press as the organization moved to the forefront of the unrest in Ireland. Reporting on Moore's speeches, the *Scotsman* advocated the arrest of women "who stomped the three kingdoms, pouring forth on the Ministry a deluge of shrill invective." Referring to her cheering of the No Rent Manifesto, the newspaper maintained that "the gullibility of the Irish people, and their readiness to confide in unworthy leaders, have been proved to be almost inexhaustible."[49] When Parnell spoke in front of a massive crowd of some six thousand people in a field in Glasgow, the local press noted her "violent and vituperative" words for Gladstone.[50] In Blackburn, the police tried but failed to stop Parnell speaking at the Exchange Hall. Outside she was booed by Liberal party supporters, and inside she reassured the audience she could handle the jeers of the Blackburn protesters, as the Scottish ones had thrown stones.[51] The *Liverpool Mercury* wrote dismissively of the Ladies' Land League, expressing hope that its outlawing would "bring to a reasonable frame of mind . . . infatuated women who are trying to do so much mischief."[52] That did not happen in Ireland or Britain, however, and meetings still attracted large crowds.

Where were the branches located in Britain, who organized them, and who attended demonstrations? Of the forty-eight Ladies' Land League branches identified in this study, the majority were located in the industrialized towns and cities of northern England and Scotland, reflecting the routes taken by Moore and Parnell on their speaking tours. Just eight branches existed south of Liverpool: at least five in London, and one each in Birmingham, Nottingham, and Newark-on-Trent. Most branches were found in the northeast (eighteen), Lancashire (twelve), Scotland (five), and Yorkshire (five).[53] There were no women's branches in Wales and only one Land League branch in Cardiff, though the Home Rule party did enjoy support there.[54] Only scant evidence for these branches has survived, but it seems that the largest branches in Glasgow, Newcastle, Dundee, London, Liverpool, and Manchester each held between one hundred to two hundred members, while some of the smaller branches could have had as few as ten members. An estimate would put membership across all branches in Britain at under two thousand women.

Some secretaries considered sending statements along with their subscriptions to the central fund, but, unfortunately, the organization resolved that just the branch name, amount, and sender's name be included in the lists published in the *Nation* and *Freeman's Journal*.[55] Nonetheless, these details still provide us with clues as to the makeup of the movement. From the names of more than one hundred committee women in Britain that accompanied subscriptions sent to Dublin, we can identify forty-four of them in the census records, giving us some perspective—albeit fragmentary—on the people involved. About 68 percent were second-generation Irish, the rest were Irish-born, with one American. There were more single than married women members, at 63 percent. For second-generation Irish members, the place of birth does not always match the place of residence, and when considered with siblings' (often different) birthplaces, this indicates a certain mobility among emigrant members in Britain. The Ladies' Land League, as was sometimes the case with female political activism more generally, was portrayed as an upper-class or bourgeois phenomenon by some contemporaries on the right and the left.

The ostensibly middle-class composition of the first branch in London reflected the numerous Irish professionals who made their home there in the Victorian era.[56] Yet the picture that emerges elsewhere in Britain is one of a primarily working-class membership. Chapter 3 takes a detailed look at the occupations of members in Dundee, the majority of whom were textile factory workers. It was possible to identify here the occupations of thirty-seven committee members from across Britain, and they included fourteen homemakers or unemployed married women, eleven textile factory workers, four dressmakers, three shop assistants, two domestic servants, two teachers, and one newsagent.[57] This profile generally corresponds with the one outlined by D. A. J. MacPherson in Jarrow, Northumberland, where many Ladies' Land League members were from "reasonably well-off working class backgrounds."[58]

Branch locations suggest that the Ladies' Land League found considerable support among textile workers in Scotland, Lancashire, and Yorkshire. In Manchester and neighboring Lancashire mill towns, the number of branches suggests that Irish women played active roles in migrant associations in the late nineteenth century, contrary to one assessment that they were "conspicuously absent."[59] In Liverpool there were comparatively fewer employment opportunities for women, which could explain the initially slow response to the league in a city with such a large Irish community. In the northeast, women textile workers were not numerous, and Irish women worked in a variety of occupations. The specific occupations for members in this region are difficult to trace in the census, but information on male family members provides a mixed picture of skilled laborers, shopkeepers, and artisans. The Newcastle branch president was second-generation immigrant Kate Scallon, whose occupation is unknown, but whose father was a local fruit and vegetable merchant. Annie Kennedy of the Stockon-on-Tees branch was the daughter of a local Irish shipyard laborer.[60] The Ladies' Land League flourished in the northeast partly because of a congenial environment and support offered by Joseph Cowen, trade unions, and the *Newcastle Chronicle*.

There was a generational dynamic in the transnational Ladies' Land League. Historian Timothy Meagher has pointed to a "generational juncture" in Irish America between Famine immigrants and their American-born children.[61] The Land War caught this post-Famine generation in their late teens and early twenties, and they overlapped with older, Irish-born migrants in diaspora branches. This was evident in the very first women's branch in New York, in which the treasurer was Irish immigrant Fanny Maguire and one of the organizers was her daughter Mary, born in the United States in 1862.[62] In one large branch in Woonsocket, Rhode Island, the majority were "young, with an average age of almost twenty-five."[63] A similar profile can be found in Britain: among the forty-four women identified here, 25 percent were aged twenty or less and 82 percent were aged thirty or less. There were more unmarried women, though the role of married women might be obscured; they could donate money through their husbands' involvement in the Land League and are not then visible on subscription lists, one of the few sources available for analyzing the movement. Younger members included both first- and second-generation migrants. At one Glasgow rally, Moore was joined on the platform by local branch president Ellen Quigley, a twenty-one-year-old seamstress from Donegal and a supporter of Henry George. This generational dynamic was not confined to the diaspora: in the central branch in Dublin, several members were in their early twenties or younger, "of an age to enjoy these activities," including the Lynch-Cantwell sisters, Katherine Tynan, Jennie O'Toole, and Hannah Reynolds.[64] In contrast, the men's Land League drew members from across generations and included many who had been active in the 1860s.[65] The Ladies' Land League differed in that it represented a more novel opportunity for women's activism in the land and nationalist movements. It appears that mobilization occurred at least partly through a generational consciousness among women born in the decade after the Famine who sought greater opportunities for political activism in both Ireland and the diaspora.

Humanitarianism was a significant element of diaspora activism in both the men's and women's leagues. Moore's speeches in Britain often referred to the "work of charity," and Frances Genevieve Sullivan described the Ladies' Land League as a "great social philanthropic movement" that was "designed to save from pauperism and starvation or compulsory emigration thousands of women and children." For Fanny Parnell it was a "work of philanthropy and humanity."[66] The Ladies' Land League emerged during a period identified by scholars when "female internationalism" expanded in the United Kingdom and when an "internationally oriented humanitarian impulse" developed in the United States, in which women took leading roles.[67] The American section of the International Red Cross, for example, was established in 1881 by Clara Barton, who, like Fanny and Delia Parnell, had volunteered to provide civilian aid during the Franco-Prussian War and returned to the United States committed to organizing relief for famine, war, and other disasters.[68] In Ireland, women's philanthropic work expanded significantly in the second half of the nineteenth century and was linked to growing numbers of women religious.[69] The Catholic Church's relief work was also globally oriented, "part and parcel of the belle époque's 'golden age' of international civil society."[70] Marguerite Moore and the Ladies' Land League reflected this expanding transnational humanitarianism as well as a Catholic rhetoric of charity.

Moore consistently spoke and wrote with admiration for the "religious sisterhoods" who worked "for the advancement and uplifting of the Irish race." In the early twentieth century, she was the guest speaker at Catholic fundraising events in New Orleans, which was off her usual East Coast circuit. She was invited by her first cousin—Margaret Anna Carroll, or Mother Austin, from Tipperary—who founded a convent in New Orleans in 1869, and whom Moore visited in her first year in the United States. Carroll published widely, including a history of the Sisters of Mercy and a biography of Catherine McAuley, founder of the order.[71] Moore's admiration for her notable cousin seems to have influenced the religious concepts of charity and sacrifice that she regularly evoked at Ladies' Land League meetings. She looked upon women religious as pioneers, a view that was shared in the organization. In 1881 in Queen's County, Ireland, for example, one member explained Ladies' Land League activities in terms of the history of Irish women religious: "Who was it that tended the wounded soldiers of ungrateful England, or who nursed both northerners and confederates during the American civil war? . . . The poor Irish nuns."[72] Writing for the American *Catholic World*, Moore singled out for praise Agnes Morrogh Bernard, who had founded a convent, a school, and later a woollen mills in Foxford, Co. Mayo, to counter hardship and high levels of emigration in the district. If Morrough Barnard had not been a nun, Moore maintained, she "would have been called a 'new woman.'"[73] Moore's Catholicism and progressive activism occasionally came into conflict, such as during the Edward McGlynn protests in New York in the 1880s. Generally, however, Catholicism partly informed her views of social reform and the roles of women within it.

Humanitarian concern about the famine conditions that appeared in 1879–80 was a major motivating factor for many members of the Ladies' Land League. The organization first emerged from the Irish Relief Fund in New York that was established in response to the crisis. When discussing the Great Famine of 1845–52, Anna Parnell remarked that, "even to persons who were not in existence when they occurred, the horrors of these years had a vividness almost as great as actual experience of them could produce."[74] Moore warned of the return of famine to Ireland and declared that in the past the "bones of thousands of her [Ireland's] children whitened the bottom of the Atlantic. And why was that? It was because the Irishman owned not the soil he tilled."[75] Jennie O'Toole later recalled that "in the autumn of 1879 it became evident that the country was confronted with another '47. Famine menaced the poorest districts, those that were most Irish and most thickly populated."[76] Collective memories of the Great Famine were prevalent among members during the Land War, and the parallels drawn with the 1840s powerfully mobilized support.

At the same time, the activities of the Ladies' Land League represented more than a form of humanitarianism. Heather Laird has emphasized the difference between charity aimed at relieving poverty within existing structures and charity that challenges the status quo.[77] The Ladies' Land League in Ireland and the diaspora engaged in a form of oppositional humanitarianism distinctive from mainstream charity. According to Jennie O'Toole, from the outset Anna Parnell "resisted a suggestion that the new league should be run on the lines of the St. Vincent de Paul Society" and viewed it as a political organization instead.[78] Their opponents often agreed. After Moore spoke along with Ellen Quigley in Glasgow, the *North British Daily Mail* accused them of hiding behind the "cloak of philanthropy" to engage in "work which cannot by any stretch of words be called charitable."[79] The same reproach was also voiced by the Catholic archbishop of Dublin, Edward McCabe, who charged the women with operating under the "flimsy pretext of charity."[80] These accusations also functioned to promote respectable relief initiatives, including the

Duchess of Marlborough Fund, yet such criticisms seem to have had little impact on the popularity of the Ladies' Land League. Its mix of humanitarianism, nationalism, and social radicalism made for a very potent force over the course of the Land War. This was also true for emigrant branches of the men's Land League, whose main activity was also fundraising. However, beyond the reproaches of Clan na Gael's William Carroll—that charity should be kept separate from politics—their actions were not typically categorized as charitable.[81]

Emigration to New York

Within weeks of her release from Tullamore in June 1882, Marguerite Moore became involved in further controversy at a large demonstration in Listowel, Co. Kerry. When the RIC and the army attempted to break up the crowd, Moore instructed her audience to reassemble one mile away, beside the train station. The RIC and the army reappeared there and charged the crowd, this time firing shots as stones flew in their direction. Between thirty to fifty demonstrators were injured, and while Moore narrowly escaped and avoided arrest, four men were imprisoned, including the nationalist editor of the *Kerry Sentinel*, Tim Harrington.[82] Afterward, Harrington wrote to the Ladies' Land League suggesting that this style of confrontation was counterproductive, and that the episode had undermined the Kerry Land League.[83]

The Listowel riot happened one month after the Kilmainham "treaty" with Gladstone and the release of the male Land League leaders from jail, and Harrington's letter highlighted new questions regarding the future of the Ladies' Land League. Already in May, Charles Stewart Parnell had told Henry George that the women "must be greatly tired," and in July he recommended that the organization be limited to distributing relief under his direction.[84] The men's executive accused the Ladies' Land League of spending more money in eight months than they had in two years, yet the women had been tasked with implementing the No Rent Manifesto, which Charles Stewart Parnell knew would be very costly when he issued it from prison.[85] Anna Parnell considered the Kilmainham treaty a surrender of principles and later wrote that "people with aims so radically different and incompatible as the Land League and the Ladies' Land League had no business in the same boat."[86] Fanny Parnell died in July, and the news plunged her sister into a period of ill health. In August the Irish Ladies' Land League disbanded, and Anna Parnell never spoke to her brother again. The new National League replaced the Land League and excluded women in Ireland, though in emigrant branches this was not always the case.[87] The money subscribed to the National League was safeguarded for parliamentary politics, while funds for evicted tenants were now collected separately in the Mansion House Fund run by Dublin's lord mayor, which Charles Stewart Parnell no longer opposed.[88] These funds would later be merged again, but the separation of the humanitarian and nationalist arms of the movement in 1882 served as a means to further minimize women's roles. Irish women's political activism continued in different forms in the late nineteenth century, but in nationalist bodies it was on a notably smaller scale than in the Ladies' Land League.[89]

Moore shared Anna Parnell's disillusion, though she did not break completely with the new National League. In August she addressed the last official convention of the Land League of Great Britain (where Peter O'Leary unsuccessfully proposed nationalization as the new policy), at Manchester's Free Trade Hall, speaking on the platform with Irish party members T. P. O'Connor, Joseph Biggar, and Andrew Commins. Her speech did not openly challenge the other speakers, but it differed markedly in tone from theirs and avoided Biggar and O'Connor's celebratory talk of "victory" and the "different spirit" in which Ireland was now administered. Moore maintained that a legal repression "more hateful and more tyrannical than dared to exist in Russia" was still in place, and singled out John O'Connor Power as a "traitor" for claiming that Irish grievances had been addressed. "Land League principles," she asserted, "would never be torn out of the hearts" of those who had experienced the Land War and declared that its main cause—poverty—had not improved.[90] In September Moore delivered her final talks for the Ladies' Land League in Scotland, during a short tour with the Georgite land reformer Edward McHugh.

In the aftermath of the Land War, Moore found herself marginalized, both as a woman and as someone affiliated with radical land reform, yet she continued to engage with nationalism. She believed Henry George "was the greatest political economist of his day" and on many occasions she shared a platform with George supporters such as McHugh, Harold Rylett, Ellen Quigley, and John Ferguson. Unlike George, however, Moore believed the land question was fundamentally intertwined with nationalist demands; it could not ultimately be solved until "the English had left [Ireland] bag and baggage."[91] In an 1883 lecture in Dublin, Moore emphasized how the history of the Young Ireland movement influenced her nationalism. She argued that the appearance of the *Nation* in 1842 was the first concrete step toward independence and spoke of her admiration for Thomas Davis's attempts "to create an educated people."[92] Davis and A. M. Sullivan's book *The Story of Ireland* (1867), which reflected the Young Ireland ethos, influenced the Ladies' Land League's emphasis on education, and in 1881 Francis Genevieve Sullivan urged British branches to "teach your children and your young friends the history of the past." A Junior Irish Literary Club was established in London, where Children's Land Leagues also appeared. After 1882 some members sought to expand this educational work, though this did not really happen until decades later.[93] Moore fully supported educational schemes and, like many of her contemporaries, viewed women as best suited to running them, "spreading lessons of hope and consolation, and in teaching the people to rely on themselves." Poetry and prose were part of this, and Moore highlighted how the poetry of Speranza—the penname of Jane Francesca Wilde—in the *Nation* during the 1840s had pointed out "the path of educating and making the people of our country fit for liberty." Education and female teachers were vital to the development of a genuine nationalist movement in her view, and Moore stressed in her 1883 lecture that nationalist societies would be better off if they utilized women.[94]

Despite giving the odd public lecture, Moore remained a peripheral figure and soon emigrated to the United States. In December 1883, her eleven-year-old daughter, Lelia, died in Dublin, and four months later Moore sailed to New York with her remaining children, except for her eldest daughter, Catherine.[95] Perhaps the family tragedy contributed to a desire for a fresh start, but it seems likely that frustrations with her limited political opportunities were push factors. In New York, Moore could continue the activism she began in the Ladies' Land League and maintain her links with Henry and Annie George. In 1884, Henry

George had toured Britain and returned for a short time to Ireland in March and April. Shipping records show that he sailed back to New York from Queenstown, via Liverpool, arriving on 21 April 1884. Just one week later, Moore arrived in New York via the same route.[96] The family rented a small apartment on West 15th Street in Manhattan, before later moving to the Bronx. Moore quickly became a familiar face at Irish political and cultural events in New York and on the East Coast.[97] By the 1890s she was a "well known Single Taxer" and also active in a range of movements and associations including the National Woman Suffrage Association, the Universal Peace Union, Henry George's 1886 mayoral campaign, the United Labor Party, the Irish National League, the Women's Single Tax Club, the New York Women's Press Club, and temperance societies.[98]

Moore's introduction to reformist and radical circles in New York came about through her links with George and former Land Leaguers. In the 1880s, there was considerable overlap between Irish nationalism and labor politics in the city through the *Irish World* and the Knights of Labor. Moore became involved in George's Single Tax Club and the United Labor Party, which was affiliated with the city's Central Labor Union. In 1886, backed by the United Labor Party, George ran for mayor of New York, coming in second with a large share of the vote. The following year, he ran in the New York state elections, but with more disappointing results. Moore played an active role in both campaigns.[99] In 1887, she collaborated with Edward McGlynn, the Irish American priest and George ally, in the Anti-Poverty Society, which combined Catholic social justice with Georgism and secular reform, continuing, as one study has observed, "the trend begun by the progressive nationalists within the Land League."[100] George acted as vice president, and weekly meetings attracted over two thousand people. Moore's speeches stressed the threat of landlordism in both rural Ireland and industrial America and the similarities behind the causes of social inequality in both places.[101] McGlynn's activities brought him into conflict with the archbishop of New York, Michael Corrigan, and he was censured and ultimately excommunicated. This antagonistic break with the church brought Moore's own relationship with the Catholic hierarchy into tension; at protests for McGlynn, her speeches expressed criticism of Catholic leaders in Irish America and in Ireland, and she encouraged audiences to make their discontent felt by spurning church fundraising.[102]

The networks established by Henry George during the Land War also brought others to New York. In the 1890s Moore revived the personal connections she had made through the Ladies' Land League in Scotland with Ellen Quigley and her husband, Edward McHugh. After the Land War, McHugh formed the National Union of Dock Labourers in Britain, and in 1896 he and Quigley moved to New York to establish an international dockworkers' federation. McHugh and Quigley were dedicated followers of George—even naming their child Henry George McHugh—and they were involved with Moore in the Manhattan Single Tax Club. McHugh threw his full weight behind George's second push for mayor of New York in 1897, but George died five days before the election. His funeral brought together supporters from across the United States.[103] In 1899 Quigley and McHugh returned to Britain, and years later a Ladies' Land League was established on the Scottish island of Barra, which, one study has suggested, took inspiration from Quigley.[104] Similar to Moore, McHugh and Quigley's experiences during the Land War had a lasting impact on their lives.

Alongside her involvement in Georgism, Moore's activities in the suffrage movement led to her becoming a recognized feminist, with one newspaper describing her as one of four "leaders in the movement that is making this the woman's age."[105] When the Ladies' Land League first started, Fanny Parnell maintained that it was not a women's rights organization, yet there were clear overlaps between the movements. Just weeks after her initial call to arms in the *Irish World* in 1880, one front-page article in the same newspaper contended that one of the radical changes of the era was the acknowledgment that "women are entitled to equal political rights with men, to equal rights to common property, to equal rights with men to the inheritance left by parents."[106] From the mid-1880s Moore contributed articles to the weekly *Woman's Journal* and addressed meetings of the New York State Woman Suffrage Association, speaking extensively on voting rights in eastern cities and often sharing a platform with the prominent campaigner Lillie Devereux Blake.[107] In 1886 Moore spoke at a demonstration in Union Square that brought together three different strands of her activism: organized by the Central Labor Union, the meeting was in support of Irish Home

Rule, and the speakers included Devereux Blake.[108] In the 1890s Moore collaborated again with Blake and Susan B. Anthony and was "busy speaking every day" in the constitutional amendment campaign for the women's vote in the state of New York.[109]

Moore's feminism took on an internationalist dimension. In 1888 she attended the first convention of the International Council of Women in Washington, DC, as the delegate of the New York branch of the Woman Suffrage Association. Lasting eight days, the convention partly resulted from the networks developed during the transatlantic tours of Elizabeth Cady Stanton and Susan B. Anthony earlier in the decade and was attended by delegates representing eight different countries—the United States, India, Canada, France, England, Denmark, Norway, and Finland—with Moore representing an American, rather than an Irish, branch. The aim was to form a confederation, exchange ideas "on the great questions now agitating the world," and give women "a realizing sense of their power of combination."[110] In her address Moore expressed her nationalist beliefs, telling fellow delegates, "I stand here as a representative of Irish women . . . having received the highest honor in the power of the English government to bestow upon an Irish woman, that of imprisonment for the love of her country."[111] Moore's attendance did not trigger new links between Ireland and the International Council of Women, however, and an Irish national branch was not formed and affiliated until 1924.[112] Feminist connections also introduced Moore to the peace movement; she became vice president of the New York branch of the Universal Peace Union, which promoted disarmament and arbitration, and cooperated with the Women's Christian Temperance Union. She also spoke at a number of meetings with Belva Lockwood, the women's rights activist who twice ran for president in the 1880s, and Clara Barton.[113]

Moore advocated equal rights, while offering a view of women's distinctive social roles. At one suffrage demonstration, she outlined that "equal rights, not women's rights, are what we want—the right to equal wages for equal work, equal right to own property and equal right to our children."[114] On another occasion, when writing for a Catholic journal, she asserted that the "new woman" was "still tender, loving, gentle, and sympathetic, whether God's will calls her to preside over house and family as queen and mother, to nursing in the hospital ward, teaching in the convent school or . . . reforming and uplifting a people by means of technical education."[115] These comments echoed her and others' speeches in the Ladies' Land League, which sometimes emphasized specific roles for women in education, charity, and in the home, reflecting the power Irish women then held in these spheres.[116]

In 1914 developments in Ireland gripped Irish America, and nationalism returned to the center of Moore's activism. In the early 1900s she had been mainly occupied by the presidential campaign of the Democratic candidate William Jennings Bryan, the Edward McGlynn Monument Association, and the Harlem Equal Rights League, and in 1905 she joined protests at the debarring of women from municipal elections. Apart from politics, her speaking talents were put to use at social events in Brooklyn and New York, where she delivered "humorous Irish sketches."[117] She had always remained involved in nationalism, and since her arrival in 1884 had participated in the American wing of the National League. Despite her associations with Henry George and Anna Parnell, she acted as the secretary and treasurer of the Charles Stewart Parnell branch of the Irish National League in New York, and they evidently held her in high regard. In 1888 a social gathering was organized in her honor in Washington, DC, for "the gratification felt by the organisation in Mrs Moore's work."[118] Following the 1891 split in the Irish Home Rule party, Moore remained a Parnellite. When referring to the anti-Parnellite Irish National Federation that emerged after the split, she lamented how it had been "made a crime to cheer for Parnell."[119] In 1891 she spoke at several public meetings to mark his death, and again on his anniversary.[120] When a Parnell monument in the form of a Celtic cross was proposed in Wicklow in 1895, Moore wrote to *United Ireland* suggesting that the memorial should take a more defiant form: that of "the Irish Wolfhound with head erect, eyes watchful, and fangs exposed to the Saxon wolves across the Channel."[121] Despite Charles Stewart Parnell's split with his sister Anna and his role in the acrimonious demise of the Ladies' Land League, Moore still greatly admired him. At the same time, she also maintained personal links to more militant Irish nationalists in New York. She had attended the same convent school in Tipperary as Mary Jane Irwin, the wife of Jeremiah O'Donovan Rossa, who organized a bombing campaign in Britain in the 1880s. The two women evidently remained friends, and in 1916 Moore delivered the eulogy at the memorial following Irwin's death.[122]

The events of 1914 refocused Moore's attention on Ireland. In March she addressed a United Irish Women rally at Carnegie Hall opposing the potential partition of Ireland suggested in the new Home Rule settlement.[123] The meeting was organized by Gertrude B. Kelly, an Irish nationalist who previously allied with Henry George and Edward McGlynn, who would help to establish the American branch of Cumann na mBan in New York later that year. Kelly invited Moore to address the organization's first meeting, and Moore's presence provided a direct link with the Ladies' Land League; indeed, Moore openly compared the new movement with the generation of female activists of over thirty years earlier.[124] In September 1914 John Redmond called for Irishmen to enlist in the British war effort in a speech that drastically diminished Irish American support for the Home Rule party. The events in Ireland over the following years mobilized huge numbers of Irish Americans in support of independence, and New York saw especially high levels of activity. Moore, who represented something of an elder stateswoman in the new movement, participated widely in rallies, protests, and boycotts. In 1915 she spoke at a meeting in New York with Francis Sheehy Skeffington and was described as a "veteran of the Ladies' Land League" by the *Irish Citizen*, the Dublin-based organ of the suffrage movement.[125] In 1916 she helped raise funds for the families of imprisoned rebels, and in 1920, then seventy-four years of age, she played a role in the American Women Pickets. This group of nationalists and suffragists staged a provocative two-week protest at the British embassy in Washington, DC, chaining themselves to gates in order to raise awareness of British violence in Ireland. In August they coordinated a boycott of British shipping on the Chelsea docks on Manhattan's West Side in protest at the arrest of the Irish archbishop, Daniel Mannix, shortly after he had sailed from New York, and the imprisonment of Cork's lord mayor, Terence MacSwiney. The boycott turned into a massive longshoremen's strike that lasted over three weeks and attracted tremendous publicity.[126] Interestingly, Moore's census return for 1920 listed Irish as her native tongue for the first time, reflecting heightened nationalist feelings on her part.[127]

After 1920 Moore faded from public view. She died in 1933, at the home of her daughter Susan in New York, aged eighty-six.[128] She appears to have returned to Ireland on just one occasion since her arrival in 1884 and later maintained that "every Irish woman who comes to America comes home. . . . I have declared my intention of becoming an American citizen and bringing up my children here in the land of liberty."[129] Moore traveled to Ireland in 1894, ten years after first emigrating, and felt slightly out of place. She found Dublin a changed city, observing that a "new generation had grown up," and that new organizations were on the rise.[130]

Emigration facilitated the development of Moore's multifaceted activism, but her blend of nationalism, feminism, and Georgism first took shape in the Ladies' Land League in Ireland, and through her encounters with Henry George and Anna Parnell. During the Land War she served as a vital link between Ireland and the Ladies' Land League in Scotland and England, and in the United States she brought together networks of nationalists, women's rights activists, and social radicals into the twentieth century. When told primarily from the perspective of Anna Parnell, the history of the Ladies' Land League is one of a short, intense period of women's activism that ended traumatically, in a long-term breach between leading male and female nationalists. Yet, when viewed through the lens of Moore's life, and in adopting a diaspora perspective, it becomes clear that the progressive alliances of the Land War were not wholly supplanted by the National League, but proved resilient. And, rather than being in tension, nationalism and feminism continued to coexist in Moore's activism, albeit this was sometimes a tense coexistence. Moore was occasionally referred to as a socialist in American newspapers, but this was not so accurate as her activities reflected more the middle-class reformism of the single tax movement than revolutionary working-class politics. Although the Ladies' Land League has sometimes been characterized as a middle-class movement and Moore could be seen to reflect this, the branches she started and visited in Scotland and England were often comprised largely of working-class members. How the transnational Ladies' Land League translated into these local settings and mobilized emigrants in new arenas of political activity is the subject of the next chapter.

Jute, Class, and Catholicism

The Ladies' Land League in Dundee, Scotland

In the summer of 1881, over two thousand people squeezed into Dundee's Kinnaird Hall to hear Anna Parnell speak. The leader of the Ladies' Land League had arrived in Scotland a few days earlier to rally emigrant communities in support of the campaign to end land-lordism in Ireland. Speaking in fields and town halls across Scotland, Parnell declared the need for urgent support to avert catastrophe in rural Ireland and pressed her audiences to start branches of the Ladies' Land League. Parnell's appearances attracted much press attention, not least for her description of William Gladstone as a "hypocritical, bloodthirsty miscreant" in front of a huge crowd in Glasgow. That city housed Scotland's largest Irish community, which turned out in large numbers to see her, but she reserved her warmest praise for Dundee, telling her audience there that "no matter what other cities in Scotland might boast of, they in Dundee would always know that they were the first to send help."[1] The following year, John Ferguson, the leader of the Irish Land League in Scotland, congratulated Dundee's Irish women on the way they had "eclipsed all other branches on this side of the water."[2] In the eyes of contemporary leaders, then, there was a striking level of political activism among Irish women in Dundee in the 1880s, yet we know almost nothing about them, and little about the Ladies' Land League outside of Ireland and the United States more generally.

Dundee provided a highly receptive environment for the Ladies' Land League. Its Irish community comprised twice as many women as men—a highly distinctive demographic in the Irish diaspora. Many of them were factory workers in the city's booming jute industry, which earned it the nickname "Juteopolis." The visits of traveling agitators, including Parnell and Marguerite Moore, in addition to the circula-tion of newspapers from Ireland and the United States, were vital in bringing local supporters in Dundee into conversation with the wider world of the Irish Land War. These supporters, who collected funds and attended rallies, are too often considered in the plural, as a mass of anonymous people grouped together by ethnic or political allegiances. Tracing the footprints of grassroots members who left behind no memoirs or speeches comes with its challenges, but the increasing accessibility of digitized genealogical records provides some means to fill out flat descriptions of memberships. These resources allow us to identify women who took on committee or administrative roles in the organization, giving a more textured picture of how the Ladies' Land League worked at the local and personal levels. The image that emerges for Dundee is one where shared employment and local Catholic networks contributed significantly to shaping the branches, and where the members held considerable agency in developing their activities.

Types of emigrant activism varied widely, and recent scholarship has emphasized the diversity and ambiguity of relations between people of Irish birth or descent and the homeland.[3] This complexity can be seen in the reception of the Ladies' Land League in a city where working-class women predominated in the Irish community. Their story contributes to our knowledge of migrant Irishwomen's experiences and political activism.[4] Due to the upper- and middle-class backgrounds of leaders in Ireland and in the major cities of Irish immigration, the Ladies' Land League is often associated with a genteel type of radicalism, yet this is challenged by the Dundee branches, which were overwhelmingly working-class and operated with some independence from the men's Land League. Historians of Irish America have argued that Irishmen's harsh encounters with modern industrial capitalism in nineteenth-century cities led to the fusion of ethnic and class grievances in the Land League, a perspective that also merits consideration with respect to the Ladies' Land League in Dundee.[5] The city's jute mills provided many Irish women with jobs, but the work came with low pay, high rents, health hazards, and congested living conditions.

The Dundee Irish and the Ladies' Land League

After Glasgow, the textile center of Dundee was home to the largest community of Irish immigrants in Scotland at the start of the Land

War in 1879. Throughout the nineteenth century, this fast-growing industrial city became one of the world's premier producers of linen and jute, a coarse fiber used to make carpets, grain bags, and sandbags for use in wartime. Dundee was also a whaling port, and the availability of whale oils used to process raw jute contributed to the industry's rapid expansion from the 1840s, with produce sold in European, Atlantic, and imperial markets.[6] By the century's end, there were over one hundred mills in the city that brought huge fortunes for the so-called jute barons. In comparison to other Scottish cities, the mills gave Dundee a distinctive workforce, with women representing about 75 percent of jute workers, about one-third of them the main breadwinners for their households.[7] The largest mill was the Cox Brothers' Camperdown Works, located in the Lochee neighbourhood, which employed nearly five thousand workers and at one point claimed to be the largest jute factory in the world. Lochee was home to many Irish and in the Whorterbank enclave over half of the residents were Irish immigrants and their children. Although it was sometimes known locally as "Little Tipperary," relatively few migrants there came from that county; most were from Ulster and the north midlands of Ireland. The Camperdown Works was their main source of employment, particularly for women.

Migration from Ireland to Dundee rose along with general movement to Scotland in the 1800s. During the Great Famine, the flows greatly intensified, and about 8 percent of the extraordinary number of emigrants who left Ireland between the Famine and the Irish Revolution arrived in Scotland, providing a ready supply of labor for the expanding mining, steel, textile, and shipbuilding industries.[8] In 1881 Irish-born people counted for about 6 percent of Scotland's population of 3.7 million, and just under one-third of those had arrived in the previous decade. By far the largest concentration could be found in Glasgow, where Irish-born immigrants numbered over 70,000, and communities of 10,000 or less lived in Edinburgh, Greenock, and Paisley.[9] In Dundee the Irish-born population had peaked at 15,000 in the 1850s, representing nearly 20 percent of the city's population—among the highest proportions in Britain at that time. By the 1880s this number dropped to 11,500, but it had been augmented by many more second- and third-generation Irish.[10]

Two-thirds of Dundee's Irish community were women, a distinctive demographic that differed from the relatively even gender balance found among Irish migrants in other British and international cities, though resembling some eastern American mill towns in the nineteenth century.[11] Irish women were attracted by opportunities in the jute mills to use skills that they had acquired at home. Domestic spinning and weaving declined in Ireland in the early nineteenth century due to market changes, which hit women harder than men. Across all sectors, job opportunities for women steadily decreased throughout the century, and they ended up emigrating in large numbers. By the mid-nineteenth century, Irish women, typically unmarried and in their early twenties, who had either emigrated alone or in small groups with parents, siblings, or friends, made up over half of the spinning workforce in Dundee.[12] These migrants and their children created fertile ground for the Ladies' Land League.

The Land War provided new impetus for Irish activism in Dundee. Previously there had been flickers during the Young Ireland and Fenian movements, and in the 1870s the local press condescendingly described the city's branch of the Home Rule Confederation as "very harmless."[13] In 1880 branches of the men's Land League were formed and immediately proved popular, with seven hundred people squeezing into a Catholic schoolhouse at their first meeting to hear John Ferguson decry the "rule of buckshot and bayonet in Ireland."[14] Prominent Home Rule politicians T. P. O'Connor and Tim Healy came to speak, and Michael Davitt, who lived briefly in Dundee, was particularly popular in the city and in Scotland more generally.[15] From the outset, local newspapers observed high numbers of women in attendance at Land League meetings.[16] Anna Parnell's rousing tour of Scotland in August 1881 led to the establishment of the Ladies' Land League in Glasgow, but the Dundee branch pre-dated her visit. Word about the organization reached Lochee through personal networks, local newspapers, and the circulation of the *Nation, Freeman's Journal,* and *United Ireland* from Dublin, as well as Boston's *Pilot* and New York's *Irish World,* all of which were available in Scotland. In July 1881 Irish women in Lochee, in correspondence with Anna Parnell, established the first Scottish branch of the Ladies Land League at the local St. Mary's Hall. By August the branch had sent £6 to Dublin, and in September the combined men's and women's branches sent the substantial sum of £50. A second women's branch—St. Andrew's—was established the following month.[17]

The visits of touring speakers were crucial to the development of Irish diaspora activism, and, in Dundee, public talks by Anna Parnell and Marguerite Moore helped to knit together the new branches. Both speakers encouraged members to organize as part of a larger community, even calling on them to not be outshone by emigrants in other locations. Advertisements for Parnell's Scottish tour proclaimed, "Harcourt says the Land League is supported from America. Tell him that 400,000 Irish of Scotland can and will support it also."[18] Parnell filled the venue, with the mainly female audience greeted outside by the St. Patrick's Temperance League flute band and two of St. Mary's Catholic flute bands, illustrating how the different strands of nationalism, temperance, and Catholic associational culture were intertwined. Typically, the male leaders introduced the speakers at demonstrations, and Edward Roche, head of the Lochee men's branch, chaired the event, but Parnell was introduced by Jane Keenan of the Lochee women's branch. Welcoming Parnell as someone who had "done so much for [Ireland's] homeless children, for her imprisoned martyrs,' her remarks reflected a mix of nationalism and Catholic humanitarianism.[19] Parnell gave her audience detailed accounts of evictions, arrests, and police brutality and called on the journalists present to truthfully report on Irish conditions. She then attacked the Liberal party, claiming that Gladstone was "a man who had sold his soul for power." A few nights earlier, the provost of Greenock had boycotted her lecture because of her anti-Gladstone comments; to laughter in the hall, she joked that it was for the better that he did, as "there might have been an unseemly dispute, and they might even have come to blows over it." After the meeting she met privately with local members.[20]

Anna Parnell was widely recognized as the leader of the Ladies' Land League, but her appeal in Scotland was rivaled by Marguerite Moore. In December 1881 Moore addressed an enthusiastic audience that gathered in Dundee's Thistle Hall on a day's notice, and local marching bands again played "national and popular airs" outside the venue. She was joined on the platform by Harold Rylett and Charles J. Dempsey, also supporters of Henry George. When Moore spoke, she was greeted with "loud cheers, the audience rising en masse to their feet and waving their hats and handkerchiefs." Moore had lived in Donegal, which no doubt added to her popularity in a city where many Irish held connections to the northwest, and she later pointed out the similarities between Scotland and Ulster.[21] Present on the platform were representatives of the various men's branches, but they were joined by Catherine Hopper and Sarah McCarron from Lochee, and Mary Gray, Annie Darcy, and Ellen Stewart from the St. Andrew's branch. All of them weavers and spinners in the jute industry, their presence was significant, an illustration of how working-class representation was part of the public face of the city's Ladies' Land League. The appearance of five unmarried women on the platform, and three at Moore's talk in Glasgow a few days earlier, was unusual by the standards of Irish nationalist meetings and indicates the changing views of women's roles in the movement.[22]

Moore's December visit came after the outlawing of the Land League and the imminent crackdown on the Ladies' Land League in Ireland. Her speech raged against the government's attempts to suppress the organization and claimed that coercion was ultimately counterproductive, because, without it, "the Land League would never have been the power it [is] today." Repeatedly poking fun at Irish chief secretary William Forster, she insisted that Irishwomen "would go gaily to their prison" if forced to, as indeed she did some months later. Without the efforts of members in Ireland and the diaspora, she maintained, the "helpless tenant farmers of Ireland would be wholly and completely in the power of the landlords." Making emotional links between land reform and emigration, she proclaimed that "still the emigrant vessel was leaving [Irish] shores laden with thousands of breaking hearts"—a statement with obvious resonance for her audience. Although the chair Edward Roche called on all those eligible to register their vote in order "to make their power felt when the time for action came," most of the audience was made up with women with no vote, and his closing remarks tempered some of Moore's more militant statements.[23]

Moore promised to return to Dundee the following April, with the caveat "Forster permitting." As she predicted, imprisonment in Ireland prevented her from coming, but on the day she was due to speak some five hundred people gathered to demonstrate—"chiefly ladies," according to the local press. To boos and hisses, John Ferguson announced that Moore had been put in Tullamore jail and read out a letter she had sent from her cell, in which she maintained that her imprisonment spoke "as eloquently to the hearts of the people as any address I could make." Resolutions were passed condemning the "cowardly and unjust imprisonment of that much esteemed lady," and one of the men present called "on every Irishwoman in Dundee and Lochee to become members" of the Ladies' Land League. Yet the women's branches had already exceeded expectations. They estimated that by that point they had collected over £200, "to succour men, women and children who had been evicted by tyrannical landlords," and Ferguson congratulated them on surpassing all other British branches.[24] Given the variegated ways in which money was collected and forwarded to Dublin, Ferguson's claim is difficult to verify and likely inaccurate, but the subscription records make it clear that Dundee was disproportionately represented, and that the local branches there stood at the forefront of the organization across Britain.

Despite Ferguson's praise, actual members of the Ladies' Land League were absent from the platform that evening, in contrast to Moore and Anna Parnell's previous visits. Ferguson focused on party politics and voter registration, aiming principally at the audience's male minority.[25] He repeated the Land League's call for "war against the Liberal party" at the next election, calling on "the men of Dundee" to vote Conservative—"a thankless task. Nevertheless it had to be done." The local Liberal MPs George Amritstead and Frank Henderson had already condemned the Land League, but at the same time Ferguson was careful not to excessively widen the divide with the Liberals.[26] He maintained it was a source of regret to him to "see a good man [Gladstone] go wrong," as Irish people simply demanded the same rights as existed in Britain and were ready to follow the "constitutional way."[27] In contrast to Anna Parnell's and Moore's confrontational lectures, the men's meetings in Dundee typically adopted a more moderate tone, which reflected the increasing differences between the Ladies' Land League and the men's organization in Ireland. At another meeting, local Land Leaguer Thomas Flanagan even stated that he "was in favour of a settlement of the land question . . . without infringing on the rights of the landlord," a sentiment clearly at odds with the spirit of the wider land movement.[28]

In Ireland, the radicalism of the Ladies' Land League surpassed that of many of the leaders of the men's organization. Local stud-

ies of branches in the United States have also identified women who
challenged conservative male leaders and aligned themselves with the
radical wing of the land movement associated with the *Irish World*.[29]
It is difficult, however, to establish the political views of members in
Dundee, as they left scant records beyond those documenting their
fundraising. Yet their activities were shaped by the Scottish context,
where, more so than in Ireland or England, the ideas of land nationalization and Henry George were firmly stamped on the Land League.
During his stay in Ireland, George grew increasingly interested in the
Scottish land question, and in the *Irish World* he called for the Irish of
"Dundee and Paisley and Glasgow [to] go out in delegations amongst
those oppressed Scotchmen, and impress upon them that their cause is
our cause, and that our common cause is the cause of God."[30] In Scotland, John Ferguson admired George, as did the key figures of Edward
McHugh, Ellen Quigley, and Richard McGhee, who built alliances
with land reformers in the Highlands.[31] Both Anna Parnell and Marguerite Moore worked closely with George, and Moore moved to New
York to continue working with him. In Scotland, the members of the
Ladies' Land League had arguably greater exposure to the radical wing
of the land movement than to the more moderate land reform policies
of Anna's brother, Charles Stewart Parnell.

The circulation of Irish and Irish American newspapers greatly
enabled the transnational networks of the Ladies' Land League. The
Irish World was sold in Scotland by three Glasgow newsagents: James
Lindsay, Thomas Lynch, and Lizzie Connolly. A second-generation
immigrant in her twenties, Connolly had joined Marguerite Moore
and Ellen Quigley on the platform at Glasgow's city hall.[32] Copies of
the paper made their way from Glasgow to Dundee through the organization's networks, and readers found news of Ladies' Land League
branches in scattered locations. The paper acknowledged their activities, observing that "In Dundee also a great Irish colony is rooted, and
they have shown their opinions and determination to cooperate with
the rest of us, in every practical way, until our nation is thoroughly quit
of the English garrisons."[33] Irish nationalist newspapers were sold by
newsagent John Green in Dundee's Scouring Burn area, near many jute
mills, and they provided news of developments in Ireland and the diaspora, while also allowing members to see their branch names in print.

Sending money to the central fund in Dublin ensured that the branch name, usually along with that of the secretary or treasurer, would be published in the fund columns in the *Nation* and the *Freeman's Journal*. By naming men and women's branches in various locations, the papers' fund columns functioned as a map of what might be called an "Irish international imagined community."[34] The lists also generated rivalries between different branches in Scotland, England, and further afield, over who could donate the most.

The Branch Members and the Jute Industry

The grassroots members of the Ladies' Land League in Britain left few statements behind about their lives, which has resulted in their anonymity in the scholarship. However, by utilizing subscriber lists and reports published in Irish and Scottish newspapers and piecing this information together with genealogical records, details can be excavated about the women who participated. Most members remain elusive, but some twenty women in Dundee have been traced who held office as secretaries, presidents, and treasurers, as well as in other committee roles, providing some insight into both the mechanics of the organization and the background of local leaders.[35]

Jane Keenan was president of the Lochee branch. She was born locally to Irish parents in 1857: her father worked as a weaver and her mother as a jute winder, a job also held by her older sister, Mary Ann. Her parents arrived in Scotland from Donegal in the late 1830s, settling first in Leith and then moving on to Dundee. By 1881, Keenan was living alone with her father. She was the odd one out in the family because she did not work in the jute industry, instead she was a schoolteacher, and presumably her family was able to support their youngest child's education while her elder sibling worked in the mills. Teaching was a valuable avenue of social mobility for Irish emigrants and their children in Britain and the United States, and the position carried some status in the community and was of considerable economic importance for the family.[36] Keenan's educated, lower-middle-class status most likely contributed to her becoming president of the Lochee branch at the age of twenty-four.

Keenan's profession set her apart from her fellow members, who worked as weavers, spinners, reelers and cleaners in Dundee's many factories and mills. They were a relatively young group: of the twenty women in this sample, most were in their early to mid-twenties, and only one was married, corresponding to the generational profile of the Ladies' Land League in Ireland. Twenty-six-year-old Lucy Paterson, a worker in the Camperdown mills, was originally named president of the Lochee branch at its inception, though she soon stepped aside for Keenan and took on another role. Paterson had emigrated to Dundee with her mother and five siblings in the 1860s and lived in the Albert Street enclave. By the time she was fifteen, she had joined her brothers and sisters to work in the jute factory. Her brother James had joined the workforce before he was eleven, indicating the expectations of children's labor at that time.

Annie Darcy, the treasurer of the St. Andrew's branch, organized the sending of subscriptions to Ireland. Like Keenan, she was twenty-four years old and second-generation Irish. Darcy's parents had emigrated together, first to England, where she was born, and then to Scotland in the 1860s. In 1881, she lived with her widowed mother, two brothers, and a lodger, Mary Byrne, a short distance away from St Joseph's Catholic church and school. She was a weaver, as was Byrne, while both her brothers worked in the textile industry. Although Keenan and Darcy were second-generation Irish, women born in Ireland were in a slight majority in our sample. Between the Lochee and St. Andrew's committees, twelve women were born in Ireland, six in Scotland, and one in England, while one—branch secretary Catherine Hopper—had no discernible family links to Ireland. The few cases with traceable counties of origin fit with general patterns of movement from Ulster and northern Leinster, with some women hailing from Monaghan, Cavan, Donegal, and Longford, similar to members of the men's branches. The census did not systematically record the Irish county of origin, yet entries included it occasionally. Perhaps, when collecting information, some determined enumerators sought to delve deeper, but it is also plausible that some migrants preferred to state their county or town as well as their country when asked where they were born. This suggests the lingering importance of regional identities in Ireland, and that participation in the land movement could have in certain cases been motivated by a desire to improve conditions in specific regions of Ireland, even though donations could only be collected on a national level.

Along with contacts made on the mill and factory floor, acquaintances made in boardinghouses near the mills provided entry points to the Ladies' Land League. Due to the housing shortage and the increasing population, Dundee's overcrowding problem was, after Paisley, the worst in Scotland. Low wages and rents often well above the national average meant that women working in the jute industry would commonly board with families in cramped rooms.[37] Lucy Paterson's family of seven, for example, shared their home with occasional lodgers, and Mary Gray of the St. Andrew's branch boarded with Kate Clarke and her family. Born in Ireland in 1835, Gray worked as a weaver at the Pleasance Works and was part of an older generation of league members. Before the Dundee branches were formally established in 1881, she had already collected money among her coworkers and forwarded it to Dublin under the factory name. Twenty-two-year-old Kate Clarke, who had come to Dundee with her father and sister in the 1870s, worked at the North Dudhope Works and similarly collected and forwarded money to Dublin under the mill name. Also living with the Clarkes was Elizabeth Murray, who came to Dundee from Ireland in the 1860s. Some branch members had emigrated with siblings, like sisters Margaret and Bridget Burbage, who boarded with the Donnelly family near the Camperdown Works. Sisters Bridget and Mary Connor boarded in a house on Lyon's Close, near St. Joseph's church, with branch secretaries Mary Hagan and Sarah Donohue. Places of work and accommodation were very much interlinked, and the boardinghouses close to the mills became part of the ancillary networks of the Ladies' Land League.

Dundee was not the final destination for all Irishwomen who moved there. In 1884, during an economic downturn, Lucy Paterson, the founder of the Lochee branch, emigrated to Paterson, New Jersey, with her two sisters, Catherine and Anne, after living in Lochee for twenty years. Perhaps attracted by the city that shared their name, the sisters were well qualified for employment in Paterson's jute mills. A look at the census returns for their new neighborhood also reveals a community littered with first- and second-generation Irish, as well as many Scottish-born residents with Irish parents and grandparents.[38] The city of origin in Scotland was not recorded, but the fact that jute mills were the principal source of employment for Irish migrants suggests that the

Paterson siblings were not the first to arrive in the New Jersey textile city from Ireland, via Dundee.

Across Britain and the United States, leadership roles in the Ladies' Land League were often taken on by the wives, daughters, and sisters of prominent male leaguers and politicians, most obviously in the case of the Parnells, the Sullivans in London, or the Blighs and Denvirs in Liverpool. In contrast, there are no discernible family connections between the organizers of the women and men's branches in Dundee. The presidents of the four men's branches in the city were Edward Roche, Thomas Flanagan, James O'Kane, and Thomas Smith, whose occupations—Roche and Flanagan were shopkeepers, and Kane was an undertaker—reflected the petit bourgeois status associated with many local leaders in Ireland, contrasting with the women's branches. Born in Ireland, these men were older than many of their female counterparts, most of them in their thirties and forties. Some members of the women and men's branches shared a platform at large events, but overall they remained separate in many respects. The women's branches functioned with a level of independence that gave them some input into managing the visits of key speakers. At the same time, this made it more difficult for them to integrate into, and to influence, the men's activities and events.

The members sent money to Ireland to alleviate poverty and hardship, but they faced grim situations of their own in their new homes. The workday lasted from 6 a.m. to 6 p.m., with additional shifts on Saturdays and many employees brought home sacks to sew at night. The cost of living was high in Dundee, but wages in the jute mills remained low compared to most other British cities because of domestic and emerging Indian competition.[39] The industry dominated the labor pool in Dundee, employing thirty-four thousand people, over 40 percent of the entire workforce, yet its exposure to international economic fluctuations brought periods of both depression and high profit, making employment unstable. In the 1880s, during an industry slump, a local Catholic priest in Lochee lamented to his bishop that "Things are very dull and bleak: so many of our poor people idle here!"[40]

Danger and difficulty came with mill work, ranging from the daily risk of accident to long-term illnesses resulting from the dust and dirt. The Cox Brothers, who owned the Camperdown Works in Lochee, sought to foster good relations with the local Catholic clergy, and in

1871, arranged a papal blessing from Pius IX for their Irish workers. In 1891, Edward Cox donated £100 to ease the debts of St. Mary's church beside the mills, writing to the local priest that "There is and has always been, although they may not know it, a warm corner in my heart for the Irish people of Lochee."[41] Given the conditions on the mill floor, Cox was almost certainly right: they did not know it. The registers of the Royal Infirmary in Dundee show high rates of admission of patients who worked in jute mills, many of them suffering from chronic bronchitis and "mill fever," respiratory problems linked to the oil fumes and heavy dust. In 1881, the register included 203 Irishwomen, 166 of them listed as "mill workers"—over four times as many as from all other occupations combined.[42] The high number reflects the centrality of employment in the mills for Irish immigrants and starkly indicates the long- and short-term health hazards associated with the work. Along with illness, there were frequent accidents, typically involving workers getting their hands caught between rollers and spinning frames, often while cleaning them. In 1896, when the Cox Brothers began recording accidents, ninety-one incidents resulted in bruised, cut, or broken fingers, and in some cases fingers and hands needed to be amputated. Fatal injuries were rare, but they did occur.[43] This situation was not unique to Dundee, and in the mill towns on the east coast of the United States, where the Ladies' Land League also proved popular, textile work was often looked down upon as less desirable than domestic service due to the health risks.[44]

Bad working conditions had provoked some protests in the 1850s and 1860s, and in the mid-1870s, Jessie Craigen, who later joined the Ladies' Land League and toured Ireland, sought to establish the Women's Protective and Provident League among Dundee jute workers.[45] In the 1880s, however, limited options existed for women's trade union participation, and the Ladies' Land League channeled some of the resentments associated with industrial labor through its calls for lower rents, improved living standards, and social and economic rights. Bad pay, high rents, overcrowding, and hazardous work generated frustrations that, as Kerby Miller has argued in regard to the United States, could be "easily translated into nationalist expressions and activities."[46] The 1879 manifesto of the Irish Home Rule Association in Scotland compared the cause of the "farmers of Ireland" with the "miners of

Lanarkshire," and the Glasgow Land League, one of the most radical branches in Britain, linked land reform in Ireland to both industrial workers in Scotland and land reform in the Highlands.[47] The Ladies' Land League may not have explicitly addressed labor grievances, but it undoubtedly offered a voice to people who did not otherwise have one, in addition to new opportunities for political participation.

The league also represented a form of humanitarian activity that arguably brought a sense of respectability for some members. In Dundee and across Victorian Britain, charity work carried associations with religion and with middle-class status.[48] The Catholic Church supported fundraising for the relief of deprivation in Ireland, and their recognition of this work may have encouraged involvement in the league, as it generated positive attention from within the Irish community. Jane Keenan held close links with the local clergy and was well positioned to organize fundraising for both Catholic charities and the Ladies' Land League. When she introduced Anna Parnell in Kinnaird Hall, she explicitly evoked the language of Catholic welfare: "Like a true sister of charity you take your stand by the poor and oppressed, bringing peace and comfort to many a well-nigh broken heart."[49] Yet Anna Parnell herself refuted the idea that the Ladies' Land League was a charity. The Dundee members' fundraising served partly as a form of Catholic humanitarianism for evicted tenants, but it was also significantly different from mainstream charity in that it was in the name of an organization that had been outlawed in Ireland by the end of 1881. Keenan's profile was also different from that of the other women in the branches, and it is more difficult to measure the extent to which their participation might have made a real contribution to social mobility in terms of employment. Improving one's social position could be frustrated by gender and class, and the employee registers of the Camperdown Works indicate that, although women filled the mill and factory floors, every middling and senior position was taken by a man.[50] As Eleanor Gordon has observed, for women jute workers "there was no opportunity for vertical mobility."[51] Marriage offered one means of social mobility, and to be a nonworking wife was a sign of respectability, but, in our sample, only one person fits that profile.

Timothy Meagher has observed how "a sense of gender solidarity" that derived from the collective taking-on of public roles in a movement dominated by men contributed to the vibrancy of the Ladies' Land League in Worcester, Massachusetts.[52] Similar gender solidarity was evident in the Dundee group, that was further shaped by the dynamics of the workplace. The main class distinction in the jute industry was between a small core of well-paid male supervisors and the mass of female workers, which hardened the realities of gender division and arguably contributed to a heightened sense of solidarity among women. Class differences also existed within the female workforce among weavers and spinners. The latter, who came from more modest backgrounds, performed the more hazardous and intensive work on the mill floors, while the weavers were slightly better paid, the work was cleaner, and the position was perceived to be more respectable.[53] Jane Keenan's mother and sister were weavers, as were treasurer Mary Gray and secretary Mary Hagan in the St Andrew's branch, suggesting that workplace distinctions sometimes translated into committee roles. However, this was not always the case: Annie Darcy was a spinner, as was Lucy Paterson. The women sharing the platform with Marguerite Moore in Thistle Hall included both weavers and spinners. Overall, the membership was dominated by working-class women whose chances to elevate their occupational status may have been slim, but outside the workplace public activities could improve their social standing in the Irish community.

Class concerns were also apparent in fundraising. Published subscription lists were a central part of Land League fundraising, and when representing a particular community, they reflected social hierarchies and Catholic clergymen's desired position in them. In 1881, the local newspaper printed the amounts given to a Land League collection by men and women, their names listed according to the amount donated. At the top of the list of some seventy names was the city's senior Catholic clergyman, Robert Clapperton, who donated £1, followed by the names of four other priests who gave smaller amounts. Donations from laypeople then followed the clergymen, from the largest downward, even if some had given more money than the clergy. John McCheyne, an Ulster Presbyterian who emigrated in the 1860s and owned a drapery in the city center, topped the list of laypeople with £1.[54] Toward the bottom of the list we find some members of the Ladies' Land League, including Annie Darcy of the St. Andrew's branch, who donated sixpence. The list revealed who supported the Land League while also representing a ladder of respectability and income, publicly marking out class and gender hierarchies in the community in both the host city and the homeland: the list was first published in A. M. Sullivan's *Weekly News* in Dublin, then in the *Dundee Courier*.[55]

The profile of the Dundee branches challenges assumptions about the bourgeois dimensions of the Ladies' Land League. In his recollections, the Land League leader Michael Davitt partly acknowledged the prominent roles of upper- and middle-class women in the organization, observing that Archbishop McCabe, who condemned the Ladies' Land League because it undermined women's "modesty," was only concerned because its members belonged "to families at least as respectable as his own."[56] Women from prominent backgrounds featured strongly on committees in Ireland, Britain, and the United States. Frances Genevieve Sullivan, wife of politician and journalist A. M. Sullivan, led the London branch, and Mary Agnes Bligh, wife of the local Land League president and surgeon, led the Liverpool branch. With her on the committee were Mary and Anne Denvir, daughters of the bookseller John Denvir, a prominent Land Leaguer and member of the Catholic Total Abstinence League. Local studies of branches in rural Ireland have highlighted the way the more vibrant ones "drew active support and leadership from middle-class and urban groups."[57] Yet branches in Scotland and northern England point to strong support among immigrant industrial workers and their children. The Dundee branches were very much rooted in the working-class culture of the jute mills, while the Glasgow branch president, Ellen Quigley, was an immigrant seamstress. The organization in England, as discussed in chapter 2, drew support among textile workers in Lancashire and Yorkshire. In the United States, too, a study of the Ladies' Land League in Woonsocket, Rhode Island, has demonstrated that many members worked in the city's cotton and wool mills.[58] The social backgrounds of members varied according to setting, and local perspectives offer a corrective to assumptions that the movement was entirely a middle-class affair. The more vibrant branches in Britain appeared in towns and cities with a large presence of industrial workers.

In studies of Irish immigration to Victorian Scotland, particularly on the west coast, sectarianism and ethnic prejudice emerge as familiar themes. These tensions were not so sharp in Dundee, where the numbers of Orange Lodges and parades were lower, but neither was the city free of anti-Irish prejudice.[59] When reporting on Anna Parnell's visit, the *Dundee Courier*, published by D. C. Thompson, described her as blind to the faults of Irish Catholics and "sees no want in them of that quality which makes Scotchmen generally so prosperous and content with fewer privileges." When Parnell famously challenged the Lord Lieutenant of Ireland on a Dublin street by grabbing the head-collar of his horse, an editorial likened her actions to those of a "maniac, or the escaped inmate of a lunatic asylum."[60] The *Dundee Advertiser* wrote of the Ladies' Land League's support for the "activity of the assassin" and their "inflammatory speeches."[61] When the Lochee branch was established, the paper published an angry letter proclaiming that "Irishmen, and those of them residing in Lochee especially, are rank cowards, or else they would not resort to such a mean dodge as mix up their sisters and daughters with a movement the outcome of which is a disgrace to the civilisation of the nineteenth century." The letter reflected a central thread of the hostility in Britain toward the Ladies' Land League, that the members were the men's stooges, not activists in their own right. The correspondent continued that he also opposed the new branch, because "the majority of the Irish people are unfit for self-government, and that no time should be lost in placing them on the same footing as the people of India."[62] For Glasgow's *North British Daily Mail*, the Ladies' Land League was a "much more objectionable body" than the men's league, the result of "an unnatural application of the doctrines of those strong minded ladies who champion the extreme form of women's rights."[63] Reports across the Scottish press indicate the hostility that involvement in the organization could bring to emigrant women. Membership also entailed other risks. Collecting and securing large sums of money until sending them off to Dublin, for example, had its dangers. In May 1882, Kate McCabe, a sixty-year-old emigrant to New York, was murdered by her sixteen-year-old stepson for the Land League money she kept in her flat.[64] Most Irish American newspapers ignored the case, presumably to avoid negative publicity, and the episode is suggestive of lesser-reported dangers associated with fundraising.

Participation in the Ladies' Land League obviously presented greater hazards in Ireland than in the diaspora, particularly after the authorities proscribed the organization in December 1881. Yet it was also a different matter to protest in Dundee against the British government, send money to an illegal organization, and cheer the imprisoned Marguerite Moore, than it was in New York or Melbourne. In Scotland, ethnic prejudice and pejorative attitudes toward women's political activism were combined in condemnations of the Ladies' Land League. Members faced considerable animosity, perhaps to a greater extent than the men. At the same time, they were left to organize and fundraise relatively free from official interference. In part this was due to the considerable support they received from the Catholic Church.

The Catholic Church

Catholic institutions and personnel were intermeshed with the Dundee branches from the outset. The Catholic hierarchy had mixed opinions of the organization, with some bishops condemning women's public political activism. Richard Gilmour, for example, the Glasgow-born bishop of Cleveland, Ohio, considered membership to be "incompatible with womanly modesty"—comments that were reprinted in the Dundee press.[65] Local clergymen did not publicly voice similar sentiments, however, and were significantly involved in the organization and Irish nationalist events more generally. In an influential essay on the Dundee Irish, historian William Walker argued that Catholic priests promoted moderate Irish nationalism in Dundee "as a distraction from the politics of class."[66] While many priests likely found Irish nationalism preferable to socialism, ethnic and class politics were not so neatly counterposed. Walker's argument also provokes questions about the agency of immigrants and the extent to which they could have been so easily marshaled by the Catholic Church.[67] While there was considerable clerical involvement in the Ladies' Land League, it was not always on the church's own terms.

From the mid-nineteenth century, the Catholic Church expanded in Scotland, with substantial growth in the numbers of men and women religious. Irish migration contributed to this expansion and, while tensions existed between Scottish and Irish Catholic personnel, there were high levels of Irish involvement in Catholic institutions in Dundee. This was partly due to the Fermanagh-born Stephen Keenan, the city's senior Catholic clergyman from the 1840s to 1862, who invited an order of the Irish Sisters of Mercy to establish a convent in Lochee in 1859. Seeking to bring a Catholic moral influence to life in the area, the order started a school for children and women under twenty-five who worked in the mills, providing an education for many Irish in the area.[68] Irish Catholics had complained to the Cox Brothers that children who worked in the mills and attended half-time schools were "compelled to learn the Protestant catechism."[69] By the end of the 1870s, there were four Catholic Churches and six schools in the city, double what had existed in the previous decade.[70] In 1878, the Catholic school in Lochee was expanded to include more rooms and a teacher's house. By the time of the Land War the influence of Catholicism in life in Dundee had significantly increased.[71]

The names of the Land League branches reflected a religious sense of place in the city. The men's organization was divided into four branches that corresponded with the four Catholic parishes of St. Andrew's, St. Joseph's, St. Mary's, and Lochee, while the women's organization was divided into the Lochee and St. Andrew's branches. Historian William Jenkins has observed that the Catholic parish offered "the ideal spatial unit for the Land League branches" in Toronto and Buffalo, and the same was true in Dundee, where social, political, and parochial worlds were very much entangled.[72] At the same time, there were also significant associations with the workplace, and funds were occasionally sent to Dublin under the names of the mills where the members worked, rather than the branch name, including the North Dudhope, Pleasance, and Camperdown Works.

When prominent Irish nationalists came to town, the church made itself visible. Catholic flute bands paraded before Anna Parnell and Marguerite Moore's talks, and when Home Rule MP T. P. O'Connor addressed the local Land League's first big event, he was joined on the platform by four local Catholic priests. When Michael Davitt spoke in 1882, no less than eight priests accompanied him.[73] In Lochee, the local curate Peter Butti was present at the founding of the Ladies' Land League branch and regularly stewarded meetings and assisted with collecting donations. Meetings were usually held in the Catholic St. Mary's hall, which he managed. Butti was popular; at one point local Irish petitioned the bishop to prevent him being switched to another parish.[74] Jane Keenan's relationship with Butti was shaded by the fact that the school where she taught in Lochee was funded by the diocese and administered by him.[75] This relationship likely complicated her ability to act independently and finds some parallels with women's charitable societies in Ireland, where "the clergy exerted a powerful control over the direction taken by women philanthropists."[76]

There were no St. Patrick's Day parades, but annual meetings were held in Lochee and central Dundee chaired by Butti and Robert Clapperton, then the city's leading Catholic clergyman. Speeches and celebrations easily spilled over into politics, with one local priest proclaiming, "Ireland for the Irish was as loud on the shores of the Mississippi as on the banks of Ireland's Shannon."[77] The Temperance League, the St. Vincent de Paul charity, the Catholic Young Women's Association, and the Young Men's Society intertwined with nationalist politics. In 1879, the Dundee Harp football team was founded, inspired by Edinburgh's Hibernian F. C. and comprised almost entirely of Catholic and Irish-born players. Senior officials in the club were local Catholic clergymen.[78] The head of the Lochee Land League also chaired the local committee of lay Catholics. Women were excluded from many male-dominated societies, yet the considerable presence of Irish women religious in the city and their promotion of charitable causes meant that some women had fundraising experience, and the Ladies' Land League branch could operate in a public space already partially carved out. In one of the first calls for a women's Land League in New York, Ellen Ford asked, "No one thinks it's wrong for women to beg for church fairs, sell tickets for lotteries, picnics, lectures, etc.; and why should they not form clubs or societies for the relief of the wives, mothers and sisters in Ireland?"[79]

Access to space for events is vital to the success of any movement. The men's and women's leagues depended on church schoolrooms and halls, holding monthly meetings in the Young Men's Hall on Tay Street, purchased by the Catholic Church in 1873, and they also regularly used St. Mary's Hall in Lochee and schoolrooms on Larch Street.[80] Access to the large venues of Thistle Hall and Kinnaird Hall was no doubt made easier through the support of Clapperton. Lack of access to buildings created difficulties for members, evident when divisions emerged down the road in Edinburgh. When heated exchanges occurred at a Land League meeting following Charles Stewart Parnell's compromise with Gladstone in May 1882, opponents of the new moderate direction were denied the use of St. Mary's Hall in the Cowgate by a "lay element in the council of the Young Men's Catholic Association." This element was James Whittet, president of the Edinburgh branch, who, interestingly, grew up working in the Dundee jute mills from the age of eleven. He later became a tailor and draper in Edinburgh, a prominent member of the Catholic Young Men's Society, and the caretaker for St. Mary's Hall.[81] In 1886, when the president of the Catholic Young Men's Society in Edinburgh was forced to resign over his support for boycotting in Ireland, Whittet replaced him and became a prominent face at Irish events in the city, including nationalist meetings, St. Vincent de Paul fundraisers, St. Patrick's Day celebrations, and Hibernian F. C. football matches.[82] Such was the overlap in the city between the National League and the Catholic Young Men's Society that the *Tablet* observed, "They almost appear as one society."[83] Close associations with the Catholic Church secured Whittet's ascent in local nationalist politics. In both Edinburgh and Dundee, church halls and Catholic networks buoyed the Land League, but providing, or denying, access to buildings gave clergymen additional influence over the types of events organized by the branches.

The presence of Irish men and women religious in Dundee likely helped to cultivate a close relationship between emigrants and the Catholic Church. Seventeen of the eighteen nuns resident at the Sisters of Mercy convent were Irish born, as were three priests in the city, though they came via a Scottish seminary.[84] A closer look, however, complicates the picture. Far from being Irish-dominated, the Catholic Church in Dundee had transnational dimensions and incorporated many priests from different European missions who had come to Britain specifically to serve working-class parishes.[85] The three parish priests who served Lochee during the 1870s and 1880s were Francis Beurms, from Belgium; Peter Butti, born in Edinburgh to Italian parents; and Alphonsus Van de Rydt, from the Netherlands.[86] The latter two were present at a number of Land League and Ladies' Land League meetings, with Butti particularly involved with the women's branches. Robert Clapperton hailed from Moray and had no links to Ireland. Stephen Keenan was born in Ireland, but was very much a product of the Scottish and Roman education system; he emigrated as a young child with his parents to the southwest of Scotland and was educated in Aberdeen and the Scots College, Rome.[87] He died in 1862, before the Home Rule movement began. Many clergymen associated with Irish politics in Dundee did not hold direct links to Ireland.

The diverse background of these clergymen raises questions, then, about their connection with diaspora nationalism and Walker's interpretation that they used moderate nationalism to stifle class politics. It seems more likely that they felt there was an expectation among parishioners that they be seen at nationalist events. In this sense, they were responding to local engagement with the Land War, rather than shaping it, and then sought to align themselves with the more moderate, and wealthier, elements within the movement. It would also be misleading to assume that all within the Catholic Church shared the same political views; rather, perspectives on nationalism and the land movement varied among men and women religious and involved radical as well as conservative positions.[88]

There are some indications that not all clergymen in Dundee were comfortable supporting the Ladies' Land League. Local priests were always eager to appear on the platform at Land League events, but they were occasionally absent from women's demonstrations. Curiously, when Annie Darcy, Ellen Stewart, Catherine Hopper, Sarah McCarron, and Mary Gray accompanied Marguerite Moore on the platform in Thistle Hall, no clergymen were present, and neither was Jane Keenan.[89] Similarly, when Moore spoke in Glasgow two nights earlier, she was joined by three local women, but no priests. Perhaps their absence reflected a discomfort with unmarried women assuming public roles, or maybe they were simply less interested in associating with low-paid jute workers. They may have been equally cautious of appearing with Moore, who held views to the left of the Land League executive in Ireland. Priests were again absent at the demonstration for the imprisoned Moore in April 1882. Whatever the reasons, uneven clerical attendance at meetings indicates that the Ladies' Land League enjoyed some autonomy, and events did not always proceed with priests in attendance. The close alliance of Jane Keenan with the Catholic Church was not representative of all members. While, in many ways, the local branches benefited significantly from the Catholic Church's material resources, clergymen did not steer the direction of the organization.

* * *

Marguerite Moore returned to speak in Dundee in September 1882. She was joined by Edward McHugh, who had just come back from a tour of the Isle of Skye, where he addressed crofters on the similarities between the Irish and Scottish land questions and was identified by police as a troublesome agitator.[90] His presence on the platform along-side Moore again linked the Ladies' Land League in Scotland with the Georgite wing of the land movement. Moore was given £6 raised by local members, yet by that stage the Ladies' Land League in Ireland had been disbanded, throwing the diaspora branches into uncertainty. Her visit constituted the last public meeting of the Lochee and St. Andrews branches, and over the following months the organization faded. In November, Michael Davitt spoke in Dundee, but he made no mention of the contribution of local women during the Land War.[91] Nonetheless, during a short lifespan of a little over one year, the branches of the Dundee Ladies' Land League were among the most vibrant in Britain. Dundee was, as the saying went, a "women's city," and the high proportions of women in the textile workforce—sometimes as their families' main breadwinners—along with their predominance in the Irish community provided a congenial environment for the organization. The city's branches rivaled those in much larger centers of Irish settlement in Liverpool, Glasgow, and London. There was no comparable mobilization of Irish women in Dundee for the rest of the century. While existing studies suggest that Irishwomen were not significantly involved in trade unionism or suffragism in subsequent decades, both areas are underresearched and merit more scrutiny.[92]

Adopting transnational perspectives on the Ladies' Land League is necessary because the organization connected people in multiple locations, and the local branches cannot be fully understood in isolation. Yet, as Lara Putnam has observed, taking a large-scale view risks "overemphasizing the importance of that which connects, and underestimating the weight of that which is connected."[93] While newspapers and mobile agitators plugged the Ladies' Land League in Dundee into wider networks of Irish activism, local situations and experiences gave the branches a distinctive stamp. Their vibrancy sprang from the interpersonal connections and class-based camaraderie developed through members' jobs and living circumstances. There was considerable over-lap in the branches with the Catholic Church and religious humani-tarianism, but priests responded to women's mobilization rather than initiating it. The local membership profile challenges perceptions of the organization as primarily a middle-class affair and suggests that the agency of working-class women as a factor in nineteenth-century Irish diaspora activism has been neglected. The Ladies' Land League disrupted gender conventions, offered emigrants an unprecedented op-portunity to publicly protest injustice in Ireland, and provided an out-let for frustrations rooted in urban industrial life.

4

John Creaghe, the *Southern Cross*, and Land Wars in Argentina

In 1883 Dublin's *Freeman's Journal* published a short letter to the National League from "Irish Exiles in the Argentine Republic," which accompanied a considerable donation. The Irish in Argentina, the letter asserted, were, "in proportion to their number, the richest amongst the various nationalities that go to make up the population . . . and they wish their countrymen at home to be, as they are themselves, free, prosperous and independent."[1] Such claims were not new. Eight years earlier, the *Southern Cross* newspaper opened its first issue with proud claims of the "large fortunes" made by Irish immigrants.[2] The organ of Irish Catholics in Argentina, the newspaper was keen to trumpet the success of the community it wanted to represent, but similar claims about Irish achievements were also voiced by Argentine officials. An 1881 parliamentary report maintained that "Amongst the most successful—if not the most successful in comparison to their numbers—of all immigrants in this country have been the Irish."[3] The "exiles" who wrote to the National League did not long to return home, but considered themselves among the most successful immigrants in a land of immigrants. Yet the emergence of the Land League prompted some critical voices to look behind the boasting of Irish-Argentine success and raise uncomfortable questions about the poverty of recent immigrants and the increasing wealth of a landowning elite that engaged in practices then being fiercely opposed in Ireland. Chief among them was John O'Dwyer Creaghe, an Irish doctor who had emigrated to Argentina in the early 1870s and later became a leading figure in Argentine anarchism, one of the most powerful labor movements in South America until 1914. In the 1880s, however, Creaghe was primarily focused on the Land League and land nationalization as the solution to Ireland and Argentina's problems.

Shortly before Henry George departed New York for his 1884 tour of Britain and Ireland, he received a letter from Creaghe inquiring about the possibility of publishing an affordable Spanish translation of his pamphlet *The Irish Land Question*. Describing himself as an "admirer and disciple" of George's work, Creaghe maintained that "Monopoly of land has been carried to such an extreme in this country that the hope is that the very excess of it will bring about the reaction."[4] Creaghe's knowledge of George and the Land War came through reading Irish and English newspapers, including the *Irish World*, which circulated in Argentina.[5] While the Land League appealed to him in part for its potential to transform Ireland, more significant for him was the prospect of deploying similar ideas of land reform and models of protest in Argentina to challenge inequities and large landowners, some of whom were Irish themselves. "Let it be known," Creaghe wrote, "that there are no worse landlords in the world than the ignorant Irishmen who in former years were able to buy land and are now millionaires."[6]

Creaghe's attacks on agrarian capitalism provoked a debate that revealed tensions within the Irish Argentine community and sheds light on the reception of the Land League in a less familiar corner of the Irish diaspora. From his home in the town of Luján, seventy miles west of Buenos Aires, Creaghe wrote numerous lengthy letters to English- and Spanish-language newspapers, including the *Southern Cross*, to promote land nationalization and connect the Land League with issues of poverty and reform in Argentina. In doing so, he clashed with influential Irish figures, including Patrick Dillon, chaplain to the Irish community in Buenos Aires and editor of the *Southern Cross*, and his successor, Michael Dinneen, who edited the paper from 1882. Both men were Catholic clerics who promoted free-market capitalism and political conservatism and glossed over the contradictions thrown up by their support for the Land League in Ireland and some Irish landlord practices in Argentina.[7] During these years a violent campaign to remove and exterminate indigenous people from the Pampa and Patagonia regions made vast tracts of land available to speculators and wealthy landowners.[8] Some were of Irish birth and descent. Irish Argentine leaders cheered the expansion of the frontier and the accompanying land boom at the same time as the agitation against landlordism in Ireland intensified.

* * *

John O'Dwyer Creaghe was born into comfortable circumstances in 1841 in Dublin, the son of a senior clerk in the General Post Office. In 1865, he completed the exams and gained a license from the Royal College of Surgeons, Dublin. He then traveled to the United States to enlist in the Union Army for the final stages of the American Civil War. In so doing, he followed almost 150,000 other Irish-born recruits, but he avoided the Irish battalions, instead joining the 122nd Colored Infantry in the South, suggesting that he was an abolitionist. When he returned to Ireland, he earned further medical qualifications and married Margaret Slattery, a Catholic woman from Wexford. Creaghe was baptized a Protestant, though in adulthood it seems he was an atheist. In 1871, he set out for Argentina as a confident economic migrant seeking opportunities in a country with long-standing links to both the Irish medical community and county Wexford. Margaret Slattery followed him once he established steady employment. He quickly found work, but his encounters as a doctor with "poverty in its worst forms" and exposure to institutional corruption and violence turned him toward radical politics, first in the Land League and Georgism, and then in anarchism.[9] From 1890 to 1892, he lived in Sheffield, England, where he started an anarchist group and newspaper. The few English-language histories that have paid Creaghe any attention have focused on these years and the extent to which his anarchism disrupted and irritated the English socialists William Morris and Edward Carpenter. From the moment Creaghe arrived in their city, Sheila Rowbotham has maintained, "the Sheffield Socialists were destined to go up in smoke."[10] In 1892, he returned to Luján, where he was known as the doctor whose services were free to the poor. Creaghe is recognized in several studies of Argentine anarchism, but typically has made no more than fleeting appearances. At different times he edited the leading anarchist daily *La Protesta* and was known within the movement as "El Viejo Creaghe." By that point, he had become more distant from Irish affairs, though he maintained close friendships within the Irish Argentine community. It was during the 1870s and 1880s that he was most engaged with Irish Argentina and events in Ireland.[11]

Irish emigrant activism in the United States and Britain dwarfed that in Argentina, reflecting its smaller Irish community, but the Land League did find a response there. Estimates place a community of less than forty thousand first- and second-generation Irish in a population of over three million at this time, although numbers are difficult to measure, due to the Irish being officially counted as *ingleses*, or immigrants from the United Kingdom.[12] The 1895 census, for example, lists both John Creaghe and his wife as *ingleses*. Irish Argentines generally did not adopt the underdog sensibility often projected by political and religious leaders in nineteenth-century Irish communities in the United States and Britain. In contrast, many belonged to the dominant national religion, Catholicism, but they were also set apart by their preference to maintain English as their primary tongue, adopting a wider Anglophone identity that largely lacked the anti-British sentiment often expressed by Irish nationalists elsewhere. Integration into a wider Anglophone community brought the benefits of participation in British capital projects and "informal" colonialism.[13] The majority of Irish migrants in Argentina originated from two counties—Westmeath and Wexford—and arrived between the 1830s and 1880s, the decade when Irish immigration slowed to a trickle as the flows from Italy and Spain surged. Between 1871 and 1914, just under six million migrants came to Argentina, contributing to the tremendous population growth and sweeping social transformation of that era. The majority of these migrants came from the Mediterranean region and included large numbers of people who stayed temporarily before moving on again to other countries. The stereotypical Irish Argentine worked in sheep farming, but the urban Irish also included dockworkers, artisans, and a clique of professionals.[14] Irish Argentine diaspora activism is an understudied topic, with some accounts maintaining that migrants to Argentina had little interest in Irish politics in the nineteenth century.[15] This was not the case. Despite their small number, Irish Argentines followed events in Ireland and were not disconnected from wider diaspora networks. From 1875, they benefited from telegraph connections to Europe and North America and a steamship journey from Ireland that had shrunk to one month.[16]

The Land League in Argentina built on existing nationalist networks. In the 1870s, branches of the Irish Home Rule League existed in Carmen de Areco, Chacabuco, Salto, Arrifices, and Mercedes, rural colonies in the north of Buenos Aires province. Creaghe was a member of the Mercedes branch that was organized by a priest named John Leahy. Land League branches were started in many of the same locations. In Salto,

William Murphy organized a branch that sent money to Dublin collected among fifty-two locals, while Patrick Mulvihill ran the Chacabuco
branch, and Michael Leahy administered the Carmen de Areco branch.
Like his brother John, Michael Leahy was a priest who had been involved
in nationalism since the 1860s. During the Land War, he sent subscriptions from "Irish priests and people" in Argentina to "express their sympathy for the Irish farmers," which were sent to Irish archbishop Thomas
Croke, who then forwarded it to the Land League. Leahy's fundraising
bypassed a Buenos Aires–based Irish Relief committee headed by Edward
Mulhall and Michael Carroll, which sent money to the Dublin Mansion House Fund organized by Edmund Dwyer Gray. Leahy avoided this
committee because he perceived Carroll to be too close to British elites
in Buenos Aires, and he was likely familiar with Parnell's hostility toward
the Mansion House fund. Nonetheless, Mulhall and Carroll succeeded in
sending over £3,500 to Ireland.[17] By 1882, a number of local Land League
branches had sprung up in Argentina, but they lacked coordination and
received mixed support from the *Southern Cross*. Editor Patrick Dillon,
who did not promote the Land League, ignored communications to start
branches in Buenos Aires. Instead, he viewed the upheaval in Ireland
as an opportunity to try and attract more Irish migrants to Argentina.
Considering Dillon's reputation as an establishment man, perhaps it is
no surprise that he did not encourage a movement that aimed to challenge ideas of property ownership. At the same time, the paper did report
news of Home Rule demonstrations in Ireland and Britain and reprinted
a number of speeches by nationalists, including the Glasgow-based John
Ferguson, who was on the Land League executive committee.[18]

When the Land War came to a close in Ireland, however, the questions it raised began to more seriously engage the Irish in Argentina. In
1882, Michael Dinneen succeeded Dillon as the editor of the *Southern
Cross* and set about more assertively promoting the National League
and Charles Stewart Parnell. He also sought to organize a limited association for Irish migrant workers in response to increasingly straitened
conditions on the *estancias*, or large estates.[19] Under Dinneen's editorship, the *Southern Cross* included, to a degree, new voices, including
Creaghe. Sharp differences emerged between them regarding how severe the poverty and inequality in Argentina was, whether it resembled
what immigrants had left behind in Ireland, and what changes were

necessary to improve the situation. The question of land nationalization versus peasant proprietorship instigated a barbed debate that played out as a microcosm of the wider clashes between the supporters of Parnell and Michael Davitt in Ireland and across the diaspora. Creaghe led the defence for nationalization and Georgism in regular letters to the *Southern Cross*, the *Buenos Ayres Herald, El Nacional* and *Libertad,* highlighting the poverty of recent arrivals in order to challenge the golden image of immigration promoted by Dillon and Dinneen.

Patrick Dillon and Assisted Emigration

Emigrant activism in Argentina was not defined solely by relations with Ireland, but was mediated by Irish America, and attempts to foment Land League initiatives came from the United States. In 1881 New York's *Irish World* praised itself for making "happy the home of many Irish rancher [in Argentina], serving, as it were, the binding link between him and the world he has left behind him."[20] It was common for Irish migrants to move to the United States after a period in Argentina, while others—known as "Irish Yankees"—had first arrived via the United States, a journey that cost less than the direct route from Ireland.[21] In one mid nineteenth-century ballad about Irish youths leaving Wexford for Argentina, the first verses describe a voyage to America and the "Land of Liberty."[22] Before coming to Buenos Aires, John Creaghe had lived in Boston, and in 1910 he left Argentina for California. Thomas Murray, the nationalist historian who wrote the first account of the Irish in Argentina in 1919, first emigrated from Kilbeggan, Co. Westmeath to the United States, then to Argentina, before returning to New York. In the 1860s, the American Fenian Brotherhood sent an emissary to Argentina to establish a new center there, but with limited results. It was the American Land League that first wrote to Patrick Dillon, encouraging him and Irish Argentines to establish new branches. The letter from the New York Branch presumably singled out Dillon because he ran the *Southern Cross*, but they had misjudged his views. Dillon brought the letter to the British ambassador, Horace Rumbold, assuring him that he took no notice of it and that the Irish community was generally uninterested. Rumbold, confident in Dillon, reported that "the Irish community are undoubtedly very much under the guidance of their clergy."[23]

Born in Mayo, Patrick Dillon trained as a missionary priest at All Hallow's College, Dublin, and the Latin American College in Rome. He was ordained in 1863 and first served in southern parts of Buenos Aires province before moving to the capital, where he became a professor of theology, and in 1870 traveled to the Vatican Council as an advisor.[24] When the popular Irish chaplain Anthony Fahy died in 1871, Dillon was well positioned to step into his role as community leader. By 1880, he had become dean of the Cathedral of Buenos Aires and the leading Irish cleric, yet he never attained Fahy's status. According to Thomas Murray, Dillon "was always much more popular with the rich than with the poor among his countrymen," and "at that time there was a very considerable number of the two classes." In 1875, Dillon founded the *Southern Cross* as an Irish Catholic newspaper to complement the *Standard*, the English-language daily edited by the Dublin-born Mulhall brothers, but generally aimed at the British community. Somewhat unusually for an Irish immigrant, Dillon was a naturalized Argentine citizen and a provincial politician, first becoming a member of the Chamber of Deputies for Buenos Aires and then later a senator.[25] He first expressed little interest in the Land League, though he supported Home Rule and later spoke at a National League meeting during an 1885 visit to Ireland.[26]

In 1881, when Dillon discussed the Land League with the British ambassador, the main reason for the meeting was an assisted emigration scheme. Dillon saw the Land War first and foremost as an opportunity to expand the Irish Argentine community through this plan, which aimed to settle Irish migrants on frontier lands. In 1880, he agreed to travel to Ireland at the direction of president Julio Roca and the immigration department, to promote Argentina as a destination for "honest and industrious emigrants."[27] The scheme originated from a conversation between Roca and the British ambassador, who had remarked that he believed "a greater flow of emigration would perhaps afford the best solution" to the unrest in Ireland. Roca took to the idea right away; he believed that opportunities to acquire land cheaply could allow Argentina to compete with the United States as a destination for European migrants, and he considered Irish settlers desirable for grasslands.[28] In the past, similar schemes had met with some success, and in 1869 an immigration department was set up in Buenos Aires with agents in

Europe to offer incentives to migrants, such as one week's free lodging and free rail transport upon arrival.[29]

The assisted emigration plan was purported to have the additional benefit of easing British "difficulties" in Ireland, by transferring would-be agitators to Argentina. According to one London-based Argentine official, the Irish who moved to the United States had a reputation for becoming ardent nationalists, but those who settled in Argentina were "animated by feelings of loyalty toward Her Majesty, the Queen of England." Having witnessed a Land League demonstrated in London, this official concluded that if supporters were "really animated by the desire of devoting themselves to the cultivation of the soil," then they should emigrate to Argentina. Unlike in the United States, they would not have to compete with "black or yellow hands" in a country where, he added incongruously, there was no discrimination, just "Christian toleration."[30] These observations demonstrated a facile understanding of Irish problems among Argentine officials, yet the plan was given the go-ahead, and Dillon departed for Ireland in April 1881.[31] The British embassy was excluded from the scheme due to Dillon's belief that their involvement would alienate "the class he was going to" and doom his mission before it began.[32] Although Rumbold took the proposal seriously enough to alert the Foreign Office, Home Office, and the Lord Lieutenant of Ireland, he did not anticipate success and derisively noted that Argentina was not "the Eldorado of the agricultural labourer which it is made out to be by the vain and self-complacent Argentinian imagination."[33] He considered nothing "more improbable" than the government offering accessible, fertile lands to new immigrants.[34]

In late 1881, Dillon returned alone to Buenos Aires, with no hordes of Irish migrants following him and no indications that they planned to. Under pressure to explain the failed mission, he published the report he had filed to Interior Minister Yrigoyen in several newspapers. In Ireland, the report recounted, Dillon had visited several Catholic bishops and urged them to assist in "vigorous propaganda" for the assisted emigration scheme, but these efforts bore no fruit. Among the tenant farmers he encountered, Argentina, it seems, was not part of their imagined map of an Irish world. Rather, it was "a country quite unknown," particularly among the rural poor, who knew "nothing, nothing whatever, of South America." Dillon claimed to have met with

Land League leaders in Kilmainham jail, who informed him that they were entirely opposed to emigration. These meetings also affected his views on the Land League; upon his return he expressed some support for the movement. Dillon had departed with the impression that the Argentine government would guarantee "pecuniary support" to induce emigrants to come over, but this was never confirmed, and he lamented that he "could offer them nothing." He recommended that, in the future, small portions of land and free passage be granted to would-be emigrants, with the costs being repaid after eight years.[35] Otherwise, it would be impossible for Argentina to compete with the chain migration and cheaper fares to the United States, or the subsidies offered to settlers in Canada and Australia. Dillon's trip coincided with the early stages of James Hack Tuke's and Bishop John Ireland's assisted emigration schemes to the American Midwest. In comparison, his offer was poor fare.

Despite his defense, Dillon came in for criticism for the cost of his mission and its lack of success. The English-language *Standard* and *Buenos Ayres Herald* were the most sympathetic papers and half-heartedly attempted to defend him, claiming that compulsory military service was an insurmountable deterrent for new immigrants and should be abolished.[36] The anticlerical *Libre Pensador* (Freethinker), however, did not show such restraint and ridiculed Dillon. Edited by Juan Silveira, the paper had already demonstrated an interest in the Land League beyond the usual press reports (often translations from London newspapers) on Parnell's parliamentary manouevers, and it cheered the "stirring up of the revolt against rents." The cause of Ireland, the paper stated, was "the cause of all oppressed people." Noting the involvement of some priests, it remarked that "maybe it is the first time the Catholic clergy have promoted a just movement."[37] The paper did not view Dillon as part of this movement, but rather portrayed him as a dandy, primarily concerned with his own appearance and "foppish hair," which was perfumed with "Rose of the Alps." Dillon promised to "inundate us with immigrants," one editorial jibed, and then he returned with nothing except a large bill for the treasury: "Now we know the importance Mr. Dillon holds in Ireland." Only in Argentina, the paper continued, could he have risen to the level of canon and become a member of the provincial parliament—an amazing feat, considering "he does not speak the language and has no track record of any kind, but just knows how to bend his spine." In short, Dillon advanced through opportunism, sycophancy, and patronage: like a "true clerical leech," he fed off the government and "swapped patriotism for religion" and back again, according to wherever the biggest personal advantage seemed to lay.[38]

Alongside these jibes lay a sharper appraisal of the reasons behind the entire affair, in which the potential immigrants were an incidental concern. President Roca financed the trip in the mistaken expectation that Dillon could corral the Irish Argentine vote—however small—behind his party. Dillon was flattered by the prestige of a European junket on which he would represent the Argentinian government; this "shepherd of the Irish sheep" was only too eager to "elevate himself to the high-life," the *Libre Pensador* concluded, and a self-important Dillon saw the trip as a means to advance his social and political status.[39] Indeed, a large banquet was held in Dillon's honor both before his departure and, despite his failure, also when he returned.[40] Had Dillon succeeded in persuading large numbers to sail to South America, shipping agents stood to profit. His brother John was a shipping agent, with an office in Cork city. John Dillon later collaborated again with the Argentine government on the disastrous *City of Dresden* affair at the end of the decade.

The Roca-Dillon plan was not the only attempt at an "Irish colonization scheme." In 1884, the Home Rule MP for Louth, Philip Callan, came to Argentina and spent months surveying land "outside the pale of civilisation" in Santa Fe province, which he described in letters to the *Southern Cross* as being "as fertile as the best of the plains of royal Meath." So attractive were these lands, Callan maintained, that Irish emigrants would no longer "persist in going to Manitoba, Dakota, Minnesota." In London, an editorial in the *Telegraph* commenting on his trip sneered, "Would an Irishman, never enthusiastic for work, toil hard in a country where intense heat at noonday supplies humanity with an excuse if not a justification for indolence?" The cold Dakota winter provided a greater incentive to work. These comments did not go unnoticed in the *Southern Cross*.[41] Callan's descriptions of lands in Santa Fe turned out to be largely fiction, and the scheme was soon forgotten. According to John Creaghe, the "unfaithful Irish member" Callan was in reality advertising lands that were no more than swamps.

But, Creaghe maintained, even if they had lived up to his description, new immigrants had no opportunities to buy land in a market dominated by a wealthy clique and should be forewarned that they would find in Santa Fe no more than a life of drudgery.[42]

Creaghe's calls for warnings about the false promises of emigration schemes were prescient in light of the miserable *City of Dresden* affair, which ended hopes of renewed Irish migration to Argentina. In 1887, John S. Dillon, Patrick's brother, and another agent named H. Buckley O'Meara were commissioned by the Argentine government to organize emigration from Ireland. In speaking tours and pamphlets, they promised that newcomers would receive official help, and they proved more successful than previous schemes. After sailing from Queenstown via Southampton, the *City of Dresden* arrived in Buenos Aires in February 1889 heavy with at least 1800 people, the majority of whom were Irish, many from poorer areas of Limerick city. Irish Argentines who came to greet them reported exhausted arrivals, accounts of infants dying on the voyage, and an absence of any organized assistance upon disembarking. City hotels were either full or unaffordable, and one letter to the *Freeman's Journal* told of families "with dying babies in their arms stretched on the ground outside a hotel where they had passed the previous night."[43] Over the following weeks, the agents transported some 800 of the new arrivals to work as laborers in the remote Napostà colony, over three hundred miles from Buenos Aires. Soon abandoned, the immigrants lacked shelter and could not communicate in Spanish or Basque. Reports of malnutrition, disease, and high infant mortality appeared in the Irish and Argentine press, and in 1891 the colony was abandoned. O'Meara and Dillon had "exported them as if they were human ballast," lamented the *Freeman's Journal*, and Francis O'Keefe, MP for Limerick, raised the migrants' plight in the House of Commons.[44] Newspapermen Michael Dinneen and Michael Mulhall organized a Buenos Aires aid committee that arranged help and accommodation for some, though some established Irish Argentines displayed haughty attitudes toward the working-class newcomers and indifference toward their situation.[45] The *City of Dresden* Irish were not alone in their predicament; newspapers in France and Belgium had warned would-be migrants to think twice due to recent, similar experiences among their countrymen. In Dublin, the *Freeman's Journal* reported on the episode with a told-you-so tone, repeating how their editorials, along with the bishops of Cashel and Limerick, had warned "strongly and authoritatively" against going. From now on, the paper predicted, Irish emigrants would only consider Argentina "with horror."[46] The affair put an end to any revival of Irish emigration to Argentina.

The "Conquest of the Desert" and Eduardo Casey

Five years before the Dresden affair, John Creaghe wrote to Henry George that "Emigrants must be prevented by all means from coming to this country," in stark contrast to the message promoted by Dillon.[47] Creaghe agreed that land was abundant, but it was not for the peon (laborer) or immigrant. His verdict—that land monopoly in Argentina was fast approaching its limits—had considerable grounds. From the 1850s to the 1880s, sheep farming and wool production for global markets became a leading sector of the economy, which transformed parts of rural Argentina. Expanding commercial agriculture required new lands, which were provided by wars undertaken to displace indigenous people in the Pampas and Patagonia. The free market dictated the sale of the territories seized by the government, and vast tracts of lands were transferred from public to private hands. In the 1870s, the government sold on frontier lands with no limitations on individual purchases, facilitating *latifundismo* and land monopolies. In 1878, new legislation did establish an upward limit of 30,000 hectares for a single purchase, but this was still high and favored large landowners and speculators who, in many cases, found ways around these limits and amassed holdings anyway.[48] Between 1878 and 1882, the state sold some 20,000,000 hectares of land in large parcels to private interests.[49] This market, Creaghe believed, was dominated by an elite that priced out anyone without access to major credit. At the same time, immigration continued to rise. In 1871, Creaghe himself was one of 20,000 new arrivals in Argentina; in 1884, almost 80,000 people came to the country. Net immigration rose to 850,000 during the booming 1880s, a decade that saw the beginning of what one historian has described as "a prodigious process of social transformation" that lasted until the First World War.[50]

One speculator who made an enormous fortune through the soaring land prices in the 1880s was Eduardo Casey, a second-generation Irishman. From the mid-nineteenth century, many Irish immigrants and their children benefited from early involvement in sheep farming and wool and, according to Devoto, gained a greater foothold in the Argentine landowning class compared to other immigrant groups.[51] Living in Luján, west of Buenos Aires, Creaghe would have known both Irish landowners and laborers involved in sheep framing. In 1875, the area around Luján belonged "almost exclusively to Irish sheep-farmers, Browns, Hams, Caseys, Garaghans, Kellys, Clavins, Murphys, Maxwells, Cooks, Kennys, Burgesses, Fitzsimmons. . . . One-half of the population of the department is Irish," and there was also a resident Irish priest.[52] For Creaghe, the rise of some Irish landlords offered the perfect explanation for everything that was wrong with the land system.[53] Few had large fortunes, but the Duggan, Gahan, and Cavanagh families were among those who consolidated extensive holdings in the provinces of Buenos Aires and Santa Fe. Michael Duggan was described by Thomas Murray as the "richest Irishman in Argentina, if not the richest Irishman in the world."[54]

The land wealth of Eduardo Casey was distinctive not only in Irish terms but by the standards of wider Argentine society. Backed by banking contacts in London and political contacts in Buenos Aires, he became one of the figures most associated with the boom of the 1880s and the huge fortunes to be made from land speculation.[55] In his letters to George, Creaghe singled out the rise of Casey, who, by the early 1880s, had acquired "110 leagues in one place alone beside probably thirty leagues in other places."[56] This estimate of Casey's land wealth—140 Argentine leagues—came to c. 350,000 hectares. In 1880, backed by British credit, he acquired huge tracts of land from government sales in Santa Fe province, where the colony of Venado Tuerto was established. Over the next few years, he auctioned off the land in parcels, and with the help of Patrick Dillon via the pages of the *Southern Cross,* he encouraged Irish sheep farmers to invest, promising favorable terms. Through sales to Irish Argentines and others, he made enormous profits off the staggering rates of property appreciation during these years.[57]

In a separate venture in 1881, Casey secured the further purchase of vast land holdings in Buenos Aires province, on which he established the vast Curumalán *estancia*, which he fashioned as a model of agricultural modernization. By this point, the land that Casey had purchased was significantly larger than the entire land area of Westmeath, the Irish county from which his parents had emigrated in 1830. By 1888, the estate employed 500 people, including Irish, French, German, Italian, and American immigrants, and had 200,000 sheep and 43,000 cattle. Across all his estates, Casey was said to own some 80,000 horses, and he also invested heavily in the development of horse racing.[58] Throughout the 1880s, the ambitious Casey continued to expand his business and seemed to personally embody the Irish Argentine success story trumpeted by the *Southern Cross*. Dillon and his successor as editor Michael Dinneen knew Casey personally and enthusiastically documented his rise. At a farewell ball to mark Dillon's return to Ireland, Casey entertained the high-profile guests with party pieces that were "interrupted at every moment with roars of laughter." Regular adverts in the *Southern Cross* called on "Colonists" to avail themselves of the "splendid and valuable lands" he had for sale. Before one "colossal" auction, Dinneen published an interview with Casey about the secrets of his success—essentially a pitch for the auction. Casey outlined his strong loyalties to Argentina, asserting that in "no other country has a foreigner more liberty than in this; he can buy up the whole Republic if he chooses without exciting any jealousy or ill will." He did not minimize his attachment to owning land and claimed, in racial tones, that "Land is gold. . . . Land is the noblest of all property as well as the safest; the owner of £1,000,000 in money is called a usurer or a Jew, the man of a million in land is called a Prince."[59]

The lands on which Casey made his fortune became available for purchase because of genocidal campaigns to remove indigenous populations in the Pampa and Patagonia regions. In 1878 Julio Roca, then minister of war and later president, led the "Conquest of the Desert" to remove Ranqueles, Mapuches, Puelches, and Tehuelches from the plains, to consolidate national borders, and to grab land and resources for expanding white settlement. The so-called desert represented an area with grasslands suited to livestock farming, but the designation suggested an uninhabited territory that required European settlers to develop it.[60] Roca's forces committed brutal acts, with one study maintaining that "physical elimination, concentration practices, deportation, enslavement, identity cleansing of children, and cultural destruction constitute mechanisms that add up to conceptualizing this political process as genocide."[61]

Eduardo Casey acquired the land for the Curumalán estate shortly after it was brought under government control. During the Conquest of the Desert, an Argentine military officer was promised the land for a nominal fee in return for supplying the army with horses. He claimed the lands, but, unable to meet the cost of maintaining them, he fell into difficulty and Casey swooped in and took them.[62] Dillon's assisted emigration plan followed the Conquest of the Desert and aimed to settle Irish migrants on lands taken violently. He did not consider the removal of the existing inhabitants significant enough to mention in his descriptions of the schemes during his tour of Ireland.

Along with many of the larger papers, the Irish-owned *Southern Cross* and *Standard* supported the Conquest of the Desert, which involved some Irish Argentine soldiers. "General Roca's march to the desert," the *Southern Cross* declared, "means more than a mere expedition against the Indians and the more we see of the business the more we like it." The paper directly linked the removal of indigenous groups from the plains to Dillon's plans for new Irish colonies, announcing that "we have no longer any hesitation in recommending the Rio Negro lands to those of our readers who have the spare cash."[63] At the same time, Dillon and the *Southern Cross* became aware of atrocities being committed by Roca's army and occasionally expressed shock at soldiers who behaved "as if the Indians were oxen," suggesting some moral reckoning was necessary for what was taking place.[64] Yet this did not seem to affect their overall support for the Conquest of the Desert. The availability of secure new territories was important for Irish and British commerce and crucial for supporting the gilded descriptions of immigration, and the campaigns reduced the likelihood of raids on frontier settlers.

John Creaghe acknowledged the provenance of Casey's new estancias and their relation to Roca's "expedition which drove out or exterminated the Indians."[65] He maintained that the historic dispossession of indigenous Americans was at the root of land inequality across South America, yet in his letters to George or the newspapers he did not go into in detail about the Conquest of the Desert.[66] He was no doubt aware of some of the army's atrocities, which were reported in the *Southern Cross* and *La Nación*, but he did not weigh in vocally on the question of violence against indigenous groups. Rather, in the 1880s, his focus was firmly on the conditions of peons and immigrants and the breaking up of land monopolies, indicating something of a blind spot for the severity of the violence and exploitation then taking place on the plains.

Creaghe, Michael Dinneen, and the Land Question

In the 1880s a lengthy debate about the conditions of rural workers and the land question in Argentina played out on the pages of the *Southern Cross*. As one of the most high-profile Irish Argentine landowners, Eduardo Casey was singled out in Creaghe's letters to Henry George, but conditions for tenants were as bad or worse on other Irish estates, and Creaghe was not alone in raising protests. One correspondent to the *Southern Cross* decried Irish "Rackrenters in the Plate" and claimed that the same land system that originally "drove us away from our native hills" had now developed in Argentina. Some Irish *estancieros*, along with agents and middlemen, had become "extortioners of the poor" on the sheep ranches around Salto and Arrecifes in Buenos Aires province, grinding huge rents out of tenant farmers for small parcels of land; some rents had increased threefold since the 1870s. Eduardo Casey claimed to offer favorable terms to Irish buyers for modest parcels of land, but another letter to the paper lamented the absence of ethnic solidarity among Irish landowners, who "never cast their memory back to the 'dear old land,'" but reverted to the "lash of the tyrant." Like Creaghe, the author argued that the time had come to form a Land League in Argentina to voice "the grievances under which [Irish tenant farmers] labour and giving substantial assistance to one another when required."[67]

The fact that the *Southern Cross* gave column space to Creaghe and others with similar views reflected the new editorship under Michael Dinneen in 1882. Dinneen's background was varied: born in Bandon, Cork, he studied in Dublin and Paris, later taught at the University of Chile, and translated some classical texts into Irish. Described by Murray as the "fighting editor," he remained head of the *Southern Cross* until William Bulfin took over in 1898, at which point the paper assumed a "sturdy Irish national spirit."[68] Dinneen forwarded collections for various National League funds to Dublin, sent regular copies of the paper to contacts in Ireland and the diaspora, and arranged the delivery of newspapers from Ireland in Argentina. He also received regular letters about missing persons, deaths and illness from Irish families unable to locate relatives. His knowledge of Ireland and Irish politics was partly formed through networks of clerics, including some who passed through South America. For example, James Foran wrote frequently to Dinneen about political developments in Ireland and England and had spent a decade as a priest in the Malvinas and later lived in Buenos Aires, before moving to the northeast of England, where he promoted Home Rule.[69] Under Dinneen, the *Southern Cross* was more openly nationalist than during Dillon's time, but this stance was not accompanied by a departure from the free market economics and association with elites that had characterized Dillon's tenure. Dinneen did take steps to organize an Irish Argentine tenants' rights league, triggered by the questions raised by the Land League in Ireland, though it did not grow on a large scale.[70] The attempt represented some acknowledgment of the challenges facing Irish immigrants to rural Argentina, but Dinneen saw no comparisons with the situation in Ireland. Instead, he persisted in promoting the rosy image that Dillon had peddled before him and, in his letters to Ireland, claimed that "poverty and want are unknown" among Irish Argentines.[71]

One incident in late 1883 focused comparisons between rural Ireland and Argentina. In Salto, a couple by the name of Higgins were imprisoned on the charge of sending threatening letters to their landlord. A steward on the estate had also recently been shot at, and the landlord, a man named Walker who originally came from Derry, interpreted the events as evidence of a conspiracy against him. Letters to the *Southern Cross*, however, questioned the couple's guilt and maintained that, even if Mr. Higgins held some responsibility, his wife's illiteracy meant that she was surely blameless. Her incarceration in Mercedes was decried as a scandal. Appeals were made for funds for a new lawyer to prevent the pair from spending years in jail without a trial, or, worse, dying from the fever then rampaging the prison. Letters to the paper took a dim view of Walker and were suggestive of tensions imported from Ireland. Walker, it was claimed, pursued the couple "with all the insatiable desire of the bloodhound" and was denigrated as having acquired wealth solely by means of marriage to a second-generation Irishwoman. One correspondent, writing under the pseudonym "Anti-Orangeman," portrayed Walker as an anti-Catholic landlord who had exaggerated, if not invented, the affair due to his own prejudices. He had enlisted a personal police escort in Salto to dramatize matters and hired "mercenaries to traduce the Irish people in the Buenos Aires newspapers," particularly *La Nación*. Letters to the *Southern Cross* urged tenants to show more support and solidarity—otherwise the Higginses' fate would be repeated.[72]

For John Creaghe, the Higgins affair underscored some of the parallels between Ireland and Argentina, and he linked the episode to Walker's plans to evict forty Irish shepherds and their families, who had no other options for work in the area.[73] Threatening letters to landlords and warning shots fired at stewards were familiar aspects of agrarian conflicts in Ireland and featured during the Land War. The English-language press reported heavily on the agitation, which perhaps inspired the letter in Salto, or, at least, Walker's interpretation of it. Many Irish emigrants in Argentina hailed from Westmeath, a county that witnessed significant Ribbon society activity after the Great Famine; James Melia, a Ribbon leader from Westmeath, arrived in Argentina in the late 1860s.[74] However, if the Higgins episode reflected the transfer of forms of rural Irish protest to Argentina, it had arrived via an indirect route. While the couple were both immigrants of Irish descent, it was later established that the wife was born in Pennsylvania and the husband in England.[75] Nevertheless, Creaghe, among others, perceived the episode as more evidence that conditions in rural Argentina matched—or were worse than—those left behind in Ireland.

Echoing Henry George, Creaghe championed the Land League as "the advance guard of the strife that will soon agitate all civilised nations." Its achievements in Ireland, he argued, have "taught us to view many things in a different light," particularly the nature of land tenure in Argentina, where the problem was even "more pernicious" than in Ireland.[76] "Every day of the week" at his medical practice in Luján, he came face to face with "cases of utter destitution." Argentina was an Irish landlord's dream, he claimed, with its tradition of large ranches, abundant livestock, and a system of rent and labor unrestrained by public opinion. Borrowing the language of slavery that Land League leaders sometimes deployed to frame the land question, Creaghe asserted that "The Argentine *peon* is much more degraded and much more a slave than the Irish labourer," such were their ties of debt and rent, and their dependence on local justices of the peace, who were "men of the worst character."[77]

The growing inequality in Argentina could only be be permanently halted, Creaghe insisted, by the equal distribution of land through nationalization. In 1883–84, such was the regularity of his letters on the topic to the *Southern Cross* under the pseudonyms "J.C.," "Homo," and ,"P.M.," that other readers wrote in with questions for him, leading Dinneen to grudgingly acknowledge that nationalization versus peasant proprietorship had become the "burning question of the day."[78] Creaghe provoked antagonistic responses from Dinneen and Irish Argentine supporters of the National League, who not only opposed land nationalization in Ireland or Argentina on ideological grounds, but also because they associated it with Michael Davitt and his supporters, who they believed were sowing division within the National League and trying to weaken Charles Stewart Parnell. Echoing the position of *United Ireland* and the *Connaught Telegraph* in Ireland, one article in the *Southern Cross* (signed with a pseudonym) warned that if Davitt "should attempt to introduce the curse of division among them [Irish people] he would be thrown overboard and future ages would execrate his memory." In this view, Davitt was stubbornly pushing against the "will of the people," and Creaghe was not a "friend of Irish nationality . . . when he speaks of Davitt leading another agitation," but merely promoting division within nationalist ranks.[79] At the same time, acknowledging the severity of land problems in Argentina would puncture the *Southern Cross's* romanticized image of immigration.

Creaghe's long letters and articles, dotted with quotations from Henry George, repeatedly made the case for a new movement for the collective ownership of land. He engaged in exchanges with other correspondents (who also signed under pseudonyms), which often slid into lumbering analyses of the successes and failures of the American Homestead Act or systems of land tenure in Europe. Creaghe maintained that peasant proprietorship "has proved a decided failure everywhere" and suggested that the growth of socialism and anarchism worldwide signaled the major challenges lying ahead for private property. The pursuit of peasant proprietorship in Ireland would perpetuate a dysfunctional land system and leave "labourers, the rank and file of the Land League struggle . . . entirely out in the cold." Instead, nationalization would guarantee the rights of all classes and future generations to land, in Ireland and Argentina.[80]

At the same time, Creaghe held an exaggerated understanding of Davitt's political influence in Ireland and misread the firmness of Parnell's opposition to nationalization. His analysis of Irish politics was shaded by his own enthusiasm, as well as his distance from Ireland. Since 1875, telegraph cables had transformed communications between Argentina and Europe, and Irish newspapers were also available. Yet the telegraph was expensive, and the number of available Irish newspapers was less compared to those available to diaspora communities in Britain or North America and took longer, about a month, to arrive. Creaghe's exchanges in the *Southern Cross* were no doubt connected to the transnational debate on the Irish land question, but they also occasionally betrayed his geographical distance from Ireland.

In mid-1884 the Spanish translation of Henry George's *The Irish Land Question* was eventually published in Argentina, completed, with George's approval, by John McKiernan, an Irish Argentine whom Creaghe had known since his arrival in the country. Sales were slow, but Creaghe remained hopeful and in the meantime enjoyed "the satisfaction of seeing it denounced as socialistic" in the mainstream press.[81] The *Southern Cross* acknowledged the publication of the book, observing that its appeal extended far wider than Ireland and merited reading.[82] Around the same time, however, George also became the focus of negative attention in *Southern Cross*, prompted by the continuing attacks by Parnellites on nationalization during his 1884 tour, which concentrated on Britain to a greater extent than Ireland. The *Southern Cross* reprinted articles hostile to George and Davitt from the *Boston Catholic Herald* and the *New York Sunday Tablet* (which Dinneen encouraged Creaghe to read) wrongly claiming that George was born in England, and therefore that was where his loyalties really lay.[83]

Nationalization was dismissed by Dinneen, who asserted that "Ireland has declared through her great spokesman, Parnell, that it is a 'wild craze' and she will have none of it."[84] Dinneen's editorials responded to Creaghe's comparisons of Ireland and Argentina by protesting that the land question in their adopted home "had not assumed the shape of a great national evil as in Ireland. The peasants are not starving on the soil," nor were they forced to emigrate.[85] Nationalization was "impracticable," and even if "Henry George had his way," and it was realized, poverty would not disappear, "*atorrantes*" (idlers/layabouts) would remain in Buenos Aires, and "there would still be men who were unwilling to work, but who are ever ready to pray on society."[86] Some others agreed. Thomas Edward Gormley, a teacher and recent arrival from Ireland, acknowledged that some immigrants worked for "starvation wages," but small landowners in Argentina were "active, prosperous, industrious, and happy" and part of a growing rural middle class. Peasant proprietorship would bring a similar class to Ireland, where owning land was a birthright that would be destroyed by "the positive evil of Nationalization," which would hand over Irish soil to an "alien and hostile government."[87] Dinneen and Gormley believed George's theories only served to distract from the paramount national question, which Irish Argentines needed to engage with more energetically. Gormley criticized the lack of familiarity with Irish nationalist literature and the popularity of London-based magazines such as *Bow Bells* and called for Irish migrants to educate their offspring with the children's magazine *Young Ireland* and the illustrated weekly the *Shamrock* (both taken over by the Land League in the early 1880s).[88]

The debate on nationalization in the *Southern Cross* politely refrained from directly naming Irish Argentine speculators and landlords, but Eduardo Casey was a silent presence. Creaghe's attacks on landlords and large estates and his warnings to new immigrants were all the more problematic because they represented a critique of one of Irish Argentina's brightest stars. At this time, Casey was perhaps the individual who most represented Irish Argentine success; his immigrant parents had done well in Argentina, and their son was one of the most wealthy and admired businessmen in the country. Casey was well connected politically and socially; he was credited with introducing modern farming techniques on lands previously considered a "desert"; he held the same views on immigration as Dillon and Dinneen, proclaiming that no other country offered migrants as many opportunities; and he called for official incentives to increase Irish and European immigration to rural areas. He was a steadfast Catholic and was considered to be loyal to the Irish community: he donated to Irish charities, including the Relief Fund during the Land War, and offered favorable terms to Irish settlers at Venado Tuerto. Yet he also relied on loans from Irish Argentine investors to purchase Curumalán when London financiers got cold feet.[89] Because Casey's success as a landowner was inextricably intertwined with the upper- and middle-class Irish Argentine community, Creaghe's radical critique of land and immigration struck a personal tone, as well as an ideological one, which contributed to tensions.

In numerous articles Creaghe responded to his critics, accusing the *Southern Cross* of wilful blindness to social problems and claiming that Dinneen was determined to "listen to nothing which is not endorsed by 'Ireland's greatest man', as you call Parnell." By mid-1884, Dinneen stopped printing Creaghe's letters, prompting him to ask if this was because of fearing "to offend your subscribers, who might take it for something 'communistic.'" Not willing to outstay his welcome, Creaghe promised to stop writing to the paper. Given Dinneen's outright rejection of Creaghe's position, why did he publish his letters and articles for so long? One explanation is that the Irish community, particularly its professional classes, was still small and integrated enough to keep Creaghe from being ignored. Dinneen, Dillon, and Creaghe had likely met each other; their personal circles overlapped. Many accounts from the time describe Creaghe as a charming and well-liked character.[90] Patrick Dillon had officiated at the marriage of Creaghe's friend Arthur Greene; Creaghe advertised his practice in the *Southern Cross* in the 1870s, and he knew the Mulhall brothers, editors of the *Standard*. Creaghe's letters also suggest he had met Eduardo Casey. These personal connections prevented outright hostility, and when Creaghe announced he would cease writing to the *Southern Cross*, Dinneen responded with "our columns are always open to 'J.C.' and always will be, and, though we do not agree with his theories, we admire his ability and respect his honest convictions, and we shall always be glad to hear from him."[91] Evidently Creaghe was not yet associated with anarchists, who, according to the paper, were "especially marked by the Church for malediction."[92] Creaghe was also esteemed for his acerbic responses to newspaper articles with a perceived anti-Irish or anti-Catholic bias. One letter published in the *Buenos Ayres Herald* that claimed the Irish were predisposed to lawlessness provoked Creaghe to write to the paper to rebuke the author as a "snivelling bigot" and "pious sneak" who used the "vilest of epithets" to describe Irish nationalists. If Irish history taught one lesson, he declared, it was that people were demoralized and lacked faith in the law because a "foreign government" used "force and fraud" to rule. The following issue of the *Southern Cross* reprinted his letter in full.[93]

During their debates on the land question, Dinneen referred to Creaghe as "an Irish nationalist: so are we."[94] Creaghe, who had been a member of the Home Rule League and the Land League, believed Ireland was deprived of "the right of every nation, to govern herself" and should be granted "legislative freedom." At the same time, he argued that the injustice of land monopoly would unite the working classes of Ireland and Britain in a common struggle. "What greater proof of that union can there be," he maintained, than to see the "noble Irish convict Davitt received with frenzied applause" in England and Scotland? "Thanks to Mr George," Creaghe wrote, "I have come to see plainly that the cause of Ireland is the cause of the people of England: that there is no real antagonism between us." The root cause of misery and injustice on the island was "the same cause which crams the workhouses in England, which produces there, also, want, misery and vice."[95] Creaghe embraced a sense of working-class unity and solidarity between Ireland and Britain, but combined this with support for some form of Irish independence.

At the end of the 1880s, however, Creaghe moved away from Irish nationalism. Instead, he became increasingly interested in anarchism and its outright rejection of the state. Dinneen's main criticism of Creaghe had been that, following years of promoting Henry George's theories and nationalization, he had still "not gained more proselytes" and stood "alone against a host," as he had at the beginning.[96] This was not entirely accurate: others had voiced support, but it was inescapable that Creaghe had failed to start a radical land movement. The absence in the country of even limited reforms or a homesteading scheme along American lines dimmed Creaghe's faith in the capacity of progressive reforms to challenge the power wielded by landed interests over government and the economy. As the 1880s progressed, increases in rents and food prices, as well as the start of a serious economic crisis, triggered strikes and considerable trade union activity that drew Creaghe in the direction of radical labor groups. Around this time he met the eminent Italian anarchist Errico Malatesta, who was then living in Argentina, and the encounter had a decisive impact. Creaghe came to view the general strike as the most effective means of revolution, by allowing workers to take control, not just of factories, but of land too, and in 1888 he helped establish one of the first anarchist newspapers in Argentina, *La Verdad.* In turn, Creaghe's knowledge of the Land League interested Malatesta..[97] In the 1890s, Creaghe grew more distant from the Irish Argentine community. On one occasion he severely damaged his links with Irish Catholic leaders, when, along with a group of anarchists in Luján, he sought to protest and disrupt the annual pilgrimage to the town in honor of the Virgin of Luján, the patron saint of Argentina—a major event for Irish Catholics, not only in Luján, but across Buenos Aires province—and ended up in jail.[98] Despite Creaghe's embrace of anarchism, however, his writings continued to echo Henry George into the twentieth century.

In 1889 Creaghe traveled to Ireland and Britain and spoke in Dublin on "Anarchism versus Democracy" to the Progressist Club, who held meetings and lectures on trade unionism, strikes, and the single tax. Reports claimed that the "advocates of Social Democracy were the more numerous" at the meeting, but "the anarchists having if anything the best of the argument." Creaghe also likely attended a lecture on the Haymarket Anarchists by Thomas Fitzpatrick, a Dublin anarchist who had gone to Chicago in 1888 to investigate the case for himself.[99] There is little more evidence for this trip, and, while the land agitation had reignited in the Plan of Campaign, there is no indication that Creaghe attempted to observe demonstrations or eviction protests firsthand. He returned to the political and economic turmoil in Argentina in 1890, when the Barings Bank crisis was in full swing, before departing again for Sheffield, England, where he remained until the end of 1892. His departure was likely motivated by a desire to be closer to London, then the international centre of anarchism-in-exile, and a city for which Malatesta was also bound.[100] The 1890 economic crisis hit hard in Argentina, not least for Eduardo Casey, who suffered a remarkable reversal of fortune when the land boom ended. Unable to access credit in London or to service the debt on his massive holdings, he was soon ruined, losing almost everything. He survived for another sixteen years, living in modest circumstances, until he fell under a train in Buenos Aires in 1906, aged fifty-nine.[101]

In Sheffield, Creaghe advocated militant tactics and expropriation, calling on the working classes to take what they needed to survive, using force if necessary. Historians have considered his militancy in the context of the "direct action" schools of anarchism that were then becoming increasingly visible in Europe.[102] But Creaghe's stance derived less from Bakuninism and more from his reading of Irish history, Fenianism, and the Land League. Previously, in the *Southern Cross*, Creaghe had praised Irish agrarian secret societies and the Fenian movement. In the *Sheffield Anarchist* he lauded the Land League as proof of the importance of "unconstitutional methods," claiming "Balfour, Gladstone and Co have been forced to consider the land question; not by the handful of Irish members, but by the brave Fenians and Hillside boys."[103] He encouraged anarchists to emulate the Fenians when commemorating the Haymarket anarchists, with a poster for one Sheffield demonstration calling on workers to follow the example of the Fenians who "meet yearly to commemorate the cowardly murders of their brave comrades, Allen, Larkin and O'Brien," the three "Manchester Martyrs" of 1867 who were executed for their role in a prison escape.[104] Creaghe was not alone in drawing these parallels; the main anarchist newspaper in Britain, *Freedom*, printed regular articles on Ireland in the 1880s and often held Irish unrest up as an example of popular resistance to government.[105] Creaghe claimed the most important question for Ireland was not Home Rule or Rome Rule, but "Home Rule or No Rule" and optimistically predicted "that Anarchy will find in Ireland a people ready to accept its teachings." Curiously, Creaghe held Charles Stewart Parnell in some regard. Despite his rejection of constitutional methods and his trenchant criticisms of peasant proprietorship, Creaghe nevertheless wrote that Parnell's death represented a major loss for Irish society.[106]

The language of Henry George and the Land League infused the *Sheffield Anarchist*. Creaghe used the paper to encourage boycotting and resistance to rent payments, and he peppered his articles with statements such as "The land owner who does nothing himself robs you of all that your labour on the soil produces." Clear echoes of the *Irish World* could be heard in the lines, "The Irish Landlord, the British Shipowner and Ironmaster, and the American Railway Boss are equally indebted to pillage and manslaughter for their money bags."[107] In 1891 Creaghe launched a "no rent strike" in Sheffield and sought to lead by example. He physically stopped a "bum bailiff" from removing furniture, in lieu of rent owed, from his dispensary, by applying "a few whacks" of a poker to force him out the door and then "laughed at him through the window." When the bailiff again attempted to remove goods from the house, Creaghe threatened "serving him as they did in Ireland" and made a speech about the Land League to the small crowd that had gathered.[108] Creaghe soon returned again to Argentina and established the anarchist newspaper *El Oprimido* in Luján. The violent language that he had become known for in Sheffield receded from view, and instead he placed organization and education at the forefront of his view of revolution. From 1897 to 1910, he occasionally edited, contributed articles and gave considerable financial help to the daily *La Protesta*, one of the most important and long-running anarchist newspapers globally in the pre–First World War era.[109]

* * *

Creaghe's activism in the 1880s had failed to generate an Argentinian Land League or a following of like-minded radicals. Yet he did force the *Southern Cross* and Irish Argentine leaders to reflect more directly on how the causes they supported in Ireland related to questions about inequalities and landlordism in Argentinian society and, in the process, brought their political and social conservatism into focus. In times of economic boom, Creaghe provided a dissenting voice that warned of the false promises made to immigrants, and his writings challenged the rosy picture of opportunity and easy prosperity promoted by Dillon and Dinneen. Creaghe's engagement with the Land League and Henry George developed his understanding of the importance of changing land rights within his vision of wider social revolution. The Land League ultimately became a stepping-stone for him into the anarchist movement, demonstrating some of the interplay between the land movement and wider revolutionary politics in the late nineteenth century.

In September 1911, a seventy-year-old Creaghe left Argentina again, animated by news of events in the Mexican Revolution and eager to escape continual police attention. He traveled to Los Angeles via Mexico in order to join up with the anarchist group that had grown around the brothers Ricardo and Enrique Flores Magón, with whom he had already been in contact, and to offer his services as a doctor.[110] After he arrived in California, their paper *Regeneración* printed an article by Creaghe addressed to his Argentinian and Uruguayan comrades, explaining that he initially doubted reports of the extent of the revolutionary atmosphere, but, after spending time in Mexico, he had become convinced of the "immense importance" of events there and the potential of the Zapata movement, and he asked for their best efforts to support the *Regeneración* group, whose rallying cry was *tierra y libertad* (land and freedom). Land remained fundamental to his concept of revolution. He viewed historic colonial dispossession to be at the root of revolutionary discontent, asserting that "There can not be peace in Mexico until the people possess what they consider to be theirs." Just as he believed Ireland had been in the 1880s, Mexico was now "the front line of this beautiful social, agrarian revolution."[111] Creaghe also collaborated in California with the British American anarchist William Owen, who produced the English-language journal *Land and Liberty*. It seems that Creaghe, then in his mid-seventies, was still inspired by Henry George and *Progress and Poverty*. The journal was highly critical of the American single tax movement, claiming that it misrepresented George's original doctrine as "trifling reform," when in reality it was "one of the most revolutionary ever preached, since it proposes to abolish landlordism entirely."[112] *Land and Liberty's* advice to revolutionaries was: "Study the land problem. It is absolutely basic, and until you understand it you cannot be an effective soldier in the revolutionary army."[113]

5

Thomas Ainge Devyr and the "Great Truth"

Writing to Karl Marx from his Brooklyn home in 1872, Thomas Ainge Devyr described himself "as a leader and editor, both in England and here," and a land reformer who had once been "one of the most active men in the Chartist movement."[1] By the time of this letter, Devyr was a veteran activist. He began campaigning for land reform in his native Donegal in the 1830s, before emigrating to England, where he became a Chartist. In 1840, he fled to the United States to escape arrest for planning an insurrection in Newcastle and was soon a familiar face in New York radical circles, with one contemporary going so far as to claim that Devyr was "entitled to the credit of having conceived this great principle of man's natural right to the soil."[2] He wrote to Marx with hopes of forming an alliance between the First International and land reformers. He had made similar attempts to forge a new land movement for decades, with few concrete results. In the 1870s, close to resignation, Devyr was reinvigorated by the *Irish World* and the Land League, which seemed to realize the type of land movement he had long campaigned for. New levels of transnationalism characterized Irish radicalism during the Land War, but Devyr's life illustrates the long historical roots of these networks; in many respects, Devyr embodied the idea of the nineteenth-century transatlantic radical.

The septuagenarian Devyr was not a leading figure in the Land League. Outside of his New York circle of reformers, which came together in an anti-rent campaign in the 1840s, he cut something of an independent figure on the fringes of various labor movements as well as Irish nationalism, which has contributed to his neglect by historians. Nonetheless, his obituary in the *Irish World*, similar to those in other New York newspapers, remembered him as "one of the founders of the Land-Reform Movement."[3] Devyr himself claimed to be an early advocate of the theories later espoused by Patrick Ford, Michael Davitt, and Henry George. This was part exaggeration, but the type of land radicalism Devyr advanced throughout his life was central to the development of new kinds of oppositional politics in the 1870s, including the Land League. His transatlantic blend of Ribbonism, Chartism, and American agrarianism, in addition to the interlinking of land and labor reform, was a precursor to the ideology espoused by the *Irish World*. Devyr connected the Land League with an older generation of reformers and the nineteenth-century tradition of agrarian radicalism. While historian Eric Foner has argued that the American Land League was shaped by Irish immigrants' embrace of American reform politics, a closer look at Devyr's life suggests that a more reciprocal process of exchange occurred across the nineteenth century that informed the new land radicalism of the 1870s and 1880s on both sides of the Atlantic, rather than a process that occurred solely in the United States.[4]

Outside of Ireland, the Land League found its strongest response in the United States, which was then home to some five million people of Irish birth or descent, rivaling the population of Ireland itself. The American Land League was formed in 1880, following a tour by Charles Stewart Parnell. By 1881 it had one thousand branches, and Kerby Miller has estimated it may have had as many as half a million members, who hailed mainly from the immigrant working classes.[5] The Land League emerged at a time of heightened industrial tension in the United States, and its anti-monopoly and anti-rent messages appealed to urban Irish Americans at the forefront of labor disputes in the 1870s. Their sense of grievance was intensified by the executions in 1877–78 of twenty men linked to the Irish secret society known as the Molly Maguires, following an unfair trial for violent crimes in the Pennsylvania coal fields. More than other Irish American newspapers, the *Irish World* responded to working-class concerns, marrying radical land and labor reform in its columns, and generating broad support for the Land League.[6] Impressed by what he read, Devyr approached Ford and joined the staff of the *Irish World* in 1876. His columns advanced his long-held doctrine on what he variously referred to as the "Divine Truth," the "Sublime Truth," or the "Great Truth": that land was a natural resource, a gift from God to humanity that could not be privately owned. This spiritual understanding of humanity's natural right to land also informed the approach of Henry George and the *Irish World*, and the paper adopted Devyr's phrase "Spread the Light" in its fundraising.[7]

Devyr's life offers a distinctive perspective on the ideological alliances, as well as some of the tensions, between Irish land reform and wider social movements in the nineteenth century. By many accounts, he was a rousing public speaker, but also an intransigent follower of his own ideas who struggled to tolerate approaches to reform not akin to his own. His interactions with the Irish community in New York were thorny before his alliance with the *Irish World*, and he never fully incorporated nationalism into his reformist worldview. His pugnacious manner contributed to abrasive encounters with other radicals and Irish nationalists, and particularly with proponents of the abolitionist movement. Historians have recognized that the *Irish World* and the Land League expressed affinity with and admiration for American abolitionists and radical Republicans, yet Devyr offers a reminder that this outlook was not universally held. He took a narrow view of abolitionism and considered it an unnecessary distraction from land reform. For Devyr, Irish tenant farmers and industrial factory workers were worse off in some respects than enslaved people in the American South. At the same time, he was no reactionary; he argued that radical land reform was the only real way to comprehensively end slavery on southern plantations and wage slavery in northern factories. His intransigence on this issue and others, however, exposed tensions in the Irish land movement's wider alliances.

Ireland

Thomas Ainge Devyr was born about 1810 in Donegal town in the northwest of Ireland. He came from a mixed religious household; his mother was an English-born Methodist, and his father, an Irish Catholic, had been active in the United Irishmen movement of the late eighteenth century. Devyr downplayed the influence of his parents, attributing his own politicization and, in his words, "chivalric" approach to reform to the novels he read in his youth, though he criticized others for not appreciating their parents' effect on their lives. His memoirs, self-published in 1882, described the hardships of his childhood and how his parents, "though in a small way of business, were very poor." They were more comfortable than others in the area, however, and at different times ran a bakery and a hotel. As a child Devyr attended school and had access to books through his sister, who worked as a governess, and he was aware of his better education compared to his peers, "all very poor and wholly illiterate." He spoke only English and noted how his lack of Irish inhibited his interactions. Although touted for the priesthood as a teenager, from a young age he claimed "no allegiance to either church or king," though strong spiritual convictions underpinned his radical views. In the early 1830s, he married Margaret McIntyre, and soon their daughter Cecilia arrived, the first of ten children and the only one born in Donegal. Devyr first found work as a clerk to a yarn dealer before setting out as a traveling hardware merchant, with a shop in Killybegs, Co. Donegal. This work required travel around counties Donegal, Sligo, and Mayo, and the poverty he encountered contributed to shaping his political views.[8]

Devyr remembered a rigid "caste" system in Donegal, where social place was carefully stewarded. In the towns, he recalled, the "shopkeeper knows his high position," while the day laborer was "the lowest down of all." Along with economic hardship, poverty carried with it a social and psychological burden, for "it was a great discredit to be poor—a disgrace, almost a crime." His experiences traveling around the northwest of Ireland left an impression, including a stay at a boatman's cabin, where Devyr passed two nights before a rough crossing: "I saw his children, from five to ten years of age, without any other covering than a piece of ragged flannel pending from the waist, and on one, a child of about three years old, I never saw a rag of clothing of any kind, although I saw it many times, both in Summer and Winter."[9] Devyr would describe how, following the potato crop failures of 1835, he saw people in the Rosses region of west Donegal "driven to subsist on seaweed, and the green garbage of the fields." These encounters gave him insight into grinding human struggles that politicians and "the men who write books, who assume to speak with authority, know or care little about."[10] Throughout his life Devyr felt his firsthand knowledge of severe poverty set him apart from middle-class reformers, even if his own hardships were relative compared to the scenes he witnessed.

The solution to such misery and inequality, Devyr resolved, was land reform. Influenced by the legacy of the United Irishmen and their rebellion, he reprinted satirical pamphlets by James Porter, the Presbyterian minister executed after 1798. The main influence on his developing radicalism came from agrarian secret societies, which had a considerable presence in Ulster. He referred to groups such as the Ribbonmen, Carders, Levellers, and "Tommy Downshire[s]", as "knights-errant in their way," and the descendants of the 1798 rebels. Thanks to these "agrarian regulators," Devyr wrote, "in no place has their [landlords'] greed been so effectually resisted as in the North." Whether all of these groups were active in Donegal in the early nineteenth century is open to question; in his 1882 memoir Devyr may have projected a wider history of agrarian radicalism back onto his youth. He alluded to being a member of a Ribbon society himself and was friends with local man Neal Gallagher, a "chief officer of the Ribbon organization," with whom he conspired to counter Orange demonstrations in Donegal.[11] Devyr's exposure to the radical ideas of Thomas Spence and others likely first came first through his Ribbon associations. As Kyle Hughes and Donald MacRaild have demonstrated, Spencean ideas circulated through the Ribbon networks that extended across the Irish Sea to England.[12] Devyr was also influenced by the temperance movement and Daniel O'Connell; he paid the Catholic Rent in the 1820s and, similar to Fergus O'Connor, first admired but then bitterly opposed O'Connell, mainly because of O'Connell's anti-Chartism and what Devyr considered his self-interest and regard for the British aristocracy. Due to his early break with the Repeal movement, Devyr even claimed to be the "oldest 'Young Irelander,'" and he decried O'Connell as "a deluder of the Irish people who wanted merely to transfer the tyranny from London to Dublin."[13] He remained implacably hostile to O'Connell and to his memory all his life.

Devyr's first public call for reform came in the 1836 pamphlet *Our Natural Rights*, published in Belfast. It set out the principle that remained central to his worldview throughout his life: that absolute ownership of land was unnatural and the cause of "mighty evils" worldwide. *Our Natural Rights* combined influences from Spence and Paine on common ownership with a biblical understanding of land, derived from a reading of Leviticus, as a natural resource that cannot be privately owned because it is the God-given inheritance of all. The existing rent system denied the tenant farmer and laborer the true value of their work. Breaking up landed estates and placing limits on the amount of land any individual or family could occupy would, Devyr professed, bring wide-ranging transformations. These reforms would "civilise and refine the people, destroy intemperance and crime, root out misery from the land, add to our strength and importance as a nation, by keeping at home the flower of our population." And, anticipating the sentiments of the Land League over forty years later, the pamphlet emphasized the relationship between an individual's economic independence and their political independence.[14]

Although Devyr considered *Our Natural Rights* his most accomplished work and evidence of his credentials as a pioneering land reformer, its vision of rural Ireland post-transformation included significant contradictions, particularly relating to the future roles of landlords. He maintained that they should perform a type of paternalist social duty within the community as "promoters of improvement and civilisation," and in return people would provide a regular payment for their "reasonable wants."[15] His thinking on this issue seems to have been steered by his admiration for William Sharman Crawford, the progressive landlord, agrarian reformer, and MP for Co. Down, whom he personally knew. Yet Crawford was an exceptional figure in many respects. This understanding of landlords' social roles betrayed an ambiguous attitude toward the rural working classes, whom Devyr described as "an uncultivated people" who would not be ready for a new society without the landlords' help.[16] These views changed, however, during Devyr's involvement in the Chartist movement in Newcastle two years later.

England

Devyr lived in England for little more than three years, but his experience of Chartism left a lasting stamp. His account of this period has been widely used by historians to analyze Chartism generally, but Devyr has received little attention as a figure in his own right.[17] Following the publication of *Our Natural Rights*, Devyr resolved to dedicate his life to campaigning against land monopolies and concluded that the place to begin was London, "that great centre of thought and action." He arrived in 1837 and found work with the *Constitutional*, a reform-leaning daily, but left when the paper would not publish his attacks on the Poor Law in Ireland. Struggling to support himself and his family, he worked for a time as a policeman on the night beat in Hackney, a time he recalled as one of the lowest of his life.[18] Downcast, he advertised for work and received an unexpected offer from the Chartist Robert Blakey to join the Newcastle-based *Liberator*, a radical weekly with a sizable circulation. Blakey was restructuring the paper after having just bought it from the New York-born Augustus Beaumont, who came to Newcastle via Jamaica, where he had managed a plantation, though he later became an abolitionist.[19] Devyr happily departed London, but would remember its "dead sea of pauperism" as a damning indictment of class exploitation through rent.[20] He became secretary to the Chartists' Northern Political Union in Newcastle, where he found the political atmosphere inspiring, along with the "zeal, activity, and singleness of purpose" of Blakey and Thomas Doubleday and the Irish Chartists James Bronterre O'Brien and Fergus O'Connor, with whom he shared a platform in 1838.[21]

Devyr immersed himself in urban labor politics, writing articles and speaking at meetings in Newcastle and other northeastern towns. He also helped set up a successful joint stock store that supplied provisions to colliers, utilizing skills from his Donegal hardware-store days. His ideas about land reform became less restrained and less forgiving toward landlords, whom he now attacked as "profligate idlers" who were part of the "unjust and manslaying aristocracy." His previous admiration for Sharman Crawford dwindled, and he now considered him a "humbug" for his O'Connellite associations.[22] Seeking to help build alliances in Ireland, Devyr jointly wrote an address with the Newcastle Chartists to "their oppressed brothers in Ireland," calling on the "descendants of the Volunteers" to reject government and "the exterminating power of the Landlord" and make common cause with Chartists for "the rights of citizenship" within the United Kingdom, using physical force if necessary. If the Chartists failed in their demands, the address promised they would then support a "purely Representative Parliament in College Green."[23] Daniel O'Connell greeted the address with hostility, which was unsurprising, due to his anti-Chartism and enmity toward Fergus O'Connor. For Devyr, this was simply more evidence of O'Connell's aristocratic worldview.[24]

A readiness to use physical force was a feature of the secret societies Devyr knew in Ireland, and he was not averse to violence as a tactic.

In Newcastle, he was involved in the militant turns of 1839–40. The "Address to the Middle Classes of the North of England" of July 1839, which seems to have been written (or cowritten) by Devyr, struck a newly confrontational tone. It first appealed "in the language of brotherhood" to the middle classes for support, but warned that "if you feel not for the myriads who annually perish of cold and hunger—still ask yourselves, are you prepared to see your own home in a blaze." Published in the *Liberator*, the address would lead to charges against Blakey and the printer.[25] Following a combative speech at a demonstration, Devyr was arrested and then released on bail for using seditious language—or as the *Liberator* put it, "stirring up routs, rebellions, riots, insurrections, and all that manner of thing."[26] As police attention on the Chartist movement increased nationally, Devyr participated in a type of insurrectionary underground in Newcastle that included the manufacture of thousands of pikes in preparation to strike in concert with the Newport uprising of November 1839, when thousands of Chartists marched on the Welsh town demanding democratic rights. When the Newcastle uprising failed to materialize, Devyr then conspired in plans for insurrections across multiple northern towns in January 1840 to coincide with the trials of the Newport Chartists, which would involve homemade explosives as well as pikes. The popular Chartist paper the *Northern Star* published last-minute denunciations of the plans, and when only seventy of the supposed seven hundred rebels turned up on the arranged night in Newcastle, Devyr called everything off. Nonetheless, some "desperate spirits" were eager to try and spark an insurrection by launching arson attacks in the city, which Devyr managed to prevent, despite threats on his own life for attempting to stop them.[27] A few days later, tipped off that his arrest was imminent and fearing a charge of treason, he decided to flee with his family to New York and sailed from Liverpool.[28]

The United States

Devyr and his family sailed into New York penniless, pawning possessions in order to rent a room in Brooklyn. Yet within two months Devyr had cofounded the *Williamsburg Democrat*, a weekly paper backed by the Democratic party.[29] This relationship soon became strained, however, due to Devyr's role at the centre of a campaign that provided a congenial environment for his land reform ideas. In the 1840s, an anti-rent movement erupted among tenant farmers in upstate New York that would have notable parallels with the Irish Land War forty years later. Both campaigns embraced boycotts, legal challenges, and electoral politics and featured divisions in leadership between advocates of peasant proprietorship and radicals who advanced concepts of land as a natural resource that could not be owned.[30] Devyr became a key figure in the latter group, and his anti-rent campaigning brought him to the attention of the group associated with George Henry Evans and John Windt in New York. In 1844, they invited him to form the National Reform Association, which Evans saw as an American iteration of a new generation of democratic movements sweeping the Atlantic world. Devyr soon became an editor on their paper, the *National Reformer*, and he represented a vehicle for Chartist and Irish influences within the organization.[31]

The land war in upstate New York aimed for more egalitarian distribution of land for tenant farmers and an end to fixed-term leases. It expanded to some sixty thousand supporters by the mid-1840s. For Devyr, the war was one between "feudalism and freedom," a struggle to replace a lease system he considered reminiscent of the United Kingdom, which had no place in a modern republic.[32] In 1842, he began speaking at anti-rent meetings in Albany and Rensselaer counties and later championed the cause in the *National Reformer*. Within a few years he moved to Albany and edited the *Albany Freeholder*, a new organ for the anti-renters. Along with land reform theories, his impact was also suggested by some of the tactics employed by the anti-renters, including civil disobedience and oath-bound cells that intimidated landlords, resembling those of the agrarian societies of Ireland. On one occasion, a local sheriff was killed in an exchange of fire and an Irish immigrant was convicted for his murder, though he was later pardoned.[33] Devyr developed his land reform ideas during the campaign, borrowing aspects of Jeffersonian agrarianism while remaining wedded to the core principles advanced in *Our Natural Rights* that land was common property, and that whatever rewards came from cultivating it belonged to the laborer. Along with the National Reformers, his vision entailed universal access to land in a republic of small farmers, with federal lands diced up into small plots and distributed by the government, with strict limits on the amount of land occupied by any one family.[34] From England, the Chartist *Northern Star* looked on admiringly at the "glorious movement" and "march of agrarianism" in the United States, and reprinted speeches by Devyr and Evans.[35]

Unlike Patrick Ford in the Irish Land War, Devyr did not advocate the policy of land nationalization. "We want no revolution," he told one meeting, but also warned it might come without any settlement.[36] Nevertheless, mainstream organs depicted him as a danger to private property. The daily *Commercial Advertiser* reported that he "denies the right of any man to own more land than he can cultivate with his own hands—utterly denies the right of ownership beyond the extent of actual culture—and makes war against the whole system of rents," concluding that the "appearance of the *National Reformer* is a warning to us . . . we must do battle against it."[37] More conservative leaders within the anti-rent campaign who were aligned with the Democrat and Whig parties viewed Devyr as too "dangerous," and he was ultimately removed from the *Albany Freeholder*.[38] Denouncing his opponents as political opportunists, he then launched the *Anti-Renter*, but he became sideined within the movement and returned to New York when his money ran out. The experience embittered him toward Democrat leaders, though over the next decades he retained some hope of steering the party toward land reform. Reeve Huston has argued that, despite the marginalization of Devyr and the National Reformers in the anti-rent campaign, their activism did cause conservative Whig and Democrat leaders to "became more radical," forcing some degree of realignment that reflected the concept of natural rights to land.[39]

The National Reformers' transatlantic agrarianism would find reflection in the radical labor politics of the late 1870s, including the activities of the Land League. Devyr provided a direct link between the two movements along with Joshua K. Ingalls, another veteran reformer who contributed to the *Irish World*.[40] It is tempting to link Devyr's enthusiastic support for the Land League in part to nostalgia for the anti-rent campaign of the 1840s, when he was in his heyday, at the center of a movement with kindred idealism. The *Irish World* and the *National Reformer* were New York-based newspapers, yet both advanced a pastoral view of social transformation, viewing land reform as a solution for urban as well as rural ills that would allow society generally to prosper. Equitable access to land would slow migration to cities, reduce overcrowding, and end the undercutting of wages, granting industrial workers far more bargaining power with employers, as there would be less cheap labor. In Ireland, Patrick Ford argued, land reform would remove the necessity for emigration and lead to less Irish crowding into American and British cities. Alternatively, without universal access to land, urban industrial labor would become a race to the bottom.[41] Yet the *Irish World* differed with the National Reformers on the issue of land nationalization. By the time of the Land War, Ford was even more explicit than Henry George in his assertion that "all control of lands should be vested in the state as trustee for its citizens, thus debarring all and any from proprietorship of land."[42] In contrast, Devyr stressed that "I by no means believe in State landlordism."[43]

The belief that political parties were irreparably corrupt, along with the intransigent view of land as a "Divine Gift" that could not be owned by individual or state, formed the basis of Devyr's rejection of nationalization and socialism. Back in the 1830s, he had envisaged "an inconsiderable levy off the land" to be paid to government, and again in the 1860s he spoke of land rents being paid to the state "for the public advantage."[44] While he favored a limited land tax, he balked at the idea of state ownership of land or industry. In the early 1870s he pivoted toward socialism with other veteran National Reformers and joined the First International in New York, but at one meeting he was shocked to hear expressions of support not only for state ownership of land, but also state cultivation. Marx and Engels had viewed the National Reform Association as a type of early socialism, and in the 1860s Devyr began to send Marx some of his writings on taxation.[45] When the New York police clubbed socialist demonstrators who expressed support for the Paris Commune, Devyr offered his support and wrote to Marx that the "'Internationals' and the Land Reformers here are to form a junction."[46] Yet his speeches on public frontier lands for industrial workers got a damp reception at meetings of the International Workingmen's Association in New York, the members having "long since passed that old opinion," and Devyr soon departed the branch.[47] In the 1880s, he criticized Henry George's "false assumption that the land is the property of the nation" and maintained that the advocates of nationalization underestimated officials' capacity to abuse the system. A single tax on land "would require a horde of men to work it, every one of which was a fallible, perhaps vicious and dishonest man." Nonetheless, he admired George in several respects and on other occasions lauded his "clear conception of the Great Truth."[48]

Devyr was in his sixties when he began writing for the *Irish World*, but it marked his first substantial engagement with Irish nationalism and was more cordial than any of his previous interactions with Irish reformers or organizations. Williamsburg had a Repeal association when he settled there in the 1840s, but he refused to join and "denounced O'Connell as a sycophant," sparking "the first cause of difference between my countrymen and myself." He further stirred animosities when he opposed an Irish-led initiative for an "Adopted Citizens Democratic Association", on the basis that it unnecessarily separated immigrants from native-born party members.[49] Later in the decade, Devyr claimed that he had attempted to organize the shipping of food to Ireland during the Great Famine but was frustrated by the excessive bureaucracy of local committees and the misuse of funds. The Famine certainly hardened his convictions that landlordism must be abolished, and he was later scathing about the exportation of food during the crisis.[50] In 1848, contemporary newspapers reported on his support for Young Ireland and appearances at rallies in New York in support of the Irish Republican Union and their plan to send an "Irish Brigade" to assist with insurrection in Ireland. Along with many Irish Americans, Devyr overestimated Young Ireland's strength and was dismayed by news of the abortive rising.[51] At the same time, he took issue with the Young Irelanders' nationalism, later asking William Smith O'Brien if his concept of a free Irish nation simply meant "that a few Irish lawyers and Irish gentleman shall 'play at government' and taxes without interference from British power? If so, a fig for it. I would not raise my finger to produce such a change."[52] He took a similar stance toward Fenianism. Initially attracted by the ideas of John O'Mahony, he contributed articles to the New York-based *Irish People*, but soon felt his radical views were being silenced. He then started his own *Fenian Brotherhood* newspaper, but it proved short-lived due to his frustrations with Fenian leaders' attitudes to the land question. As he put it to O'Mahony, "Nationality per se is not Freedom."[53]

The *Fenian Brotherhood* was a one-man operation that included some eye-catching articles, one of which gives a glimpse of the misogyny of the time. One front-page piece recounted the conviction and hanging of an Irish American man in New Jersey for strangling his wife to death. Devyr contested the jury's quick decision, accepting the man's defence that his wife was an "irreclaimably drunken" woman, and that, one day, in frustration with finding her drunk and no dinner on the table, he had punched her, and she fell over, hit her neck on the side of their child's cradle, and died. Drunkenness, the article argued, was the main cause of her death, not the punch, as it made her lose her balance. Despite delivering the blow, the "good and virtuous and brave and religious man" was innocent of murder, or even manslaughter. "Who might not strike a blow under the sudden impulse of anger at this repeated and criminal drunkenness of his wife," Devyr opined. "The best natured man in the world might do it." Following the jury's decision, Devyr concluded that "no man's life is safe in New Jersey."[54] That Devyr printed (and most likely wrote) the article indicates how he judged his readership. Despite the existence of the Fenian Sisterhood for respectable nationalist women, Devyr's sense that this article would find sympathetic readers is revealing of attitudes toward women during this period.

Devyr returned to Ireland in 1860, prior to the rise of Fenianism, encouraged by news of the "tenant right" movement and hoping to "see what I could do to help it." He landed in Dublin but found his arrival to be ill timed, coming in the middle of the clamor surrounding the Irish Papal Brigade's expedition to Italy, which he felt temporarily dominated politics and sidelined the land question. He attempted but failed to meet with William Sharman Crawford, who had been a significant formative influence on him, indicating that he evidently still respected him, despite his earlier disenchantment. After a short stay in Donegal, Devyr traveled on to England and Scotland, where he contacted Joseph Cowen and former Chartists Bronterre O'Brien and Thomas Doubleday, and stayed for a time with the freethinker and cooperative advocate George Jacob Holyoake.[55] This trip proved to be Devyr's only return visit to Ireland, and, following his brief fling with Fenianism in 1866, it was not until the mid-1870s that he resumed an active interest in Irish diaspora nationalism.

The reasons for Devyr's fractious relationship with the Irish community were partly ideological, but they also stemmed from his headstrong, belligerent personality. He needled and exasperated former friends and would-be allies. The *Irish World* noted that "There was no such word as *toleration* in Mr. Devyr's vocabulary," and, for one fellow-Donegal writer, Devyr was "as 'odd' as the title he gave his book."[56] After Devyr attended a lecture by the nationalist Thomas Francis Meagher, for example, he wrote a public letter to complain about its poor quality. He reminded William Smith O'Brien that he was "an 'estated' gentleman," whereas Devyr had real insight into the issues, as he had known an "early struggle with poverty."[57] Difficult relations with Irish nationalists carried over to wider reform and radical circles as well. At one point, Devyr was jailed over a libel suit. In 1850, he alienated New York trade unionists by criticizing strikes and insisting that only land reform could resolve class conflict. George Holyoake hosted him for some time in London but found him an "ungrateful" guest.[58] The newspaper editor and reform politician Horace Greeley offered to publish Devyr's report of his 1860 trip to Ireland and Britain, and in return requested that he assist the Republican party in the election of Abraham Lincoln. Devyr refused and, in a lengthy published response, detailed the many errors he felt Greeley had made in his career, telling him that his "opponents are corrupt, mean, selfish and dishonorable. . . . I have only to add that your party is WORSE—beyond all comparison." Greeley ended their exchange, stating, "You have ceased personally to infect me," yet Devyr seemed surprised, claiming, whether naïvely or disingenuously, that he was acting with "chivalry" and honestly trying to set Greeley back on the right track.[59]

Always ready to call out the faults of others, Devyr himself was easily offended. In England he came to know the novelist William Thackeray, who later wrote a sketch about "Tom Diver, the Irish lad who set out to reform the world." Devyr wrote in response, "The difference between you and me is that you started out all right, but fell in with thieves by the wayside and became one of them, whereas I have never surrendered but kept on battling with the thieves even to this day."[60] When the English republican Charles Bradlaugh published *The Land, the People, and the Coming Struggle*, Devyr wrote to him to propose an alliance and was puzzled when no response came. He concluded that Bradlaugh's silence could only be explained by the fact he was not a genuine radical, but someone who enjoyed the high life and mixing with people with questionable business dealings, a view he then pressed on Karl Marx.[61] Throughout his life, Devyr was intolerant of views about social reform that diverged from his own, but his spiky approach was perhaps most evident in his response to the abolitionist movement.

Slavery, Antislavery, and the Land League

The American antislavery movement was a hugely significant point of reference for the Land League. Irish nationalists had long demonstrated an interest in the abolition of slavery, but the Land League generation borrowed explicitly from the language of the antislavery movement in the United States. The American Civil War loomed large in the nationalist imagination because so many Irish fought in it—some 150,000 for the Union and 20,000 for the Confederates, and many veterans later became involved in nationalist organizations.[62] The *Irish World* framed the Land War as part of a global wave of reform that followed in the wake of the abolition of slavery in the United States, a turning point for nineteenth-century progressive politics. Patrick Ford had been an abolitionist, working on William Lloyd Garrison's *Liberator*, and he enlisted in the Union army. Historians have noted his "tireless efforts to connect Irish nationalism with the African American struggle for equality," efforts buoyed by support from the abolitionists James Redpath, Wendall Philips, and Henry Ward Beecher, while Frederick Douglass spoke in favor of Irish Home Rule in 1883.[63] Redpath made three lengthy trips to Ireland during the Land War to report for American newspapers and was credited with popularizing the term "boycotting." Ford even attempted to bring Phillips, a vocal ally of the Land League in the United States, to Ireland in 1881, but ill health prevented him from traveling.[64] Analogies with abolitionism brought a righteous tone to the *Irish World*, which presented the land question and Irish distress as a moral emergency more than an economic issue.

At Land League meetings in Ireland, references to slavery and emancipation were commonplace. One branch meeting in Carlow resolved "not to relax their efforts until landlordism, like slavery, had ceased to exist as an institution," and a Belfast branch stated that its aim was to "emancipate the soil."[65] For the Irish Party MPs and leading Land Leaguers John Dillon and T. P. O'Connor, who both spent time in the

United States, the Land War "elevated the Irish people from slavery to freedom" and ensured that "the tenant was no longer to be the patient slave, but was resolved to fight doggedly for his rights."[66] Abolitionism was a "constant topic of discussion" at home for Anna, Fanny, and Charles Stewart Parnell when growing up in Wicklow, and the Ladies' Land League was partly modeled on women's aid activities in the US Sanitary Commission during the Civil War.[67] Peter O'Leary believed Fanny Parnell was the Irish Harriet Beecher Stowe, and he hoped the *Hovels of Ireland* would "have a similar effect" to *Uncle Tom's Cabin*.[68] William Upton, O'Leary's ally in unionizing agricultural laborers, took the analogy further when he published a novel about Irish laborers' conditions entitled *Uncle Pat's Cabin*, which depicted landgrabbers and graziers as well as landlords as the villains and told the story of the titular character Pat, who died when his cabin was destroyed by bailiffs. It ended with the departure of his niece for the United States, "from which a new race will yet spring to raise again your Uncle Pat's cabin."[69] Not all Land Leaguers drew analogies to slavery; Michael Davitt memorably cast the Land War as a struggle against feudalism. Nonetheless, slavery was regularly evoked in speeches and columns throughout the unrest.

These references to slavery were expressed in two principal ways: first, that the enslaved Irish nation required emancipation from colonial rule, and, second, that Irish people were enslaved by a system of landlordism, which rendered them dependent and took away their agency. The two were interrelated, but the second sense was far more prevalent in the late nineteenth century. For T. P. O'Connor, it was the "system of rack-renting which kept the peasantry at once enslaved and pauperized."[70] O'Connor, who was closer to British radical politics than many in the Irish Party, deployed concepts of slavery in ways similar to how the contemporary labor movements of Europe and North America described the condition of the industrial working classes. Bishop Thomas Nulty of Meath took an active interest in the Land League and maintained, as one study has noted, that landlordism was "akin to slavery because it fostered dependency, both economic and mental," and in doing so he echoed "distinctly republican conceptions of liberty."[71]

Direct comparisons between Ireland and the American South were less frequent, but when they were made, they suggested some sort of equivalence of experience between Irish tenant farmers and enslaved people that demonstrated a wilful blindness to the horror of American slavery. William Upton's novel described Irish laborers as "a class of men no better than slaves" who lived "in hovels that the southern slave-owner would not house his slaves in."[72] Such parallels were drawn not only by Irish activists. In his first public speech in Ireland, Henry George told his audience that "He did not believe that in the Southern States of the Union they could at any time find negroes who were housed, fed and clad like some of the people of this country."[73] James Redpath told American readers in his dispatches from Ireland that "the landlords of Ireland are just as bad a lot as ever the worst of our southern slaveholders were."[74] Devyr, among others, argued that enslaved people in the American South had been better off in some respects than tenant farmers and industrial workers, because they were supposedly guaranteed food and shelter. He believed that "Disinheritance is Slavery," that the denial of man's natural rights to land in Ireland or elsewhere always led to dependence and slavery, a view widely shared in the Land League.[75] Where Devyr differed from many in the land movement was in his views of the Civil War and the antislavery movement, which stemmed from his ideological intransigence as well as his thinking about race.

Devyr had long voiced his opposition to slavery and was an admirer of the abolitionist John Brown, but he never wavered from the view that the destruction of land monopoly was the only true means of ending slavery, because it would bring about the downfall of plantations and create access to land for all people. Emancipation without land reform, in his view, would create a scenario where formerly enslaved people would find themselves trapped in a different form of exploitation with landless laborers and industrial workers. In the 1840s, this view was shared among National Reformers, but not by most abolitionists, who rejected the idea of "wages slavery" regularly advanced by Devyr, George Henry Evans, and others.[76] During the anti-rent campaign in upstate New York, Devyr contended that the enslaved person "is not in a position one quarter as bad as are those men who are ground down and enslaved by the short lease."[77] Although Devyr's circle of agrarian radicals became more active in antislavery politics in 1850s, he remained hostile. He complained that "progressives" in New York were too preoccupied with southern slavery and was admonished by Horace Greeley for his lack of support for the cause. When the Civil War began, he refused to volunteer for the Union effort, arguing that the southern states were partners in the Union and therefore had a right to secede, and he had a "good riddance" attitude when they did. In the war's aftermath, he maintained that southern slaveowners had gotten what they deserved, but that the "Northern slave-owners of the factories . . . were even more detestable—adding hypocrisy to inhumanity." Throughout the 1860s, his position brought him into conflict with former allies and even one of his closest backers, the Brooklyn politician Philip S. Crooke.[78]

Opposition to the war and the abolitionist movement revealed Devyr's own attitudes to race. He complained to Greeley that the *New York Tribune* excessively covered crimes against Black people, and "yet, when your white brother is murdered, you are essentially dumb!"[79] Referring to abolitionism as the "moral epidemic," he castigated Gerrit Smith, a reformer who had once argued along with Devyr that only land reform could truly end slavery, but later dedicated himself entirely to abolitionism. Writing in the 1860s, Devyr claimed that Smith had deserted land reform and "set about instructing the Creator that He was very wrong for making any distinction in the human families"; in the process, Smith had left behind "his brothers of the white race."[80] In the 1870s, he continued to send angry letters to an aging Smith, lamenting that if he "had done for the white man as much as he did for the negro . . . Land Monopoly would have been killed stone dead in this country." Surprisingly, Smith always responded graciously, encouraging Devyr to keep up the fight.[81] Later in the decade, when the Molly Maguire trials and executions took place, Devyr argued that the Pennsylvania coal miner was a "less protected slave than ever was the negro."[82] Around this time he supported a resolution at a reform meeting that "Wages Slavery," in many respects, was "worse than Chattel Slavery; more easily worked and more profitable to the slave driver—more crushing, and even exterminating, to the slave."[83] Devyr also spoke frequently about settling people on the "unproductive land in the nation," but he did not reflect on the removal of indigenous groups, except to note that Europeans had no right to buy land "off some Indians who had no right to sell it."[84] Despite his claims to universalism, there was also a narrowness to Devyr's vision of land and labor reform.

Devyr later wrote for the *Irish World*, but his attitude toward abolitionism was in marked contrast to Patrick Ford's. He likely represented part of the "attitude of seeming hostility" that Ford lamented among elements of Irish America toward the antislavery movement.[85] At the same time, Devyr was hardly alone in his views of the abolitionist movement, which encountered considerable opposition among Irish immigrants, though this did not necessarily equate with proslavery sentiment. Neither could his views be classed as extreme on the spectrum of Irish nationalist opinion in Irish America and Ireland. Devyr strongly differed, for example, from the reactionary proslavery position of Young Ireland exile John Mitchel, who supported the Confederate war effort from Virginia. In Ireland, Home Ruler and influential newspaperman A. M. Sullivan sympathized with the Confederacy in the *Nation*.[86] Ultimately, Devyr opposed the Confederacy and sought to end slavery, albeit by different means to abolitionists. The argument that Irish nationalists' self-interested preoccupation with independence resulted in a blinkered view of other causes, including antislavery, does not apply in Devyr's case, as his nationalism always remained in the background. Rather, it was his utter refusal to countenance any cause that might sidetrack land reform that brought him into conflict with abolitionism, along with racial prejudice and his contrary, cantankerous streak. It also seems likely that his visceral animosity for Daniel O'Connell, who was associated with abolitionism more than any other Irish leader, was also a factor.

The *Irish World* and Devyr

The *Irish World* was founded in 1870, but it was not until the middle of decade, following the Panic of 1873, that radical politics became familiar in its columns. In 1878, it became the *Irish World and American Industrial Liberator*, a newspaper advocating for a range of progressive causes including trade unionism, temperance, women's franchise, African American rights, land nationalization, the Greenback-Labor party, and indigenous rights. Ford complained that the paper's positions were "howled at, again and again, as 'communism' or 'socialism,'" but he did not explicitly express either support or opposition to Marx or socialism during these years. However, he did promote labor radicalism and reported sympathetically, for example, on the influential Irish socialist

Joseph Patrick McDonnell, who advanced land and labor reform as editor of the *Labor Standard,* and who was a familiar face at the *Irish World* office.[87]

The intersection of class tensions with Irish immigration was brought home in this period by the Molly Maguire unrest in Pennsylvania, where twenty coal miners were executed for violence against supervisors and foremen, partly on the basis of dubious evidence supplied by the Pinkerton detective agency.[88] For Ford, the "Slaughter in Pennsylvania" was "wound up in the great Labor Question," which was "as universal and as enduring as is the human race itself." Even if the men were guilty, which he doubted, he maintained their crimes were understandable products of the "grinding tyranny of the coal ring."[89] Devyr was similarly outraged, protesting that "Nothing else could show up so clearly the murderous ruffians that now hold power of life and death over the workingman." Most of the Molly Maguires were, like him, from Donegal, and Devyr wrote at length about the case, seeing it as a harbinger of a "War of Classes" that could only be prevented by sweeping reforms.[90]

Devyr had first contacted the *Irish World* to express support for the Greenback-Labor Party and, more predictably, to promote the idea that land was the natural inheritance of all humanity: "Here is the grand Truth that must root out the great Lie. Teach it, Mr. Editor." He described himself as an exile, forced out of Ireland by landlords, "the men whose crime blighted my childhood with poverty, and sent me to explore other regions for the means of life, which they had feloniously taken away." In 1876 he joined the staff of the *Irish World,* which, interestingly, introduced him to readers as a "veteran in the war for Human Rights" rather than for workers' rights or land reform.[91]

At this time, the *Irish World* adopted an increasingly militant approach to Irish republicanism and Ford was formulating plans for "skirmishing," or the bombing campaign in British cities that came to pass in the 1880s.[92] Ford, along with the British Home Office's Fenian watchers, took some of Devyr's more ardent comments as a show of support for dynamite attacks.[93] This was not the case, but Devyr did prove consistently ambivalent toward political violence. On the one hand, he wished to revive the old 1848 rifle clubs with the aim of sending a "fleet of emigrants" and "lead and steel to the Irish people," and asserted that violent resistance to evictions was fully justified.[94] On the other, he argued that the time for revolution had not come and, in spiritual language, maintained that "it is from a flood of light from Heaven, not from a torrent of blood on the earth, that man's earthly redemption must come."[95] When he spoke of "weekly volleys from the *Irish World*" that "boomed across the ocean," he was referring to a war of ideas rather than a dynamite campaign, and he appealed for reformers "to go to Ireland and England for the purpose of teaching the people the true doctrine on the Land question."[96] Forty years earlier he had fled England after planning an insurrection, but now he considered that similar action was only justifiable and possible in specific circumstances in Ireland, and was more unlikely in the United States.

Devyr linked the Land League and the *Irish World* to the agrarianism of the National Reform Association, an antecedent for Georgism and the movement that came in the wake of *Progress and Poverty*. In fact, many veteran National Reformers remained active into the late-nineteenth century in currency and tax reform, the Greenback-Labor party, socialism, as well as in the Land League and among followers of Henry George. In 1876, Devyr, with Joshua Ingalls, John Commerford, and other allies from the 1840s, attempted to have a "colossal bust" of Thomas Paine erected at the 1876 Centennial Exhibition in Philadelphia. The effort failed, but their interpretation of Paine's theories of common inheritance still resonated.[97] There were clear similarities between the National Reform platform of the 1840s and George's theories, even if he, as one study has observed, "feigned an ignorance we know he did not have" when shown the writings of earlier land reformers.[98] Some contemporaries in Ireland associated George's ideas with the writings of James Fintan Lalor, who was of Devyr's generation and linked natural rights in land to national independence in the 1840s, yet George never referred to him. "Lalor's idea," the writer Standish O'Grady pointedly remarked, "from America has come back upon Europe, advertising itself as 'Progress and Poverty.'"[99] George Jacob Holyoake maintained that Devyr's "prior advocacy" of the land theories espoused in the *Irish World* was not properly acknowledged by Ford, a complaint that surely originated with Devyr himself when he met with Holyoake in New York.[100] Devyr also maintained that much writing on land reform in the *Irish World* was left to him, since Ford "had so many subjects pressing on him," but Devyr, always prone to hubris, was surely exaggerating.[101] This tendency for hubris was evident when the *War of Classes* was published, and he expressed confidence that it would "circulate by millions."[102] There is no evidence that Henry George read anything by Devyr before *Progress and Poverty*, but the influence of Thomas Spence and Thomas Paine on both men highlights the sustained significance of an earlier agrarianism on radical politics in the late nineteenth century. Devyr met with George, and, while they disagreed on the single tax, he admired him and believed George had been "sent by Providence" because he provoked a new global debate, which was all for the good of the "Great Truth."[103]

Along with the National Reformers' ideas, Devyr was also keen to engage a new generation with the United Irishmen, their songs and satirical pamphlets, his own pamphlet *Our Natural Rights*, and popular poems about land and inequality by Oliver Goldsmith and Robert Burns.[104] He connected the *Irish World* readership with an earlier radical politics in Ireland, as well as with Chartism. He was not alone in this; for example, the Dublin-born Samuel McEvatt was active in Ireland before moving first to London and becoming a Chartist in 1848. He returned to Ireland and was involved in Fenianism, and then he moved to the United States, where he remained politically active.[105] The *Irish World*'s London correspondent, Thomas Mooney (or "TransAtlantic"), born in the insurrectionary year of 1798, was a former Young Irelander, and served as another link to an earlier generation of radical Irish politics.

Devyr saw Patrick Ford as a kindred spirit with "a great deal of my own ardor," though the feeling was not exactly mutual. Devyr was heartened that an Irish newspaper editor shared his belief that "railroad thieves, or other monopolists here, and thief landlords in Ireland, own no lands in either hemisphere," and he was further impressed by Ford's acerbic assessments of the "propertied aristocrats" of the Home Rule party in the 1870s. The *Irish World*, Devyr maintained, "opened a communion of mind to Reformers all over the world. . . . And have they not inaugurated the Great Movement that now shakes the earth?" From Devyr's New York-centric perspective, Ford and the *Irish World* circle led the Land League, with Davitt and Parnell "merely their disciples."[106] This admiration was not entirely reciprocated by Ford, who offered a very qualified endorsement for Devyr's 1882 memoir: "I do not endorse all the headlong opinions of Mr. Devyr. I believe that he has fallen into errors and made mistakes. But he has labored so long in Land Reform, and so sincerely, that I accord to him the privilege of having letters addressed to him, at the office of the *Irish World*." This was not high praise, but the fact Devyr included the half-hearted testimony on the title page of his book indicates the weight he gave to his association with Ford and, arguably, his marginalization within wider radical circles.[107]

These "headlong opinions" with which Ford took issue were manifold. The two men differed on land nationalization and economic protectionism, and Devyr had not shed his bitterness toward abolitionists. When Charles Stewart Parnell visited Brooklyn in 1880, Devyr was thrown out of the hall for heckling Henry Ward Beecher, who was otherwise received very warmly at the event. Devyr's 1882 memoir included lengthy and vexed recollections of the antislavery movement.[108] He also nursed a grudge against Ford for funding Henry George's transatlantic travels and Davitt's 1882 tour, thinking that he would have made a better envoy. *Progress and Poverty* was "kept before the readers of the *Irish World*," while his memoir was not.[109] In 1884, a major breach occurred when the *Irish World* supported the Republican James Blaine in the presidental election. Devyr turned his temper on Ford, accusing him of backing the party of corporations "that instituted the Land thieves," and he took further aim at Patrick Egan and other Land League figures.[110] Devyr was fiercely critical of the Democratic Party, but he still always found them preferable to the Republicans. When Henry George ran for mayor of New York in 1886, Devyr attacked his writing on land reform, which "only muddles, mixes up and mystifies the subject" and suggested that George's campaign and the "arrant renegade" Ford were somehow linked to the Republicans, despite the fact that Theodore Roosevelt was running as the Republican candidate.[111] With Devyr's track record, it seemed inevitable that he would fall out with Ford and the *Irish World* sooner or later.

In the final years of his life, Devyr turned to old allies and to Newcastle, a city he had remained fond of since he left it over forty years before. His memoir received positive coverage in the Newcastle papers, mainly for the historical light it shed on the Chartist movement there. Heartened by this attention, he considered moving to Newcastle permanently. He had become disillusioned with the United States for many reasons, and in the 1870s he was on the brink of bankruptcy, with his sole earnings coming from journalism and book sales. The move was not possible, but he did return briefly in 1884 to give some public lectures when he was seventy-six years old. In one talk on "The Land and the People," his utopian agrarianism remained evident in claims that "gaols and policemen and poor-laws would eventually become things of the past" if land was redistributed equitably. Curiously, he also seemed to reconsider his old 1830s view that landlords could perform a type of paternalist role in society. The lecture hardly mentioned Ireland, and privately he conceded that, after the Land War calmed in 1882, he had "little hope for Ireland" but held out some optimism for radical change in England, and particularly Newcastle.[112] He wrote to Joseph Cowen inviting him to join a new transatlantic land movement that would incorporate England. Cowen responded that he might assist in some way, but could not engage fully.[113]

Two years later, Devyr died in Brooklyn, leaving behind a large family, including his son and namesake Tom Devyr, who was a supporter of Henry George, a municipal politician in Brooklyn, and a well-known baseball player. His other children were also familiar figures in Brooklyn and New York as journalists, poets, and novelists.[114] In New York Devyr was remembered for his associations with the Land League and land reform more widely, but further afield he was soon forgotten. In 1894, Dublin's *United Ireland* asked, "Can any of our readers enlighten us as to the life or doctrines of Thomas Ainge Devyr?" when it noted George Holyoake's observation that Devyr was an "originator of the land theories that afterwards became famous."[115] Devyr's neglect can be explained in part by his lifelong ambivalence toward Irish nationalism. Despite his association with the *Irish World* and brief Fenian spell, his activism was always driven by land reform before a desire for Irish independence, which he struggled to integrate into his worldview. At the same time, his combative personality and undying commitment to his own perspective ultimately left him with few friends or allies who might have ensured he featured more prominently in some of the early histories of the Land League.

Devyr's vision of land reform held some utopian aspects, but he did not advocate a revolutionary transformation of systems of government. Rather, he believed every individual had a right to a small amount of land, which he typically set at forty acres, a figure that echoed the frustrated hopes for "forty acres and a mule" and land redistribution in the American South after the Civil War. For Devyr, the guaranteed right to a small amount of land resembled a type of universal basic income, an idea that everyone should have enough to support themselves and the people who depend on them. For this to be possible, monopolies had to be abolished. The amount of land any person could occupy, Devyr argued, must be strictly defined and limited. He also championed limitations on taxes, but he never really answered questions of who would do the limiting or how restrictions on land would be set. At the same time, Devyr did offer a radical challenge to accepted ideas of private property and linked different generations of transatlantic radicals. His story is significant in demonstrating both the affinities and tensions produced by encounters between different strands of radicalism and reform. Associations with Devyr contributed to the *Irish World* circle's sense that they were advancing a well-established tradition of reform on both sides of the Atlantic, rather than something entirely new or untested, and that, therefore, it was more acceptable.

Conclusion

The radicalism and the internationalism of the Land War had a mixed legacy among the revolutionary generation of the early twentieth century, reflected in some of the early histories of the period. In 1908, Francis Sheehy Skeffington published a study of Michael Davitt, who had died in 1906, which included a long section on the Land War. Too young to directly remember the agitation himself, Sheehy Skeffington portrayed the Land War as a turning point in which the Land League left behind the "Nationalists of the old school" and embraced "sentiments of international brotherhood." He likened the agitation to a "war of classes" that "sprang from a deeper and more vital principle of human nature than the war of nations."[1] In his 1919 history of Irish labor, the Gaelic Leaguer and socialist W. P. Ryan argued that the Land League was "the greatest example of combination and direct action in Irish history," but it also represented for him a lost opportunity for social revolution, a moment when land nationalization was abandoned too easily, and laborers were deserted.[2] Ryan edited the *Irish Peasant*, which claimed to be the "only paper that advocates the redress of the grievances of the Peasant Farmers," and to some extent took on the mantle of the more radical elements of the Land League. At the same time, the paper took a critical view of the Land League's internationalism, which Sheehy Skeffington had praised. The Land War, the *Irish Peasant* claimed, embodied a time when "the national ideal got well nigh irretrievably lost."[3] Ryan observed that the "development of a friendly understanding with British democracy and all democracies is a wholesome thing," but "the prime business of Irish leaders is with their own democracy and their own nation."[4] He criticized the lack of "Gaelicism" during the Land War, which arguably reflected a wider view among some of the revolutionary generation, whose references to the Land League were often muted.[5] Their engagement with the history of the Land War was also limited, of course, due to its associations with the elder statesmen of Home Rule—Dillon, Redmond, O'Connor—whom republicans aimed to remove.

This book has explored some of the complexities of emigrant engagement with Ireland and the entanglement of land reform activism with a much wider range of social and political causes. Approaching the Land League and the Ladies' Land League through less familiar figures presents an alternative perspective to histories that have linked the fortunes of these organizations to a handful of well-known names such as Anna Parnell, Michael Davitt, and Charles Stewart Parnell. The emigrant activists investigated here reveal the depth of radical thinking within the land reform movement and the extent to which it connected people in Ireland and the Irish diaspora with wider oppositional movements that included Georgism, labor radicalism, and feminism. The abolition of land monopoly was central to the worldviews of figures as diverse as John Creaghe, Marguerite Moore, Thomas Ainge Devyr and Peter O'Leary in locations from Argentina to Ireland and the United States to Scotland. While the Land War represented a crucial period in the development of Irish nationalism, a methodological focus on nationalism has often obscured the significance of radical ideas and activities and their transnational dimensions during these years. The Land League and the Ladies' Land League may not have adopted the language of Marxist revolution, but their attempts to change prevailing ideas of land ownership constituted a form of radicalism nonetheless. In some cases this radicalism could entail contradictory perspectives; Peter O'Leary saw no tensions between supporting radical land reform in Ireland while simultaneously being indifferent toward, or supportive of, the settlement of Irish emigrants on lands seized from indigenous groups.

Support for the Land War was not confined to Ireland and its diaspora, and the individual stories in this book intersect with wider histories of transnational radicalism in an era of expanding mass politics. O'Leary, Moore, Creaghe, Devyr, and the other figures examined here helped to bring together networks that are often considered separately from one another. The Land War was part of a broader ideological movement characterized by changing ideas of land and fundamental challenges to established concepts of private property. Different oppositional groups, according to their own lights, saw the agitation in Ireland as another dimension of their own battles against industrial capitalism,

aristocracy, patriarchy, or colonialism. The Land War resonated outward and influenced groups including, for example, the Social Democratic Federation in Britain, the Knights of Labor, radical Ukrainian
nationalists, and European anarchists, who sought to emulate some of
the Land League's tactics.[6] The interest of these groups in the Land War
was sparked not only by broad, and sometimes ill-defined, ideological
affinities, but also by a practical interest in models of collective action
and the innovative use of boycotting.

Emigrants had long contributed to locating the Irish land question
in wider contexts, but particular circumstances contributed to a new
intensity of emigrant activism during the Land War, including huge
numbers of Irish-born people living overseas, improved communication technologies between disparate locations, and the fact that many
members of the Land League were just one generation away from the
Great Famine and considered the catastrophe central to explaining why
they lived overseas. The prospect of a new famine in 1879 brought a
sense of emergency to the Land League's challenge to landlordism. The
massive emigrant mobilization during the Land War would prove un-
sustainable, however, and when the land question erupted again just
four years later in the 1886–91 Plan of Campaign, neither political nor
humanitarian activism approached the levels of 1879–82. Diasporic engagement with the homeland was characterized by peaks and troughs
of intensity, and the Land War represented a peak rivaled only by the
years 1916–21.[7]

The Land League and the Ladies' Land League consciously sought
emigrant support and appealed to the imagined geography of an "Irish
world" that encompassed homeland and diaspora. Yet they also contributed to mapping that imagined world. Their branches marked international locations connected though traveling agitators, speaking tours,
newspapers, and published fundraising lists. Investigating this world
and the relations between different places and groups requires local,
national, and transnational approaches. The Land League and the Ladies' Land League shared similarities across borders, but their message
took on different meanings for people in different places and when
mixed with other ideologies and social realities. The case of Dundee,
for instance, demonstrates how local settings contributed distinctive
dynamics and memberships. The lives of O'Leary, Moore, Creaghe, and

Devyr recapture some of the complexity of relations between homeland and diaspora, the diversity of emigrant activism as well as its limitations. Their activities demonstrate that relationships with the homeland were not static, but continually changing and sometimes contradictory. Their migration stories were not ones of departure, dislocation, and gradual assimilation in a new country that then produced a blend of old-world nationalism and new-world progressivism. Rather, these figures negotiated a range of influences and points of reference. Their histories contribute to a picture of emigrant activism as a multifaceted phenomenon that was much more than a story of the place of origin and adopted home.

ACKNOWLEDGMENTS

During the time researching and writing this book, I have benefited from the support of many people. This project began life as a Marie Skłodowska-Curie fellowship application, and I feel fortunate and privileged to have had the generous support provided by this grant. Without it, the book would not exist. The University of Strathclyde gave me the time and support to complete this research, which is much appreciated, and many thanks and support to my colleagues there. This project started at the University of Edinburgh, and my thanks to colleagues there as well. I am indebted to the anonymous manuscript reviewers for their insightful feedback and to the people who kindly read earlier draft sections and offered helpful suggestions, including Richard McMahon, Eoin McLaughlin, Enda Delaney, Laura Kelly, Irial Glynn, Timothy Meagher, Ksenia Wesolowska, Matt Eisler, David Wilson and Jesse Gryn-Olzynko. Many thanks to the Glucksman Irish Diaspora Series editors Kevin Kenny and Miriam Nyhan Grey, who read sections of the manuscript and provided helpful comments, and to Clara Platter at NYU Press, as well as Emily Shelton and Martin Coleman for their great editing work and help with American English. For their help at different times over the years I was working on this book and for conversations about different issues, my thanks to Fearghal McGarry, Mathias Thaler, Carole Holohan, Alison Cathcart, Alvin Jackson, Richard Finlay, Mihaela Mihai, Joe Lee, Brian Hanley, Arthur McIvor, Kirstie Blair, Ewen Cameron, James McConnel, Roseanna Doughty, Joost Augusteijn, Sophie Cooper, Julyan G. Peard, John Cunningham, Michael de Nie, Joe Curran, Susan Wilkinson, Jonathan Wright, Sarah Roddy, Ciaran O'Neill, Kevin O'Sullivan, Houri Berberian, Andrew Newby, Jules Hackett, Lindsey Earner-Byrne, Breandán Mac Suibhne, Donald MacRaild, Patricia Barton, Emma Newlands, Erin Farley, Jerome Devitt, John Quinn, and Brian Casey. Thanks also to the students who took my Irish history classes at Strathclyde and whose discussions helped me develop ideas in this book. I am indebted to the archivists and librarians in different places who assisted me with my research, particularly the fantastic staff at the National Library of Ireland, at the National Library of Scotland, and at the International Institute of Social History. Chapter 3 has previously appeared in a different version in the *History Workshop Journal*, 90 (2020).

The period of writing this book has crossed the brightest moments life has to offer and some of the darker ones. My thanks to the Whelehans for all their support and to the Casañas Adams. Above all, my thanks and my love to Eli and our children; where would I be without them. This book is dedicated to E. and O. with all my love and hopes for the world they will grow up in.

The aims of the Land League seem as relevant as ever today (though beware charlatans using the name). Many of these aims were widely viewed as reasonable at the time. It is shocking that similar demands today for security of housing and regulation of rent and private property are met with greater hostility from landlordism and government than they were in the late nineteenth century.

NOTES

INTRODUCTION

1 *Irish World and American Industrial Liberator* (*Irish World*), 4 March 1882.

2 McLaughlin, "Competing Forms of Cooperation?," 86–9; Ó Gráda, *Ireland*, 252.

3 Mortality figures for the years 1877, 1878, 1879, and 1880 were 93,543; 99,629; 105,089; and 102,906, respectively. Figures taken from the annual reports of the Registrar General, which start in 1864. The annual rates of excess mortality were 1877: 48; 1878: 158; 1879: 237; and 1880: 184. Excess mortality is calculated by comparing mortality in the year with the average mortality in the preceding ten years and is based on the methodology employed in Eoin McLaughlin and Christopher Colvin, "Death, Demography, and the Denominator: Age-Adjusted Influenza-18 Mortality in Ireland," *Economics and Human Biology* 41 (2021): fig. 2, 4. Note that the mortality figures for 1877–80 do not employ age standardization.

4 *Sixteenth Detailed Annual Report of the Registrar-General of Marriages, Births, and Deaths in Ireland, 1879* (Dublin, 1880), 15.

5 John O'Connor Power had lived in England and John Ferguson was based in Scotland. Thomas Brennan emigrated to the United States in 1882, as did Patrick Egan, who was also involved in organizing the meeting. Moody, *Davitt and the Irish Revolution*, 288–90.

6 The Land War was typically dated between 1879 and 1882, though some studies have adopted a longer periodization incorporating the Plan of Campaign of 1886–91. Donnelly Jr., *Land and the People*, 251–376; Casey, *Class and Community*, 161–228; Curtis, *Depiction of Eviction*, 81–129.

7 Curtis, "Landlord Responses."

8 Davitt to Devoy, 16 December 1880, in O'Brien and Ryan, eds., *Devoy's Post Bag*, pp. 22–24.

9 Moody, *Davitt and the Irish Revolution*, 271–533; Adam Pole, "Sheriffs' Sales during the Land War, 1879–82," *Irish Historical Studies*, 34 (2005): 386–402; Donnelly, *Land and the People*, 256–57; Clark, *Social Origins*, 334–36; Mulholland, "Land War Homicides," in Pašeta, ed., *Uncertain Futures*, 81–96; Conley, *Melancholy Accidents*, 183.

10 Hoppen, *Governing Hibernia*, 220; Allen Warren, "Gladstone, Land, and Social Reconstruction in Ireland, 1881–1887," *Parliamentary History*, 2 (1983): 153–73.

11 *Freeman's Journal*, 11 February 1880.

12 Parnell to Davitt, May 1880, MS9378/1088, Davitt Papers (DP), Trinity College Dublin Archives (TCD).

13 In 1881, the population of Ireland was 5,175,000, and the number of Irish people in the United States, Canada, Britain, and Australia came to 3,035,000. These figures do not take account of Irish emigrants in Argentina, New Zealand, and South Africa, though they would not alter the picture dramatically. *Commission on Emigration*, 126; David Fitzpatrick, "Emigration, 1871–1921." In W. E. Vaughan, ed., *A New History of Ireland, Vol. 6: Ireland under the Union, 2, 1870–1921* (Oxford, 1996): 606–52, 640.

14 Kenny, "Diaspora and Comparison," 135.

15 Anderson, *Spectre of Comparisons*, 58.

16 Delaney, "Our Island Story?"

17 For recent reflections on earlier studies, see the essays in Campbell and Varley, eds., *Land Questions in Modern Ireland.*

18 Ó Tuathaigh, "Irish Land Questions," 6.

19 Bagenal, *American Irish and Their Influence*, 164, emphasis in original.

20 Alice Stopford Green, *Irish Nationality* (Cambridge, MA: 1911), 241.

21 Donnelly, *Land and the People*; Lee, *Modernisation of Irish Society*, 67–140; Bew, *Land and the National Question*; Moody, *Davitt and the Irish Revolution*; Solow, *Land Question and the Irish Economy*; Clark, *Social Origins*; Jordan, *Land and Popular Politics*, 197–313; Bull, *Land, Politics, and Nationalism*; Vaughan, *Landlords and Tenants*.

22 Davitt, *Fall of Feudalism in Ireland*, 376.

23 On Davitt's radicalism and wider activism, see Marley, *Michael Davitt*; and King, *Michael Davitt.*

24 Lane, *Origins of Modern Irish Socialism*; Boyle, *Irish Labour Movement*; O'Connor, *Labour History of Ireland*, 47.

25 Margaret Ward, "Gendering the Union: Imperial Feminism and the Ladies' Land League," *Women's History Review*, 10 (2001): 71–92.

26 Janis, *Greater Ireland*; McCarthy, *Respectability and Reform*; Foner, *Politics and Ideology*, 150–200; Miller, *Emigrants and Exiles*; Meagher, *Inventing Irish America.*

27 Newby, *Ireland, Radicalism.*

28 Deacon, Russell, and Woollacott, eds., *Transnational Lives*; Foster, *Vivid Faces.*

29 Whelan, "Transatlantic World"; Leerssen, ed., *Parnell and His Times*; Marley, *Michael Davitt.*

30 I have preferred to use the term "transnational," rather than "global," to describe the space of emigrant activism and radical politics. The networks investigated here primarily circulated in English-speaking territories of the British empire, the United States, and Argentina, and the term "global" seems to imply wider geographical and cultural diversity. "Internationalism" is employed here to describe an outlook, an openness to associations across borders to advance common visions of progress. Sluga, *Internationalism*, 3–5.

31 Sluga and Clavin, eds., *Internationalisms*; Laqua, *Age of Internationalism and Belgium*, 5–6; Conrad and Sachsenmaier, eds., *Competing Visions of World Order.*

32 Meaney, O'Dowd, and Whelan, *Reading the Irish Woman*, 13–53; Graham Gargett and Geraldine Sheridan, eds., *Ireland and the French Enlightenment, 1700–1800* (Bas-

ingstoke, 1999); Brown, *Irish Enlightenment*; Fergus Whelan, *May Tyrants Tremble: The Life of William Drennan, 1754–1820* (Dublin, 2020); Kevin Whelan, *The Tree of Liberty: Radicalism, Catholicism, and the Construction of Irish Identity, 1760–1830* (Cork, 1996).

33 Hughes and MacRaild, *Ribbon Societies*, 64–91.

34 Osterhammel, *Transformation of the World*, 63; Eric Hobsbawm, *The Age of Empire, 1875–1914* (London, 1987).

35 Sebastian Conrad, "Colonizing the Nineteenth Century: Implications of a Paradigm Shift," *Central European History* 51, no. 4 (2018): 674–78, 676. See the contributions to "Discussion Forum: The Vanishing Nineteenth Century in European History?," *Central European History* 51, no. 4 (2018): 611–95; Donald Bloxham and Robert Gerwarth, eds., *Political Violence in Twentieth Century Europe* (Cambridge, 2011), 3.

36 Hoppen, *Governing Hibernia*; W. E. Vaughan, ed., *A New History of Ireland, Vol. VI: Ireland under the Union, II: 1870–1921* (Oxford, 1996); Alvin Jackson, "Ireland's Long Nineteenth Century of Union," *Journal of Modern History* 86, no. 1 (2014): 124–41.

37 Bartlett, ed., *Cambridge History of Ireland, Vol. IV*.

38 Earlier accounts (including my own) suggested a circulation of twenty thousand in Ireland, but a higher figure is more likely. *Irish World*, 28 August 1880 and 16 February 1884; Janis, *Greater Ireland*, 116, 122; Sheehy Skeffington, *Michael Davitt*, 106.

39 Marx to Jenny Longuet [Marx], 29 April 1881, in Marx and Engels, *Ireland and the Irish Question*, 331.

40 *Irish World*, 23 July 1881.

41 George, *Irish Land Question*, 82; O'Donnell, *Henry George*, 105–6; Phemister, "Grandest Battle Ever Fought."

42 Lee, *Modernisation of Irish Society*, 91.

43 *Freeman's Journal*, 11 February 1880; *Irish World*, 14 January 1882; *Newcastle Weekly Chronicle*, 20 August 1881.

44 George, *Progress and Poverty*, 503.

45 Parfitt, *Knights across the Atlantic*, 8–9.

46 Engels to Bernstein, 12 March 1881, in Marx and Engels, *Ireland and the Irish Question*, 329–30.

47 Ilham Khuri-Makdisi, *The Eastern Mediterranean*, 9.

48 Douglas, *Land, People, and Politics*, 46–48.

49 O'Donnell, *Crisis of Inequality*, 259–61.

50 George, *Progress and Poverty*, 364, 409–10.

51 *Report of the International Council of Women*, 44.

52 J. L. Joynes, *Adventures of a Tourist in Ireland* (London, 1882), 4.

53 Berger and Scalmer, eds., *Transnational Activist*.

54 *Manchester Guardian*, 17 October 1888.

1. PETER O'LEARY, LAND NATIONALIZATION, AND VISITORS DURING
THE LAND WAR

1 *Irish World*, 29 October 1881; George to Ford, 10 November 1881, Letterbooks, Series 1, B, Vol. 1, Henry George Papers (HGP), New York Public Library (NYPL). Annie Fox's maternal grandparents were from Limerick and Ennis. George Jr., *Life of Henry George*, 106–7.

2 *Evening Telegraph* (Dublin), 17 September 1881; *Irish World*, 8, 15 October 1881.

3 For example, Joynes, *Adventures of a Tourist*.

4 *South London Press*, 31 August 1889; 22 March 1890; 24 November 1894; *Reynold's Newspaper*, 25 December 1887.

5 Lane, *Origins of Modern Irish Socialism*; Newby, *Ireland, Radicalism*; Ward, "Gendering the Union."

6 George, *Irish Land Question*, 23.

7 O'Leary, *Travels and Experiences*, v–vi; *Irish American*, 2 September 1871; *Irishman*, 8 November 1879; *Freeman's Journal*, 8 November 1872.

8 Horn, "National Agricultural Labourers' Union," 346–77, 49; Boyle, "Marginal Figure," 324; Lane, "P. F. Johnson." Thomas Mooney (TransAtlantic) also wrote for the *Irishman* in the 1870s. John Devoy believed he was the "chief attraction" in the *Irish World* (*Gaelic American*, 23 June 1906).

9 Fitzpatrick, "Disappearance"; Boyle, "Marginal Figure."

10 *Irishman*, 16 August 1879; 29 May 1880; O'Leary, *Travels and Experiences*, 3.

11 Gerard Moran, "'Shovelling out the poor': Assisted Emigration from Ireland from the Great Famine to the Fall of Parnell," in *To and From Ireland: Planned Migration Schemes c. 1600–2000*, ed. Patrick J. Duffy (Dublin, 2004), 137–54, 141–42. On the Argentinian scheme, see chap. 4 in this book.

12 The fund was set up with Patrick Boyle, editor of the *Irish Canadian*, Michael P. Ryan, an Irish Canadian businessman, and Philip Johnson as trustees. Johnson became an emigration agent in Cork, and he also supported O'Leary's tour. O'Leary, *Travels*, vi.

13 This claim is difficult to test, as the description "labourer" was used ambiguously in statistical records. In the second half of the nineteenth century, Irish laborers outnumbered farmers to all major emigrant destinations. In Britain, the large majority of Irish settlers worked in unskilled manual jobs. Fitzpatrick, "Peculiar Tramping People," 640.

14 O'Leary, *Travels*, vi, 74; *Irish World*, 26 August 1876.

15 Harper, "Enticing the Emigrant," 44.

16 O'Leary, *Travels*, 167, 174, 215; *Morning Star and Catholic Messenger* (New Orleans), 3 December 1876; Gerard Moran, "'In Search of the Promised Land': The Connemara Colonization Scheme to Minnesota, 1880," *Éire-Ireland* 31, no. 3 (1996): 130–49.

17 *Freeman's Journal*, 14 July 1874. The *Irishman* described his reports as "clap trap," but the Fenian-leaning paper was also averse to the portrayal of Canada thriving under Home Rule. *Irishman*, 18 July 1874.

18 O'Leary, *Travels*, 191; *Irish World*, 13 September 1879.

19 O'Leary, *Travels*, 132, 150–53, 159.

20 *Irish American*, 21 February 1880.

21 Quoted in Moody, *Davitt*, 289.

22 O'Leary, *Travels*, 159.

23 *South London Press*, 16 April 1892.

24 Qureshi, "Dying Americans," 270.

25 *Freeman's Journal*, 9 February 1880. He was not alone in traveling to investigate conditions in Ireland in a broader context: the Chicago-based journalist Margaret Sullivan toured Ireland and Europe to research a comparison of Irish, Belgian, and French societies. Sullivan was the wife of Alexander Sullivan, the controversial leader of the Clan na Gael. Sullivan, *Ireland of To-Day*, 146.

26 *Irishman*, 16, 30 August 1879; *Irish American*, 24 May 1879.

27 *Irish American*, 6 December 1879, 21 February 1880; *Freeman's Journal*, 3 June 1880; Mary Francis Cusack, *The Nun of Kenmare: An Autobiography* (London, 1998), ix, 118.

28 Keyes, *Funding the Nation*, 122; Côté, *Fanny and Anna Parnell*, 116–17, 286; William O'Brien, *The Great Famine in Ireland*, 277. For an interesting study of the Victorian "brand" of "Mansion House" charity, see Roddy, Strange, and Taithe, *Charity Market*, 121–42.

29 Moran, "Giving a Helping Hand," 136.

30 Mark R. Frost, "Humanitarianism and the Overseas Aid Craze in Britain's Colonial Straits Settlements, 1870–1920," *Past and Present*, 235 (2017): 1–37, 25–27.

31 *Irish World*, 21 February 1881; Davitt to Devoy, 6 February 1880, in *Devoy's Post Bag*, vol. 1, 483.

32 *Irish Canadian*, 17 December 1879; *Boston Pilot*, 20 December 1879; *New York Herald*, 16 December 1879.

33 *Irish World*, 20 February 1875; 15 April 1876; 20 January 1877.

34 *Irish World*, 10 April, 28 August, 18 December 1875; 26 August 1876; 4 August 1877. He sometimes wrote under the pseudonyms Celt and Hibernian.

35 Moloney, *American Catholic Lay Groups*, 85.

36 *Irishman*, 3 October 1874; *Irish Nationalist*, 14 August 1874

37 *Irish World*, 6 March 1875.

38 *True Witness and Catholic Chronicle* (Montreal), 2 March 1877; *Irishman*, 16 August 1879. There was competition between Canadian federal and provincial immigrantion agents. Harper, "Enticing the Emigrant," 55.

39 *Pilot*, 15 January 1881.

40 *Freeman's Journal*, 20 June 1881. In this year he published the pamphlet *The Irish Labourer in America*.

41 *Chicago Tribune*, 24 July, 13 August 1881; *Irishman*, 24 July 1880; *Times (London)*, 12 August 1881.

42 *Brooklyn Daily Eagle*, 29 August 1881.

43 O'Connor, *Memoirs*, 209.

44 Parnell to Collins, 25 September 1881; 10 November 1881, Patrick Collins Papers, Burns Library, Boston College.

45 *Pilot*, 21 January, 4 February 1882.

46 *Brooklyn Daily Eagle*, 29 August 1881.

47 O'Leary, *Travels*, vi.

48 Northcote referred him to the Irish executive. *Irishman*, 8 November 1879; 24 July 1880.

49 *Irish Times*, 9 July 1881; *Drogheda Argus*, 16 July 1881. The *Irish Times* dismissed O'Leary's claims on laborers' conditions as exaggeration.

50 *United Ireland*, 17 February 1883; *Freeman's Journal*, 9 February 1883.

51 *Irishman*, 29 May, 5 June 1880; *Freeman's Journal*, 7 June 1880, 20 June 1881; *United Ireland*, 8 October 1881.

52 *Irishman*, 16 July 1881.

53 Lane, "Rural Labourers, Social Change, and Politics," in *Politics and the Irish Working Class*, ed. Fintan Lane and Donal Ó Drisceoil (Basingstoke, 2005), 113–39, 128–29; Donnelly, *Land and the People*, 238–39.

54 O'Leary to Byrne (Land League of Great Britain), 7 November 1881, reprinted in the *Boston Globe*, 18 December 1881. This was only a partial picture of the provenance of the Land League subscriptions.

55 *Evening Telegraph*, 17 September 1881; *Irish World*, 8, 15 October 1881.

56 Parnell to Collins, 17 September 1881, Patrick Collins Papers, Burns Library, Boston College; *Evening Telegraph*, 17 September 1881; *United Ireland*, 15 October 1881; *Irish World*, 1, 8 October 1881; Boyle, "Marginal Figure," 331.

57 Egan to O'Leary, 12 November 1881, reprinted in the *Boston Globe*, 18 December 1881; *Irish American*, 26 November 1881.

58 O'Leary to George, 25 April 1882, General Correspondence, Box 2, HGP, NYPL; *Irish World*, 4 April 1875.

59 *Freeman's Journal*, 9 June 1881,

60 *Freeman's Journal*, 21 July 1881; *Irish World*, 3 December 1881.

61 Engels to Bernstein, 3 May 1882, in Karl Marx and Frederick Engels, *Marx and Engels on Ireland*, 333; Lane, *Origins of Modern Irish Socialism*, 35. Marx and Engels were not convinced by Hyndman's socialist credentials, and later James Connolly expressed reservations about him. *Worker's Republic*, 4 November 1899.

62 Harold Rylett, "Parnell," *Contemporary Review*, 1 January 1926, 475–81, 477; "The Late Harold Rylett: An Appreciation," *Manchester Guardian*, 13 August 1936; Adam Pole, "Harold Rylett," in *Dictionary of Irish Biography* (Cambridge, 2009): https://www.dib.ie/; *Manchester Guardian*, 23 April 1881; *Irish Times*, 18 June 1881.

63 *Irish World*, 9 July 1881.

64 *Irish World*, 25 June 1881; Thompson, *End of Liberal Ulster*, 174–75, 201.

65 *Irish Times*, 5 August 1881; *Irish World*, 23 July 1881; Thompson, *End of Liberal Ulster*, 276–77. The Democratic Federation called on its members in Tyrone to vote for Rylett.

66 George to Ford, 14 January 1882, Letterbooks, Series 1, B, Vol. 1, HGP, NYPL; *Freeman's Journal*, 15 November 1881; *Irish Times*, 12 June 1882.

67 *Irish Times*, 23 July 1881.

68 Lane, *Origins of Modern Irish Socialism*, 41–42.

69 Clark, *Plea*, 6, 15; *United Ireland*, 17 February 1883.

70 Holton, "Silk Dresses."

71 *Freeman's Journal*, 20 July 1881.

72 *Irish World*, 3 December 1881; *Freeman's Journal*, 21 July 1881.

73 Craigen, *Report on a Visit*, 60, 63.

74 Jessie Craigen, *The No Rent Manifesto*, Pamphlets 1122, National Library of Ireland (NLI).

75 *Freeman's Journal*, 24 October 1881.

76 Smith, "Helen Taylor's Work," p. 792; Holton, "Silk Dresses," 138. On tensions in the early twentieth century, see Sharon Crozier-De Rosa, "Divided Sisterhood? Nationalist Feminism and Feminist Militancy in England and Ireland," *Contemporary British History* 32, no. 4 (2018): 448–69.

77 *Nation*, 11 November 1882; *Glasgow Herald*, 4 November 1882. The Irish suffrage movement also had mixed views of Home Rule and believed it might impede their progress. Crawford, *Women's Suffrage Movement*, 257.

78 Craigen to Taylor, 19 August 1882, Mill/Taylor Papers, 18, London School of Economics Archives (LSEA); Ward, "Gendering the Union," 82.

79 Parnell to Taylor, 6 January 1881, Mill/Taylor Papers, 18, LSEA.

80 O'Brien to Parnell, 4 November 1881, Letters to Anna Parnell, MS17701, Land League Papers, NLI,.

81 *Freeman's Journal*, 3 November 1881; *Irish World*, 12 November, 10 December 1881.

82 *Freeman's Journal*, 27 October 1881.

83 Lee, *Modernisation of Irish Society*, 89.

84 *Irish World*, 3 December 1881.

85 David N. Haire, "In Aid of the Civil Power, 1868–1890," in *Ireland under the Union: Varieties of Tension*, ed. F. S. L. Lyons and R. A. J. Hawkins (Oxford, 1980), 115–47, 127; Richard Hawkins, "An Army on Police Work, 1881–82: Ross of Bladensburg's Memorandum," *Irish Sword* 11 (1973–74): 75–117.

86 Parnell, *Tale of a Great Sham*; *Irish World*, 5, 12, 19 November 1881; Ward, "Gendering the Union," 83–84.

87 *Freeman's Journal*, 15 November 1881. McDonnell had previously lived in London and was active in the Fenian Amnesty campaign of the late-1860s with Peter O'Leary. *Irish Times*, 25 October 1869.

88 Parnell to Taylor, 26 October 1881, Mill/Taylor Papers, 18, LSEA,; George to Ford, 10 November 1881, Letterbooks, Series 1, B, Vol. 1, HGP, NYPL.

89 George to Ford, 10 November 1881, Letterbooks, Series 1, B, Vol. 1, HGP, NYPL; *Freeman's Journal*, 12 November 1881.

90 Parnell to Taylor, 5 November 1885, Mill/Taylor Papers, 18, LSEA.

91 George to Ford, 28 December 1881, Letterbooks, Series 1, B, Vol. 1, HGP, NYPL.

92 Smith, "Helen Taylor's Work," 780–86.

93 Taylor, *Nationalisation of the Land*, 7.

94 George to Grey, 26 September 1881, General Correspondence, Box 2, HGP, NYPL.

95 Hyndman to George, 9 January 1882, General Correspondence, Box 2, HGP, NYPL.

96 Gutiérrez and Ferretti, "Nation against the State."

97 Davitt to McGhee, 13 October 1888, 5 December 1888, 9328/181, DP, TCD; Kropotkin to Davitt, 17 October 1888, 9448/3599, DP, TCD; *Cork Constitution*, 18 October 1888.

98 *Freeman's Journal*, 15 November 1881; *Irish Times*, 25 October 1869; Ó Gráda, "Fenianism and Socialism."

99 *Irish World*, 18 March 1882.

100 George to Ford, 9 March 1882, Letterbooks, Series 1, B, Vol. 1, HGP, NYPL; Gould, *Hyndman*, 72, 86; George, *Life of Henry George*, 367–79.

101 Morris to Allingham, 26 November 1884, in Kelvin, ed., *Collected Letters of William Morris*, vol. 2a, 339.

102 Thompson, *William Morris*, 291.

103 *Athenaeum* (London), 16 February 1884.

104 George, *Progress and Poverty*, 364, 383, 386, 405, 409–10.

105 *Freeman's Journal*, 29 June 1881.

106 Bradlaugh, *Land, The People*. The conference was also attended by Joseph Arch and Edward Aveling.

107 *Freeman's Journal*, 11 February 1880.

108 *Newcastle Weekly Chronicle*, 12 February, 19 March 1881.

109 Hansard, House of Commons Debates (HC Deb), 30 August 1880, vol. 256 cc719–20. Peter O'Leary provided evidence to the Richmond Commission.

110 Cowen to Mitchell, (n.d.) 1881, Cowen Papers, F43, Tyne and Wear Archives; *Newcastle Weekly Chronicle*, 12, 19 February 1881; Allen, *Joseph Cowen*, 99–101, 129.

111 *Freeman's Journal*, 18 April 1881; Cooter, *When Paddy Met Geordie*, 166–68.

112 *Newcastle Weekly Chronicle*, 7 May 1881.

113 1881 Census of Ireland, General Report, 8, 104. O'Leary claimed there were ninety-five thousand mud cabins in the 1870s (O'Leary, *Travels*, 3). Enda McKay, "The Housing of the Rural Labourer, 1883–1916," *Saothar*, 17 (1992): 27–38.

114 *Irish World*, 6 August 1881. The author wrote under the name Mrs. A. McDougall.

115 *Newcastle Weekly Chronicle*, 7 May 1881. Thomas Devyr reported similar practices in Donegal in the 1830s. Devyr, *Odd Book*, 181.

116 Hansard, HC Deb, 19 May 1881, vol 261 c794.

117 *Freeman's Journal*, 29 June 1881.

118 "Report of the Deputation of Cleveland Miners on the State of Ireland" (Dublin, 1881), MS D-TU 1/2/96/ff, 6, 13, Oldham Local Studies and Archives.

119 Hansard, HC Deb, 15 July 1881, vol. 263 cc1004–6; *Irishman*, 16 July 1881.

120 *Newcastle Chronicle*, 7 November 1881; *Irish World*, 10 December 1881.

121 Gould, *Hyndman*, 71.

122 *Newcastle Weekly Chronicle*, 7 May 1881; *Freeman's Journal*, 29 June 1881.

123 Cooter, *When Paddy Met Geordie*, 170.

124 *Newcastle Weekly Chronicle*, 20 August 1881; *Freeman's Journal*, 29 June 1881.

125 *United Ireland*, 29 October, 19 November 1881, 27 May 1882; *Newcastle Weekly Chronicle*, 20 August 1881.

126 Connolly, *Labour in Irish History*, 211–12.

127 *Newcastle Weekly Chronicle*, 26 February 1881.

128 Moody, *Davitt*, 481; Lyons, *Parnell*, 173.

129 Hansard, HC Deb, 11 March 1881, vol. 259, cc830–1.

130 *Nation*, 19 August 1882; *Freeman's Journal*, 14 August 1882.

131 Newby, *Ireland, Radicalism*.

132 It seems the patrol that usually accompanied W. E. Forster was not continued for his successor. Hansard, HC Deb, 19 June 1882, vol. 270, cc1603–1605.

133 Davitt to McGhee, 11 January 1883, 9328/172, DP, TCD.

134 Marley, *Michael Davitt*, 61–62.

135 Davitt to McGhee, (n.d.) 1884, 9328/180/5, DP, TCD; Marley, *Michael Davitt*, 63–64.

136 Davitt, *Fall of Feudalism*, 376.

137 *Irish World*, 26 August, 28 October 1882.

138 Ó Tuathaigh, "Irish Land Questions," 6.

139 Clark, *Social Origins*, 301–2.

140 Lee, "Land War," 115.

141 Marley, "Georgeite Social Gospel."

142 *Single Tax* (London), February, March 1899; Harold Rylett, "Nails and Chains," *English Illustrated Magazine*, 75 (1889): 163–75. Rylett was the editor of the *New Age* from 1899 to 1907. He retired in Ireland. Pole, "Harold Rylett."

143 *Freeman's Journal*, 7 April 1884.

144 *Freeman's Journal*, 15 April 1884.

145 Davitt to McGhee, 12 March 1884, 9328/180/13, DP, TCD; Barker, *Henry George*, 401.

146 Biagini, *British Democracy and Irish Nationalism*, 128–29.

147 *United Ireland*, 26 August 1882; Lane, "Rural Labourers," 132-3; Parnell quoted in Bagenal, "Uncle Pat's Cabin," 937.

148 *Irishman*, 21 April 1883; William Morris to Jenny Morris, 7 May 1883, in Kelvin, ed., *Collected Letters*, vol. 2a, 188–89.

149 *South London Press*, 23 November 1889; 28 March 1891; 2 September 1893.

150 *Times*, 6 April 1883, 24 April 1885; *St. Paul Sunday Globe*, 26 October 1884; on Graceville, see Bridget Connelly, *Forgetting Ireland: Uncovering a Family's Secret History* (St. Paul, MN, 2003).

151 *Irish American*, 1 September 1888; *Freeman's Journal*, 10 November 1894; *Irishman*, 10 June 1882; 21 April, 24 November 1883; 5 July 1884; 24 January 1885.

152 W. P. Ryan, *The Irish Literary Revival*.

153 *Irish World*, 9 September 1876; *Nation*, 22 October 1881; *Pilot*, 4 February 1882; *Irishman*, 10 June 1882.

2. MARGUERITE MOORE

1 *Report of the International Council of Women*, 44.

2 *New York Evening World*, 5 June 1894.

3 Aiken, "'Sinn Féin Permits," 107.

4 Marguerite Moore has received little more than brief mentions in existing accounts of the Land War, but recently aspects of her activities in the United States have been brought to light in McCarthy, *Respectability and Reform*; and Hodges, "Transatlantic Profile of Marguerite Moore."

5 *People* (New York), 12 April 1891.

6 Offen, *European Feminisms*, 144.

7 Luddy, *Women in Ireland*, 239–42.

8 Côté, *Fanny and Anna Parnell*, 50–51, 78–79, 136–39; *Irish World*, 21 August 1880; Katherine Tynan, *Twenty-Five Years: Reminiscences* (London, 1913), 75; Janis, *Greater Ireland*, 142; Whelan, "Transatlantic World"; Foster, *Charles Stewart Parnell*.

9 Parnell to Davitt, 9 November 1880, 1091, DP, TCD.

10 George to Ford, 22 November 1881, Letterbooks, Vol. 1, 44, HGP, NYPL.

11 Janis, *Greater Ireland*, 143; Ward, *Unmanageable Revolutionaries*, 4–39.

12 She was also described as American by Ward (*Unmanageable Revolutionaries*, 15), who was perhaps using Michael Davitt's "History of the Land League," serialized in *United Ireland*, which refers to "Mrs. Moore, an American" (*United Ireland*, 5 August 1882). Moore did not move to the United States until 1884, and there is no evidence that she lived there before this.

13 *Waterford News*, 27 February 1857, 17 July 1863, 3 July 1868; *Waterford Chronicle*, 25 June 1869; "Garret Nagle," *Calendars of Wills and Administrations, 1858–1922*, National Archives of Ireland, www.willcalendars.nationalarchives. ie; "Garret Nagle," *Griffith's Valuation, 1847–1864* (1848), www.askaboutireland.ie. Moore's children were Susan Catherine, Philomena, Lelia Matilda, Margaret, Thomas St. Patrick, and Clare Mary Pia: *Ireland Births and Baptisms, 1620–1881*, www.familysearch.org and Catholic Parish Registers at the NLI, https://registers.nli.ie/; 1910 and 1920 US Federal Census; *Times-Picayune* (New Orleans), 24 June 1900; Hodges, "Transatlantic Profile of Marguerite Moore," 38; Sheila Lunney, "Margaret Anna Carroll," in McGuire and Quinn, eds., *Dictionary of Irish Biography*, https://dib.cambridge.org/; on average marriage age, see Maria Luddy and Mary O'Dowd, *Marriage in Ireland, 1660–1925* (Cambridge, 2020), 91–101.

14 In 1857, one house that was part of her father's estate burned down and was uninsured, removing a large part of the inheritance, but she may have inherited other properties. *Waterford Chronicle*, 24 October 1857.

15 *New York Passenger Lists, 1820–1957*, the *Arizona*, 28 April 1884. The 1910 US Federal Census described Moore as a widow who had married in 1863 and was married for twenty years. One short biography from 1897 indicates she emigrated to the United States without her husband. "Mrs. Marguerite Moore," in *Great American Women of*

the Nineteenth Century, ed. Francis E. Willard and Mary A. Livermore (New York, [1897] 2005, 1897), 524–25.

16 *Irish World*, 11 June 1881; Hansard, HC Deb, 18 August 1881 vol. 265 cc311–317; Marguerite Moore, "Dawdlings in Donegal," *Catholic World*, 62 (1895): 167–78, 169. The Ladies' Land League certainly had more than the "negligible impact" in Ulster observed in R. W. Kirkpatrick, "Origins and Development of the Land War in Mid-Ulster, 1879–85," in Lyons and Hawkins, eds., *Ireland under the Union*, 201–35, 232.

17 *United Ireland*, 13 August; 10 September; 15 October; 5, 19 November; 10 December 1881.

18 Binckes and Laing, *Hannah Lynch*, 9; Tynan, *Twenty-Five Years*, 77–78; *Philadelphia Inquirer*, 5 December 1887.

19 *United Ireland*, 17 September 1881; *Irish World*, 29 April 1882.

20 *United Ireland*, 12 November 1881; *Irish World*, 24 September; 28 January 1882.

21 Moore sometimes told "Irish witticisms" to audiences in New York (*Brooklyn Life*, 27 May 1899).

22 Copies of these forms can be found in MS8291, Land League Papers, NLI. Anna Parnell later lamented that these grants were regularly used by tenants to pay arrears, rather than sustain rent strikes.

23 Côté, *Fanny and Anna Parnell*, 182, 204. There are photographs of the huts at the NLI: http://catalogue.nli.ie.

24 National Folklore Commission, the Schools' Collection, Vol. 0195, 143–44, Dúchas, www.duchas.ie.

25 Parnell to Collins, 10 November 1881, Patrick Collins Papers, Burns Library, Boston College.

26 O'Brien, *Charles Stewart Parnell*, 329. Henry George also believed the Ladies' Land League proved more successful at running the movement.

27 Jennie Wyse-Power, "Lecture on the Ladies' Land League," included with Nancy Wyse-Power's witness statement to the Bureau of Military History (BMH), WS0541.

28 *Manchester Guardian*, 17 October 1888; *United Ireland*, 20 October 1888.

29 Wyse-Power, "Lecture," WS0541, BMH.

30 Henry George in the *Irish World*, 26 August 1882.

31 *Freeman's Journal*, 24 December 1881; 2 January 1882.

32 George de Mille, *Henry George*, 101; *United Ireland*, 31 December 1881.

33 *United Ireland*, 31 December 1881; *Irish World*, 21 January 1882; *Freeman's Journal*, 21 January 1882.

34 Entry for Anne Kirk, 21 April 1882, General Register of Prisoners, Limerick, Book 1/24/13, Ireland's Prison Registers, www.findmypast.co.uk; Hansard, HC Deb, 23 May 1882, vol. 269, c1404; 10 August 1882, vol. 273, c1415; Clifford Lloyd, *Ireland under the Land League*.

35 *Irish World*, 28 January 1882.

36 *Irish World*, 28 January 1882; Ward, *Unmanageable Revolutionaries*, 24.

37 *Irish Times*, 31 March 1882.

38 *Birmingham Daily Post*, 22 March 1882.

39 *Freeman's Journal*, 24 April, 11 May, 8 June 1882; *Irish Times*, 31 March, 24 April 1882; *Irish World*, 15 April 1882.

40 *Irish World*, 21 January 1882.

41 *Dundee Courier*, 12 April 1882.

42 *Irish World*, 25 June 1881.

43 *Newcastle Weekly Chronicle*, 23 February 1881.

44 O'Brien to Parnell, 4 November 1881, Letters to Anna Parnell, MS17701, Land League Papers, NLI; *Liverpool Mercury*, 14 November 1881; *Freeman's Journal*, 14 March 1881.

45 Kearney to Parnell, 6 November 1881, Letters to Anna Parnell, MS17701, Land League Papers, NLI; *Pilot* (Boston), 3 December 1881; Schneller, *Anna Parnell's Political Journalism*, 176. The short-lived "North of England Land League" overlapped with the Land League of Great Britain from 1879 to 1881. Cooter, *When Paddy Met Geordie*, 163.

46 *Jarrow Express*, 25 November 1881; *North-Eastern Daily Gazette* (Middlesbrough), 21 November 1881; *Northern Echo* (Darlington), 21 November 1881; *United Ireland*, 26 November 1881; *Freeman's Journal*, 7 December 1881; *Leeds Mercury*, 15 November 1881; 1881 Census of England; MacPherson, "Domesticity and Irishness Abroad," 107; Frank Neal, "Irish Settlement in the North East and North West of England in the Mid Nineteenth Century," in Swift and Gilley, eds., *Irish in Victorian Britain*, 75–100.

47 *Dundee Courier*, 22 December 1881; *Hull Packet*, 11 November 1881; *Jarrow Express*, 5 November 1881.

48 *Glasgow Herald*, 21 December 1881.

49 *Scotsman*, 24 December 1881; *North British Daily Mail*, 21 December 1881.

50 *North British Daily Mail*, 29, 30 August 1881; *Glasgow Herald*, 29 August 1881.

51 *Blackburn Standard*, 12 November 1881.

52 *Liverpool Mercury*, 4 January 1882.

53 Branch names compiled from subscription lists in the *Freeman's Journal*, 19 March 1881–9 August 1882. It seems likely there were more branches in London than the five identified in this study.

54 Paul O'Leary, *Immigration and Integration: The Irish in Wales, 1798–1922* (Cardiff, 2000), 268.

55 Mary Doherty (Salford) to Kathleen Burke, 1 November 1881, Letters to the Ladies' Land League, MS 17704, Land League Papers, NLI.

56 Foster, "Irish Power in London."

57 This profile is compiled from the names attached to subscriptions in the *Freeman's Journal*, information on age and background derived from England and Scotland Census of 1861, 1871, and 1881.

58 MacPherson, "Domesticity and Irishness Abroad," 110.

59 Steven Fielding, *Class and Ethnicity: Irish Catholics in England, 1880–1939* (Buckingham, 1993), 83.

60 MacPherson, "Domesticity and Irishness Abroad," 108–10; Scott, "Anglo-Irish Relations," 74–75, 90, 219; W. J. Lowe, "The Irish in Lancashire, 1846–71: A Social History," PhD diss., Trinity College Dublin, 1974, 126.

61 Meagher, *Inventing Irish America*, 6–9.

62 *Irish World*, 30 October 1880; biographical information drawn from 1880 US Federal Census. Fanny was the wife of Andrew Maguire, a Fenian and member of the Land League.

63 Janis, *Greater Ireland*, 156.

64 Wyse-Power, "Lecture," WS0541, BMH.

65 Whelehan, "Youth, Generations," 953–54.

66 *Pilot*, 12 August 1882; Janis, *Greater Ireland*, 148.

67 Summers, "British Women"; Abigail Green, "Humanitarianism in Nineteenth Century Context: Religious, Gendered, National," *Historical Journal* 57, no. 4 (2014): 1157–75; Tyrrell, *Reforming the World*, 43.

68 Julia F. Irwin, *Making the World Safe*, 15, 20.

69 Luddy, *Women and Philanthropy*.

70 Viaene, "Nineteenth-Century Catholic Internationalism," 104.

71 *Times-Picayune* (New Orleans), 24 June 1900, 24 February 1901; Carroll, *Leaves*; Carroll, *Life of Catherine McAuley* (New York, 1866).

72 Quoted in Carter, *Land War and Its Leaders*, 110–11; Maria Luddy, ed., *The Crimean Journals of the Sisters of Mercy, 1854–56* (Dublin, 2004).

73 Marguerite Moore, "A New Woman's Work in the West of Ireland," *Catholic World*, January 1897, 458.

74 Parnell, *Tale of a Great Sham*, 49.

75 *Irish World*, 24 September 1881.

76 Wyse-Power, "Lecture," WS0541, BMH.

77 Laird, "Decentering the Irish Land War," in Campbell and Varley, eds., *Land Questions in Modern Ireland*, 175–93, 183.

78 Wyse-Power (O'Toole), "Lecture on the Ladies' Land League," *Sinn Féin*, 16 October 1909.

79 *North British Daily Mail*, 22 December 1881.

80 *Irishman*, 19 March 1881.

81 Janis, *Greater Ireland*, 48.

82 *Freeman's Journal*, 5, 8 July 1882.

83 Lucey, *Land, Popular Politics*, 91.

84 *Irish World*, 13 May 1882.

85 Keyes, *Funding the Nation*, 139; Parnell, *Tale of a Great Sham*, 116.

86 Parnell, *Tale of a Great Sham*, 96.

87 In the early 1900s, several of the early National League generation were in the front ranks of the Irish Parliamentary Party and opposed women's suffrage. Pašeta, *Irish Nationalist Women*, 32; Côté, *Fanny and Anna Parnell*, 216.

88 Keyes, *Funding the Nation*, 146. Some Ladies' Land League emigrant branches continued to function into 1883 and sent subscriptions to this fund (*Irishman*, 12 May 1883).

89 Pašeta, "Feminist Political Thought."

90 *Freeman's Journal*, 14 August 1882; *Manchester Times*, 19 August 1882; *Manchester Guardian*, 14 August 1882.

91 *Philadelphia Inquirer*, 5 December 1887; *Manchester Guardian*, 14 August 1882.

92 *Freeman's Journal*, 8 December 1883; James Quinn, *Young Ireland and the Writing of Irish History* (Dublin, 2015), 134.

93 *Irishman*, 22 October 1881; Riona Nic Congáil, "Young Ireland and *The Nation*: Nationalist Children's Culture in the Late Nineteenth Century," *Éire-Ireland* 46, no. 3 (2011): 37–62; Pašeta, *Irish Nationalist Women*, 101.

94 *Freeman's Journal*, 8 December 1883. Jane Francesca Wilde was Oscar Wilde's mother.

95 *Dublin Weekly Nation*, 5 January 1884; *New York Passenger Lists, 1820–1957*, 28 April 1884, Ship: the *Arizona*; 1910 US Federal Census.

96 *New York Passenger Lists, 1820–1957*, 28 April 1884, ship: the *Arizona*; 21 April 1884, ship: the *Oregon*, www.ancestry.com.

97 For example, she spoke at an Emmet event in 1885 (*Boston Globe*, 4 March 1885).

98 *Brooklyn Eagle*, 6 February 1898.

99 McCarthy, *Respectability and Reform*, 97–98.

100 O'Donnell, *Henry George*, 249.

101 *Washington Post*, 2 April 1888; McCarthy, *Respectability and Reform*, 98.

102 O'Donnell, *Henry George*, 251.

103 *Single Tax* (Glasgow), March 1898; Newby, *Edward McHugh*, 148–53.

104 Newby, *Edward McHugh*, 180, 219. Ellen McHugh died in 1941 in Birkenhead.

105 *People* (New York), 12 April 1891. The other three were Lillie Devereaux Blake, Sara Jane Lippincott, and Kate Fields.

106 *Irish World*, 30 October 1880.

107 Tara M. McCarthy, "Woman Suffrage and Irish Nationalism: Ethnic Appeals and Alliances in America," *Women's History Review*, 23 (2014): 188–203, 193.

108 *New York Times*, 6 July 1886. Blissert was married to the labor agitator Robert Blissert.

109 *New York World*, 25, 27 February; 8 March 1894.

110 International Council of Women, *Women in a Changing World*, 3, 14; *Boston Globe*, 22 March 1888; Offen, *European Feminisms*, 157.

111 *Report of the International Council of Women*, 44.

112 International Council of Women, *Women in a Changing World*, 278.

113 *Peacemaker* (Philadelphia), October 1887; *Warren Mirror*, 2 December 1887; *Wellsville Daily Reporter*, 15 May 1889; Jill Norgren, *Belva Lockwood: The Woman Who Would be President* (New York, 2007), 169.

114 *New York World*, 27 February 1894.

115 Moore, "New Woman's Work," 458.

116 Pašeta, *Irish Nationalist Women*, 22–23.

117 *Brooklyn Daily Eagle*, 12 October 1905; *New York Times*, 21 September 1903; *Brooklyn Life*, 20 May 1899.

118 *Washington Post*, 3 April 1888.

119 *New York Times*, 20 May 1893; *United Ireland*, 23 April 1892.

120 *New York Times*, 16 November 1891; *United Ireland*, 20 October 1892.

121 *United Ireland*, 12 October 1895.

122 Hodges, "Transatlantic Profile," 48; Campbell, "Bold Fenian Wife," 61–72; Whelehan, *Dynamiters*.

123 *New York Daily Herald*, 25 March 1914.

124 Nyhan Grey, "Dr. Gertrude B. Kelly," 81–82.

125 *Irish Citizen* (Dublin), 2 October 2015.

126 Doyle, "Striking for Ireland", 362; McCarthy, *Respectability and Reform*, 122–25.

127 1920 US Federal Census, Bronx Assembly District 6, Bronx, New York.

128 Hodges, "Transatlantic Profile," 49.

129 *Report of the International Council of Women*, 44.

130 *United Ireland*, 23 November 1895.

3. JUTE, CLASS, AND CATHOLICISM

1 *Dundee Courier*, 6 September 1881; *North British Daily Mail* (Glasgow), 30 August 1881.

2 *Dundee Courier*, 12 April 1882.

3 Delaney, "Our Island Story?," 104.

4 For overviews of the literature on Irish women's migration, see, among others, MacPherson and Hickman, eds., *Women and Irish Diaspora Identities*; Swift, "Identifying the Irish"; O'Sullivan, ed., *Irish Women and Irish Migration*.

5 Foner, *Politics and Ideology*, 150–200; Miller, *Emigrants and Exiles*, 550.

6 Walker, *Juteopolis*; Tomlinson, *Dundee and the Empire*.

7 Gordon, *Women and the Labour Movement*, 142.

8 Collins, "Origins of Irish Immigration."

9 1881 Census of Scotland, vol. 2, 390–94, 426–28, 431.

10 Walker, *Juteopolis*, 115–16. Two detailed studies of the Irish in Dundee are Brenda Collins, "Aspects of Irish Immigration into Two Scottish Towns (Dundee and Paisley) during the Mid-Nineteenth Century" (master's thesis, University of Edinburgh, 1978); and McCready, "Social and Political Impact."

11 1881 Census of Scotland, vol. 2, 426–27. Gender balance fluctuated between different time periods and host communities, but from 1870 to 1900 the outflow from Ireland was relatively even. The United States was the most popular destination for women, followed by Britain. MacRaild, *Irish Diaspora in Britain*, 141; Kerby Miller, David N. Doyle, and Patricia Kelleher, "'For Love and Liberty': Irish Women, Migration, and Domesticity in Ireland and America, 1815–1920," in

Patrick O'Sullivan, ed. *Irish Women and Irish Migration, Vol. 4:* 41–65, 43; Whelan, "Women on the Move," 903.

12 Collins, "Proto-Industrialization and Pre-Famine Emigration," 145; Collins, "Aspects of Irish Immigration," 50.

13 *Dundee Courier*, 16 January 1872, 20 March 1873; notes on the Brotherhood of St. Patrick, DD2, 11, 1863, Michael Condon Papers, Scottish Catholic Archives.

14 *Dundee Advertiser*, 10 December 1880; *Dundee Courier*, 17 January 1881.

15 *Weekly News* (Dublin), 4 November 1882; McCready, "Irish in Dundee," 202; Ó Catháin, "Michael Davitt and Scotland."

16 *Dundee Advertiser*, 10 December 1880.

17 *Dundee Evening Telegraph*, 11 and 23 August, 15 September 1881; *Nation*, 25 March, 1 July 1882; *Dundee Courier*, 6 August 1881.

18 *United Ireland*, 27 August 1881.

19 *Nation*, 10 September 1881; *Dundee Courier*, 6 September 1881.

20 *Dundee Courier*, 6 September 1881; *North British Daily Mail*, 19 October 1881.

21 Marguerite Moore, "Dawdlings in Donegal," *Catholic World*, 62 (1895): 167–78, 174.

22 *Dundee Advertiser*, 24 December 1881; *Glasgow Herald*, 22 December 1881.

23 *Dundee Courier*, 22 December 1881.

24 *Dundee Advertiser*, 12 April 1882; *Dundee Courier*, 12 April 1882.

25 *Dundee Courier*, 12 April 1882. Women ratepayers could vote in municipal elections in Scotland from the 1880s.

26 *North British Daily Mail*, 20 October 1881.

27 *Dundee Courier*, 12 April 1882; *Nation*, 22 April 1882.

28 *Dundee Courier*, 14 March 1881.

29 Meagher, *Inventing Irish America*, 184–85; Janis, *Greater Ireland*, 155–56.

30 *Irish World*, 18 March 1882; 10 June 1882.

31 Newby, *Ireland, Radicalism.*

32 *Irish World*, 28 January 1882; *The Post-Office Annual Glasgow Directory, 1879–80* (Glasgow 1879); Census of Scotland, 1881; *Glasgow Herald*, 21 December 1881.

33 *Irish World*, 21 January; 15 April 1882.

34 McMahon, *Global Dimensions of Irish Identity*, 174.

35 The information on other committee members is gathered from the following sources: *Dundee Advertiser*, 6 August 1881; *Weekly News* (Dublin), 12 February 1881; *Dundee Courier*, 18 February 1881; *Nation*, 12 February, 1 and 8 July 1882; *Freeman's Journal*, 23 March 1882; *United Ireland*, 10 December 1881. The genealogical records used for this section are the Census of Scotland, 1841, 1851, 1861, 1871, 1881, and 1891.

36 Nolan, *Servants of the Poor.*

37 Gordon, *Women and the Labour Movement*, 143–44.

38 1900 and 1910 US Federal Census. They moved to Slator Street in the 8th Ward, Paterson, New Jersey.

39 Gordon, *Women and the Labour Movement*, 145–46; Walker, *Juteopolis*, 87–96.

40 Butti to Rigg, 20 January 1886, DD3, Rigg Papers, 82, Scottish Catholic Archives (SCA).

41 Cox to Van de Rydt, 8 July and 20 August 1891, MS66/2/10/59, Cox Brothers Papers (CBP), University of Dundee Archives (UDA); McCready, "Irish in Dundee," 81, 85.

42 Dundee Royal Infirmary Admissions Register, 1879–85, 1/5/1 (6), THB, UDA.

43 The recording of accidents followed the 1895 Factory and Workshop Act. Register of Accidents 1896, MS66/iv/7/1, CBP, UDA. In 1900 a mechanic died following an accident.

44 Diner, *Erin's Daughters in America*, 75–76.

45 Holton, "Silk Dresses," 136; Gordon, *Women and the Labour Movement*, 212–60; Walker, *Juteopolis*, 2, 143.

46 Miller, *Emigrants and Exiles*, 550; Ó Tuathaigh, "Irish in Nineteenth-Century Britain," 173.

47 McBride, "John Ferguson," 422.

48 Lorraine Walsh, *Patrons, Poverty, and Profit: Organised Charity in Nineteenth-Century Dundee* (Dundee, 2000).

49 *Dundee Courier*, 6 September 1881.

50 Employee returns, 1872, MS6/1/7/1, 2, CBP, UDA.

51 Gordon, *Women and the Labour Movement*, 148.

52 Meagher, *Inventing Irish America*, 186.

53 Gordon, *Women and the Labour Movement*, 156–57.

54 McCheyne filed for bankruptcy the following year (*Edinburgh Gazette*, 2 May 1882).

55 *Dundee Courier*, 18 February 1881.

56 Davitt, *Fall of Feudalism in Ireland*, 314.

57 Carter, *Land War and Its Leaders*, 114; Jordan, *Land and Popular Politics*, 295–97, 299–300. Outside of the Ladies' Land League, women played important roles in eviction protests. TeBrake, "Irish Peasant Women in Revolt," 250.

58 Janis, *Greater Ireland*, 156.

59 McCready, "Irish in Dundee," 91–92, 110; J. E. Handley, *The Irish in Scotland* (Cork, 1947), 93–121; Tom Gallagher, *Glasgow, the Uneasy Peace: Religious Tension in Modern Scotland* (Manchester, 1987).

60 *Dundee Courier*, 12 August, 6 September 1881; 16 June 1882.

61 *Dundee Advertiser*, 22 April 1882.

62 *Dundee Courier*, 12 August 1881.

63 *North British Daily Mail*, 22 December 1881.

64 *Brooklyn Daily Eagle*, 16 May 1882.

65 Côté, *Fanny and Anna Parnell*, 169–177; *Dundee Courier*, 5 June 1882.

66 Walker, "Irish Immigrants in Scotland," 663.

67 Mitchell, "Irish Catholics in the West."

68 Kehoe, *Creating a Scottish Church*, 104; Bernard Aspinwall, "Catholic Devotion in Victorian Scotland," in Mitchell, ed., *New Perspectives on the Irish in Scotland*, 31–43, 33.

69 Peter Grant to George Cox, 23 November 1869, MS6, 1/3/2/12, 13, CBP, UDA.

70 Walker, "Irish Immigrants in Scotland," 656.

71 *St. Mary's, Lochee, Dundee: Souvenir Brochure, 1866–1966* (Glasgow, 1966), 51–52; Elliot, *Lochee*, 71.

72 Jenkins, *Between Raid and Rebellion*, 205.

73 *Dundee Advertiser*, 10 December 1880; *Dundee Courier*, 2 November 1882.

74 Smith to Clapperton, 7 February 1888, DD4, Clapperton Papers, SCA; *Dundee Courier*, 6 August 1881.

75 Butti to Rigg, 16 October 1880, DD3, George Rigg Papers, SCA.

76 Luddy, *Women and Philantropy*, 23.

77 *Dundee Evening Telegraph*, 18 March 1881; 18 March 1882.

78 Wilkie, *Across the Great Divide*, 23.

79 *Irish World*, 25 September 1880.

80 *Nation*, 20 August, 17 December 1881.

81 *Scotsman*, 26 June 1882; Census of Scotland 1851, 1861, 1871, 1881. Advertisements for his shop appeared regularly in the 1880s.

82 *Scotsman*, 7 August 1882; 19 March 1889.

83 *Tablet*, 18 August 1888.

84 Census of Scotland 1881: report, vol. 1, 185; Census of Scotland 1871: report, vol. 1, 178; "A History of St Andrew's, Dundee," DD19/2, SCA.

85 John. F. McCaffery, "Politics and the Catholic Community since 1878," *Innes Review*, 29 (1978): 140–55, 145.

86 *St. Mary's, Lochee, Dundee*, 23–29.

87 *St. Mary's, Lochee, Dundee*, 14.

88 Gerard Moran, ed., *Irish Radical Priests, 1660–1970* (Dublin, 1998); Bell, *Rebel, Priest, and Prophet*.

89 *Dundee Courier*, 12 April 1882.

90 *United Ireland*, 9 September 1882; *The Nation*, 30 September 1882; Peter Speirs, Sheriff Substitute, Portree to Sheriff Ivory, 31 May 1882, GD1/36/1/38, Papers of Sheriff William Ivory (1825–1915), National Records of Scotland; Newby, *Life and Times*, 42–50.

91 *Dundee Courier*, 2 November 1882; *Freeman's Journal*, 2 November 1882.

92 Gordon, *Women and the Labour Movement*, 212–13; Walker, *Juteopolis*, 2, 143; Norman Watson, "Daughters of Dundee—Gender and Politics in Dundee: The Representation of Women, 1870–1997," PhD diss., Open University, 2000, 62.

93 Putnam, "Transnational and the Text-Searchable," 377–78.

4. JOHN CREAGHE, THE *Southern Cross*, AND LAND WARS IN ARGENTINA

1 *Freeman's Journal*, 4 September 1883. The donation was £300.

2 *Southern Cross*, 6 January 1875. The issue opened with "In no part of the world is the Irishman more estimated and respected than in the province of Buenos Aires, and in no part of the world, in the same space of time, have Irish settlers made such large fortunes."

3 Quoted in Sabato, *Agrarian Capitalism*, 91.

4 Creaghe to George, 26 January 1884, Series 1, Box 4, HGP, NYPL.

5 *Irish World*, 23 July 1881.

6 Creaghe to George, 26 January 1884, Series 1, Box 4, HGP, NYPL.

7 The economic and political conservatism of Irish-Argentine leaders has been highlighted in recent studies: see Speight, *Irish-Argentine Identity*; and Sarah O'Brien, *Linguistic Diasporas, Narrative, and Performance: The Irish in Argentina* (Basingstoke, 2017), 157.

8 Delrio et al., "Discussing Indigenous Genocide."

9 All existing accounts state that Creaghe was from Limerick, but it seems this is mistaken. He lived in Dublin at least until he was ten years old, and it is possible he then moved to live with extended family in Limerick or Tipperary, but I have not found evidence for this. Baptismal register, St Peter's Parish, 1841, www.irishgenealogy.ie; "Minute Book of the Court of Examiners, 1864–1918," Archives of the Royal College of Surgeons, Ireland; "Compiled Military Service Records of Volunteer Union Soldiers Who Served the United States Colored Troops," 56th–138th USCT Infantry, 1864–66, www.Fold3.com; *Commonweal*, 4 January 1890; *Southern Cross*, 6 June 1884; O'Toole, *With the Poor People*, 3.

10 Rowbotham, *Edward Carpenter*, 161–62; Thompson, *William Morris*, 678, 681–82; O'Toole, *With the Poor People*, 9–27; Máirtín Ó Catháin, "Dr. John O'Dwyer Creaghe (1841–1920): Irish Argentine Anarchist," *Irish Migration Studies in Latin America* 2, no. 5 (2004): 59–61.

11 Suriano, *Anarquistas*, 207; Arthur Pageitt Greene, *Recollections of an Irish-Born Doctor in Nineteenth-Century Argentina*, ed. Susan Wilkinson (Tyne and Wear, 2015); Dorronzoro, *Pago, villa, y ciudad*, x.

12 In 1885 Patrick Dillon estimated there were thirty-five thousand to forty thousand Irish in Argentina at a National League meeting in Ballinasloe (*United Ireland*, 24 October 1885); Patrick McKenna, "Irish Migration to Argentina," in *The Irish World Wide: History, Heritage, Identity, Vol. 1: Patterns of Migration*, ed. Patrick Sullivan (Leicester, 1992), 63–83, 80; Coghlan, *El Aporte*, 18–20; Healy, "Migration from Ireland," 15, 333–35; Rock, *Argentina*, 141; Kelly, *Irish "Ingleses."*

13 Murray, *Devenir Irlandes*; Korol and Sabato, *Cómo Fue*. On the debates about the designation "informal" empire, see Cohen, "Love and Money in the Informal Empire"; and Rock, *British in Argentina*.

14 Devoto, *Historia de la Inmigración*, 234–35.

15 "Political developments in Ireland received little notice among Irish migrants in Buenos Aires": Healy, "Migration from Ireland," 80, 356. The revolutionary era has received more attention: see Keogh, *Independencia de Irlanda*; and William Bulfin, *Rambles in Éirinn* (Dublin, 1907).

16 Dwayne R. Winseck and Robert M. Pike, *Communication and Empire: Media, Markets, and Globalization, 1860–1930* (Durham, NC, 2007), 71–72.

17 *Irishman*, 5 August 1876; *Freeman's Journal*, 17 November 1881; Murray, *Story of the Irish*, 238, 242, 258, 445.

18 *Southern Cross*, 13 September 1878; 28 March 1879.

19 Murray, *Irish in Argentina*, 445.

20 *Irish World*, 23 July 1881.

21 Murray, *Irish in Argentina*, 64; Healy, "Migration from Ireland," 315–17.

22 "Song Written by Walter McCormack," Schools' Collection, vol. 0879, 49–53, National Folklore Collection, UCD, www.duchas.ie.

23 Rumbold to Granville, 16 April 1881, Home Office (HO) 45/9598 96680A, National Archives (NA).

24 Patrick Maume, "Patrick Dillon," in *Dictionary of Irish Biography*, ed. James McGuire and James Quinn (Cambridge, 2009), https://www.dib.ie/.

25 Murray, *Irish in Argentina*, 397; Maume, "Patrick Dillon"; Kelly, *Irish "Ingleses,"* 115.

26 *United Ireland*, 24 October 1885.

27 Del Viso (Ministry of the Interior) to Dillon, 16 April 1881, reprinted in Murray, *Irish in Argentina*, 431–32.

28 Rumbold to Pauncefote, 8 November 1880, HO 45/9598 96680A, NA.

29 Rock, *Argentina*, 141.

30 H. G. Roms, *Financier*, 29 June 1882; Rumbold to Pauncefote, 8 November 1880, HO 45/9598 96680A, NA.

31 *La Nación*, 7 April 1881.

32 Rumbold to Granville, 16 April 1881, HO 45/9598 96680A, NA.

33 Rumbold to Pauncefote, 8 November 1880, HO 45/9598 96680A, NA.

34 Petre to Granville, 11 January 1882, HO 118–184, NA.

35 *Standard* (Buenos Aires), 8 January 1882; *Buenos Ayres Herald*, 8 January 1882; Murray, *Irish in Argentina*, 431–32.

36 *Buenos Ayres Herald*, 4 January 1882.

37 *Libre Pensador*, 4 and 25 December 1881.

38 *Libre Pensador*, 29 December 1881; 22 January 1882.

39 *Libre Pensador*, 6 August 1882.

40 Murray, *Irish in Argentina*, 433; *Libre Pensador*, 22 January 1882.

41 *Daily Telegraph*, 26 December 1883; *Southern Cross*, 8 and 29 February 1884.

42 Creaghe to George, 26 January 1884, Series 1, Box 4, HGP, NYPL.

43 *Buenos Ayres Herald*, 19 February 1889; *Freeman's Journal*, 27 March 1889.

44 *Southern Cross*, 14 February 1890; *Freeman's Journal*, 27 March 1889, 25 January 1890; Hansard, HC Deb, 17 February 1890, vol. 341 cc430–1.

45 *Irish Times*, 30 March 1889; Murray, *Irish in Argentina*, 441. Assisted emigrants also encountered some hostility from Irish Americans in the 1880s. Moran, "Shovelling Out the Poor," 148.

46 *Freeman's Journal*, 25 January 1890; Murray, *Irish in Argentina*, 443–44.

47 Creaghe to George, 26 January 1884, Series 1, Box 4, HGP, NYPL.

48 Sabato, *Agrarian Capitalism*, 292–93; Rock, *Argentina*, 139–41.

49 Roy Hora, *The Landowners of the Argentine Pampas: A Social and Political History 1860–1945* (Oxford, 2001), 42.

50 Ezequiel Gallo, "Argentina: Society and Politics, 1880–1916," in *The Cambridge History of Latin America, Vol. V*, ed. Leslie Bethell (Cambridge, 1986), 359–92, 359. Immigration numbers found in Rock, *Argentina*, 142, 153.

51 Devoto, *Historia de la Inmigración*, 221–22.

52 Mulhall and Mulhall, *Handbook*, 126.

53 Creaghe to George, 26 January 1884, Series 1, Box 4, HGP, NYPL.

54 Kelly, *Irish "Ingleses,"* 82; Murray, *Irish in Argentina*, 448.

55 María Sáenz Quesada, "Eduardo Casey," in *Argentina del Ochenta al Centenario*, ed. Gustavo Ferrari and Ezequiel Gallo (Buenos Aires, 1980), 541–53, 552.

56 Creaghe to George, 26 January 1884, Series 1, Box 4, HGP, NYPL. Over five thousand hectares was considered a large property in Argentina at the time.

57 Land values increased massively in parts of Buenos Aires province in the 1880s, sometimes in the space of a year. From 1878 one Argentine league was measured as 2500 hectares. Quesada, "Eduardo Casey," 543–46; *Southern Cross*, 11 March 1881.

58 Peard, *American Teacher in Argentina*, 218–21; Quesada, "Eduardo Casey," 545–46; José Bernardo Wallace, "Casey, Eduardo (1847–1906)," in *Dictionary of Irish Latin American Biography*, ed. Gonzalo Cané, www.irlandeses.org.

59 *Southern Cross*, 15, 29 May, 19 June 1885.

60 Briones and Delrio, "Conquista del Desierto"; Healy, "Migration from Ireland," 389; Kristine L. Jones, "Conflict and Adaptation in the Argentine Pampas, 1750–1880," PhD diss., University of Chicago, 1984, which includes a comparative chapter on the US high plains; Jones, *Invention of Argentina*; María E. Argeri, *De guerreros a delincuentes: La desarticulación de las jefaturas indígenas y el poder judicial; Norpatagonia, 1880–1930* (Madrid, 2005).

61 Delrio et al., "Discussing Indigenous Genocide," 139.

62 Quesada, "Eduardo Casey," 545–56.

63 *Southern Cross*, 16, 23 May 1879.

64 *Southern Cross*, 15 December 1882; Speight, *Irish-Argentine Identity*, 77–78.

65 Creaghe to George, 14 April 1884, Series 1, Box 4, HGP, NYPL.

66 When writing on the causes of the Mexican Revolution, Creaghe later referred to the historic "dispossession of indigenous tribes of their lands": *Regeneración* (Los Angeles), 27 January 1912.

67 *Southern Cross*, 8 February, 21 March 1884.

68 Murray, *Irish in Argentina*, 446, 456; Coghlan, *Irlandeses en la Argentina*, 250.

69 Foran to Dinneen, 26 November 1889, 13 April 1893, MS13813, William Bulfin Papers, NLI; Harrington to Dinneen, 30 January 1887, MS13813, William Bulfin Papers, NLI; Eduardo Murray, "The Irish in Falkland/Malvinas Islands," *Irish Migration Studies in Latin America* 3, no. 6 (2005): 77–79, www.irlandeses.org.

70 Murray, *Irish in Argentina*, 445.

71 *Freeman's Journal*, 4 September 1883.

72 *Southern Cross*, 18 and 25 January, 29 February, 7 March 1884.

73 Creaghe to George, 26 January 1884 Series 1, Box 4, HGP, NYPL.

74 Niall Whelehan, "Labour and Agrarian Violence in the midlands, 1850–1870," *Saothar: Journal of the Irish Labour History Society*, 37 (2012): 7–18.

75 *Southern Cross*, 18 January 1884.

76 *Southern Cross*, 2 November 1883; 22 February 1884.

77 *Southern Cross*, 30 May 1884; Creaghe to George, 14 April 1884, Series 1, Box 4, HGP, NYPL.

78 *Southern Cross*, 6, 13 June 1884. Creaghe's letters elsewhere acknowledged the pseudonyms "J.C." and "Homo." Locations and references mentioned in P.M.'s letters indicate this was also Creaghe.

79 The article was signed Spartacus, with no clues as to the author's identity. *Southern Cross*, 4 July 1884.

80 *Southern Cross*, 4, 11, 18 January; 30 May; 6 June; 18 July 1884.

81 Creaghe to Henry George, 27 July 1884, Series 1, Box 4, HGP, NYPL.

82 *Southern Cross*, 14 March 1884.

83 *Southern Cross*, 4 April 1884; 13 June 1884.

84 *Southern Cross*, 30 May 1884.

85 *Southern Cross*, 2 November 1883.

86 *Southern Cross*, 30 May 1884.

87 *Southern Cross*, 9 November 1883. Gormley wrote under the initials "T.E.G." Argentina, National Census, 1895, City of Buenos Aires, www.familysearch.org.

88 *Southern Cross*, 7 March 1884; Laurel Brake and Marysa Demoor, eds., *Dictionary of Nineteenth Century Journalism in Great Britain and Ireland* (Gent, 2009), 569.

89 Quesada, "Eduardo Casey," 542–50; Murray, *Irish in Argentina*, 429.

90 For example, see Pageitt Greene, *Recollections*, 59.

91 *Southern Cross*, 6 June, 18 July 1884.

92 *Southern Cross*, 11 July 1884

93 *Southern Cross*, 22 February 1884.

94 *Southern Cross*, 30 May 1884.

95 *Southern Cross*, 2 November 1883; 22 February, 27 June 1884.

96 *Southern Cross*, 30 May 1884.

97 *Commonweal*, 2 February 1889; Zaragoza, *Anarquismo Argentino*, 105.

98 *El Perseguido* (Buenos Aires), 11 November 1893.

99 *Commonweal*, 9 November 1889; Lane, "Practical Anarchists, We."

100 *Commonweal*, 26 April, 20 September 1890.

101 Quesada, "Eduardo Casey," 551–52; Peard, *American Teacher in Argentina*, 229–30.

102 Thompson, *William Morris*, 678, 681–82.

103 *Sheffield Anarchist*, 6 September 1891; *Southern Cross*, 22 February 1884.

104 "'Murder!' 'Vengeance!',' BG L3/60, International Institute of Social History, Amsterdam (IISH).

105 Federico Ferretti, *Anarchy and Geography: Reclus and Kropotkin in the UK* (London, 2018), 112–14.

106 *Sheffield Anarchist*, 18 October 1891.

107 *Sheffield Anarchist*, 28 June 1891; "Murder! Vengeance!," BG L3/60, IISH.

108 *Commonweal*, 4, 11 July 1891; Quail, *Slow Burning Fuse*, 97, 101; O'Toole, *With the Poor People*, 18–19.

109 Suriano, *Anarquistas*, 207.

110 *Regeneración*, 20 January 1912. Large parts of the *Regeneración* archive are available at www.archivomagon.net.

111 *Regeneración*, 27 January 1912; Rama, "Revolución Mexicana," 169.

112 *Land and Liberty* (Hayward, California), September 1914.

113 *Land and Liberty*, August 1914.

5. THOMAS AINGE DEVYR AND THE "GREAT TRUTH"

1 Devyr to Marx, 16 January 1872, D 1028, Karl Marx/Friedrich Engels Papers, IISH.

2 *Working Man's Advocate* (New York), 5 September 1846.

3 *Irish World*, 18 June 1887; *Brooklyn Daily Eagle*, 26 May 1887.

4 Foner, *Politics and Ideology*, 150–200.

5 In 1880 there were over 1.8 million Irish-born residents in the United States alongside some 3.2 million second- and third-generation Irish Americans. Janis, *Greater Ireland*, 9, 72–75; Miller, *Emigrants and Exiles*, 540, 548; Meagher, *Inventing Irish America*, 180–93; McCarthy, *Respectability and Reform*, 65–105.

6 Foner, *Politics and Ideology*, 168–79; Janis, *Greater Ireland*, 121–66.

7 Devyr, *Odd Book*, American Section (AS), 189, 212.

8 Devyr, *Odd Book*, Irish and English Section (IES), 34, 38–40, 86, 89, 101, 107. The 1880 US Federal Census gives his date of birth as 1810, but it was noted as 1808 in the *Newcastle Weekly Chronicle*, 5 July 1884. Devyr was probably a variant of Diver. Doherty, *Inis-Owen and Tirconnell*, 434; *Brooklyn Daily Eagle*, 12 February 1912; *Donegal Democrat*, 3 October 1969; Breandán Mac Suibhne, *The End of Outrage: Post-Famine Adjustment in Rural Ireland* (Oxford, 2017), 8; Gamble, *Society and Manners*, xxxiii.

9 Devyr, *Odd Book*, IES, 42–44, 132. This quotation is from the pamphlet *Our Natural Rights*, which is reprinted in the *Odd Book*, IES, 110–35.

10 Devyr, 18, 165.

11 Devyr, 61, 93, 129.

12 Hughes and MacRaild, *Ribbon Societies*, 68.

13 Devyr, *Odd Book*, IES, 58, 70–72, 101; AS, 34.

14 Devyr, *Our Natural Rights*, reprinted in *Odd Book*, IES, 110–12, 123.

15 Devyr, 124–55, 132; Huston, "Thomas Ainge Devyr," 147–49.

16 Devyr, 132.

17 Chase, *Chartism*; Dorothy Thompson, *The Chartists* (London, 1984); Dorothy Thompson, "Ireland and the Irish in English Radicalism before 1850," in *The Chartist Experience: Studies in Working-Class Radicalism and Culture, 1830–60*, ed. J. Epstein and D. Thompson (London, 1982), 120–51.

18 Devyr, *Odd Book*, IES, 135, 140, 143–44.

19 Beaumont was born in New York to an Irish mother and English father. William H. Maehl, "Augustus Hardin Beaumont: Anglo-American Radical (1798–1838)," *International Review of Social History* 14, no. 2 (1969): 237–50.

20 Devyr, *Odd Book*, IES, 155.

21 *Northern Star* (Leeds), 7 July 1838; Devyr, 157–58, 160–61.

22 *Northern Liberator*, 10 August 1839; Devyr, 162, 175, 195; "Apostacy of Mr. Sharman Crawford," *Northern Liberator*, 4 May 1839. In 1837 Crawford had collaborated with the Chartists.

23 "Address of the Northern Political Union to Their Oppressed Brothers in Ireland," *Northern Liberator*, 17 November 1838; Devyr, 164–68.

24 Devyr, 168–69.

25 *Northern Liberator*, 13 July 1839; Chase, *Chartism*, 98; Roger Hawkins, "Robert Blakey, 1795–1878," Dictionary of National Biography, www.oxforddnb.com

26 *Northern Liberator*, 17 August 1839.

27 These threats were made by a person later discovered to have been a spy. Devyr, *Odd Book*, IES, 177, 194–206; Chase, *Chartism*, 135.

28 *Freeman's Journal*, 29 January, 15 February 1840; *Dublin Morning Register*, 13 February 1840.

29 Devyr, *Odd Book*, AS, 25–26; The *Williamsburg Democrat* ran until 1848. Devyr also edited a number of short-lived papers in Brooklyn. Stiles, *Kings County*, 933–39.

30 Huston, *Land and Freedom*, 139–42.

31 Lause, *Young America*, 1; Bronstein, *Land Reform*, 124; Wilentz, *Chants Democratic*, 340.

32 *New York Herald*, 3 January, 4 June 1845.

33 Devyr, *Odd Book*, AS, 45–46; Bronstein, *Land Reform*, 124.

34 *Working Man's Advocate*, 14 June 1845; Huston, *Land and Freedom*, 138–42.

35 *Northern Star*, 27 April, 1 June 1844; 19 April 1845.

36 *New York Herald*, 4 June 1845.

37 *Commercial Advertiser* (New York), 10 September 1844.

38 *Working Man's Advocate*, 9 August 1845; *New York Evening Express*, 23 August 1845; Devyr, *Odd Book*, AS, 43, 50.

39 Huston, *Land and Freedom*, 164, 170–74.

40 *Irish World*, 19 May 1877; Lause, *Young America*, 130.

41 Rodechko, *Patrick Ford*, 68–69, 71–73.

42 *Irish World*, 3 April 1880.

43 Devyr, *Odd Book*, IES, xvii.

44 Devyr, *Natural Rights*, reprinted in Devyr, *Odd Book*, IES, 118; *Fenian Brotherhood* (New York), 5 May 1866.

45 Thomas Ainge Devyr, "Statement of Facts" (1860), S 11, Karl Marx/Friedrich Engels Papers, IISH; Lause, *Young America*, 130.

46 Devyr to Marx, 16 January 1872, D 1028, Karl Marx/Friedrich Engels Papers, IISH. If Marx responded, his response has not survived.

47 Devyr, *Odd Book*, AS, 147–48.

48 *Newcastle Weekly Chronicle*, 15 March 1884; Devyr, *Odd Book*, IES, xvi–iii.

49 Devyr, *Odd Book*, AS, 34–38.

50 Devyr, *Odd Book*, IES, 25–27; AS, 53–54.

51 *New York Evening Express*, 18 August 1848; *Cork Examiner*, 25 September 1848.

52 Devyr to O'Brien, 16 March 1859, reprinted in Devyr, *Odd Book*, AS, 64.

53 *Fenian Brotherhood*, 5 May 1866; *World* (New York), 29 March 1866; Devyr, 122, 129.

54 *Fenian Brotherhood*, 5 May 1866.

55 Devyr, *Odd Book*, AS, 83–88.

56 Doherty, *Inis-Owen and Tirconnell*, 434; *Irish World*, 18 June 1887, emphasis in original.

57 Devyr, *Odd Book*, AS, 62, 64.

58 Holyoake, *Sixty Years*, 178–79; *Commercial Advertiser*, 18 May 1846; Devyr, *Odd Book,* AS, 37; Wilentz, *Chants Democratic*, 369.

59 Devyr, *Odd Book,* AS, 101, 107.

60 *Irish World*, 18 June 1887.

61 Devyr to Marx, 16 January 1872, D 1028, Karl Marx/Friedrich Engels Papers, IISH.

62 Shiels, *Irish in the American Civil War*, 6.

63 Brundage, *Irish Nationalists in America*, 122; Janis, *Greater Ireland*, 116.

64 *Irish World*, 16 April 1881, 16 February 1884; Foner, *Politics and Ideology*, 183–84; Brundage, *Irish Nationalists*, 120.

65 *United Ireland*, 27 August 1881; *Belfast Morning News*, 24 September 1881.

66 *United Ireland*, 3 September 1881; O'Connor, *Gladstone-Parnell*, 180.

67 Parnell, *Memoir*, 125; Côté, *Fanny and Anna Parnell*, 50–51.

68 *Irish American*, 27 March 1880.

69 Upton, *Uncle Pat's Cabin*, 283.

70 O'Connor, *Memoirs*, vol. 1, 178.

71 Phemister, "Our American Aristotle," PhD diss., University of Edinburgh, 2016, 178–79.

72 Upton, *Uncle Pat's Cabin*, 283. For an interesting comparison of Ireland and the American South, see Cathal Smith, "Second Slavery, Second Landlordism, and Modernity: A Comparison of Antebellum Mississippi and Nineteenth-Century Ireland," *Journal of the Civil War Era* 5, no. 2 (2015): 204–30.

73 *Freeman's Journal*, 15 November 1881.

74 McKivigan, *Forgotten Firebrand*, 156.

75 Devyr, *Odd Book*, AS, 191.

76 Foner, *Politics and Ideology*, 68–72.

77 Quoted in Huston, *Land and Freedom*, 160.

78 Devyr, *Odd Book*, AS, 101, 110–11, 122.

79 Devyr, 101.

80 *Fenian Brotherhood*, 5 May 1866.

81 Devyr to Smith, 26 August 1872, reprinted in Devyr, *Odd Book*, AS, 106, 113–18, 153. Devyr wrote thirty letters to Smith from 1856–1874; Devyr approached Smith a few

times to financially support his campaigning (Godine, "Abolitionist and the Land Reformer," 30).

82 Devyr, *Odd Book,* AS, 173.

83 Devyr, 191.

84 Devyr, 144.

85 *Irish World*, 15 January 1881.

86 Gleeson, "Failing to 'Unite with the Abolitionists,'" 628; Ian Delahanty, "The Transatlantic Roots of Irish American Anti-Abolitionism, 1843–1859," *Journal of the Civil War Era* 6, no. 2 (2016): 164–92.

87 The links between these two papers continued into the twentieth century. *Irish World*, 9 December 1876, 4 August 1877; 11 March 1899; 21 June 1902. Ó Gráda, "Fenianism and Socialism." The *Irish World* later described Marx as a "thoughtful social philosopher" whose "profound and conscientious analysis" furthered social change (*Irish World*, 28 June 1890).

88 Bulik, *Sons of Molly Maguire*; Kenny, *Making Sense.*

89 *Irish World*, 30 June 1877. The Pinkerton detective investigating the Mollies was also Irish-born.

90 Devyr, *War of Classes*, 126–31, 152–55; Kenny, *Molly Maguires*, 13–14.

91 *Irish World*, 25 September 1875; 27 May 1876.

92 Whelehan, *Dynamiters.*

93 *Irish World*, 20 May 1876; Fenian Brotherhood correspondence, 1876, vol. 21, Foreign Office FO5/1556, NA.

94 *Irish World*, 7, 14 August 1875.

95 Devyr, *Odd Book*, AS, 188.

96 *Irish World*, 27 May 1876.

97 *Colossal Bust, of Thomas Paine, the Author-Hero of the American Revolution*, Portfolio 160/5, Printed Ephemera Collection, Library of Congress, http://hdl.loc.gov.

98 Lause, *Young America*, 135.

99 O'Grady, *Story of Ireland*, 199; Sheehy Skeffington, *Michael Davitt*, 76. Historian Desmond Ryan also emphasized Lalor's influence on George, but downplayed George's impact in Ireland. Ryan, "The Social Ideal and National Movements," n.d., LA10/396, Desmond Ryan Papers, UCD.

100 *Newcastle Weekly Chronicle*, 23 April 1881; George Jacob Holyoake, *Travels in Search of a Settler's Guide-book of America and Canada* (London, 1884), 30.

101 Devyr to "S.F.L.," August 1882, reprinted in the *Newcastle Weekly Chronicle*, 27 August 1887.

102 Devyr, *War of Classes*, 135.

103 *Newcastle Chronicle*, 15 March 1884; *Brooklyn Daily Eagle*, 15 December 1886.

104 Devyr, *War of Classes*; *Irish World*, 13 November 1875.

105 McEvatt (1813–1901) was the father-in-law of J. P. McDonnell, editor of the *Labor Standard*. *Irish World*, 1 June 1901.

106 *Irish World*, 24 July, 25 September 1875; 20 May 1876; Devyr, *War of Classes*, 124, 140; Devyr, *Odd Book*, AS, 182–86, 201.

107 A similar quote from Ford was included in his 1878 *War of Classes*.

108 Devyr, *Odd Book*, AS, 199; *Irish American*, 17 January 1880.

109 Devyr to "S.F.L.," August 1882.

110 *Cork Constitution*, 4 November 1884.

111 *Brooklyn Daily Eagle*, 13 November 1886.

112 *Newcastle Weekly Chronicle*, 5 July 1884; Devyr to "S.F.L.," August 1882 and June 1884, reprinted in the *Newcastle Chronicle*, 27 August 1887.

113 Cowen to Devyr, 21 April 1885, F56, Joseph Cowen Papers, Tyne and Wear Archives, Newcastle.

114 *Irish American*, 27 January 1896; *Brooklyn Daily Eagle*, 12 February 1912. Tom Devyr played baseball in the 1860s and 1870s for the New York Mutuals and the Brooklyn Chelseas.

115 *United Ireland*, 23 June 1894; Holyoake, *Sixty Years*, 107.

CONCLUSION

1 Sheehy Skeffington, *Michael Davitt*, 82–83, 135.

2 W. P. Ryan, *The Irish Labour Movement*, 134–35.

3 *Irish Peasant*, 28 February 1903; 9 February 1907. Sheehy Skeffington also occasionally contributed to the *Irish Peasant*.

4 *Peasant*, 27 June 1908.

5 Several witness statements to the Bureau of Military History, collected in the late 1940s and 1950s, included references to relatives who participated in the Land War, but these references often seem consciously framed to set out the credentials of a nationalist family background. Interestingly, a popular film about the Land War, *Captain Boycott*, was released in 1947, which may have revived interest and influenced some of these references. On the sidelining of Michael Davitt by the 1916 generation, see King, *Michael Davitt*, 557–58.

6 *Il grido del popolo* (Naples), 24 December 1881; *L'Agitazione* (Ancona), 7 October 1897; Anna Shukalovich, "What Ukrainians Knew about Irish Moderates and Irish Radicals," paper presented at the Ireland, Ukraine, and Empire Conference, Kiev, 16 November 2019; Parfitt, *Knights across the Atlantic*, 109–10.

7 Brubaker, *Ethnicity without Groups*, 4; Mannion, *Land of Dreams*, 7.

SELECTED BIBLIOGRAPHY

ARCHIVE AND MANUSCRIPT SOURCES

Archives of the Royal College of Surgeons, Ireland
 Minute Book of the Court of Examiners, 1864–1918
Burns Library, Boston
 Patrick Collins Papers
Catholic University of America, the American Catholic History Research Center and University Archives.
 Fenian Brotherhood Collection
International Institute of Social History
 Karl Marx/Friedrich Engels Papers
 Misc. BG L3/60
London School of Economics Archives
 Mill/Taylor Papers
National Archives, UK
 Home Office 45/9598 96680A
 Foreign Office 5/1556; 118/184
National Folklore Commission, University College Dublin
 The Schools' Collection, https://www.duchas.ie/
National Library of Ireland
 Irish National Land League Papers
 William Bulfin Papers
 Pamphlets, 1122
National Records of Scotland
 Papers of Sheriff William Ivory (1825–1915)
New York Public Library
 Henry George Papers
Oldham Local Studies & Archives
 Report of the Deputation of Cleveland Miners on the State of Ireland
Scottish Catholic Archives
 Michael Condon Papers
 Robert Clapperton Papers
 George Rigg Papers
 "A History of St Andrew's, Dundee," MS DD19/2
Trinity College Dublin Archives
 Michael Davitt Papers

Tyne and Wear Archives
    Joseph Cowen Papers
University College Dublin Archives
    Desmond Ryan Papers
University of Dundee Archives
    Cox Brothers Papers
    Dundee Royal Infirmary Admissions Register
    Minutes of Police Commissioner's Meetings, 1880–1883
Census material for Scotland, England, Argentina, and the United States, as well as civil
    registers and passenger lists, were consulted in the following databases:
    https://registers.nli.ie
    www.findmypast.co.uk
    www.askaboutireland.ie
    www.familysearch.org
    www.willcalendars.nationalarchives.ie
    www.ancestry.ie
    www.genealogybank.com

NEWSPAPERS

Newspapers in hardcopy or microfilm are denoted with *; the rest were consulted
in digital collections.

Belfast Morning News
Boston Globe
Brooklyn Daily Eagle
Brooklyn Life
Buenos Ayres Herald
Chicago Tribune
Commercial Advertiser (New York)
Commonweal (London)*
Cork Constitution
Cork Examiner
Donegal Democrat
Dublin Morning Register
Dundee Advertiser *
Dundee Catholic Herald
Dundee Courier
Dundee Evening Telegraph
El Perseguido (Buenos Aires)*
Evening Telegraph (Dublin)
Fenian Brotherhood (New York)*
Freedom (London)*
Freeman's Journal (Dublin)

Glasgow Herald
Irish American (New York)
Irish Nationalist (San Francisco)
Irish Peasant (Dublin)*
Irish Times (Dublin)
Irish World and American Industrial Liberator (New York)*
Irishman (Dublin)
Jarrow Express
Land and Liberty (Hayward, California)*
Leeds Mercury
Libre Pensador (Buenos Aires)
Liverpool Mercury
Manchester Guardian
Nación (Buenos Aires)
Nation (Dublin)
New York Evening Express
New York Herald
New York Times
New York World
Newcastle Chronicle
North British Daily Mail (Glasgow)*
Northern Star (Leeds)
Northern Liberator (Newcastle)
Peacemaker (Philadelphia)
People (New York)
Philadelphia Inquirer
Pilot (Boston)*
Regeneración (Los Angeles)*
Scotsman
*Sheffield Anarchist**
Single Tax (Glasgow)*
Sinn Féin (Dublin)*
South London Press
Southern Cross (Buenos Aires)*
Standard (Buenos Aires)
Tablet (London)
Times-Picayune (New Orleans)
United Ireland (Dublin)*
Washington Post
Waterford News and Star
Weekly News (Dublin)
Williamsburg Democrat (Brooklyn)
Working Man's Advocate (New York)

PUBLISHED PRIMARY SOURCES

Bagenal, Philip H. *The American Irish and Their Influence on Irish Politics.* Boston, 1882.

———. "Uncle Pat's Cabin." *Nineteenth Century* 12 (1882): 925–38.

Bradlaugh, Charles. *The Land, The People, and the Coming Struggle.* 3rd ed. London, 1880.

Bulfin, William. *Rambles in Éirinn.* Dublin, 1907.

Carroll, Austin. *Leaves from the Annals of the Sisters of Mercy.* 3 vols. New York, 1888.

Clark, Gavin Brown. *A Plea for the Nationalisation of the Land.* Glasgow, [1881] 1918.

Clifford Lloyd, C. D. *Ireland under the Land League: A Narrative of Personal Experiences.* Edinburgh, 1892.

Commission on Emigration and Other Population Problems, 1948–1954: Reports. Dublin, 1955.

Connolly, James. *Labour in Irish History.* Dublin, 1914.

Craigen, Jessie. *Report on a Visit to Ireland in the Summer of 1881.* Dublin, 1882.

Cusack, Mary Francis. *The Nun of Kenmare: An Autobiography.* London, 1998.

Davitt, Michael. *The Fall of Feudalism in Ireland; or, The Story of the Land League Revolution.* London, 1904.

Devoy, John. *Recollections of an Irish Rebel.* New York, 1929.

Devyr, Thomas Ainge. *The Odd Book of the Nineteenth Century, or "Chivalry" in Modern Days: A Personal Record of Reform—Chiefly Land Reform, for the Last Fifty Years.* Greenpoint, NY, 1882.

———. *A War of Classes. How to Avert It.* New York, 1878.

Doherty, William James. *Inis-Owen and Tirconnell: Being Some Account of Antiquities and Writers of the County of Donegal.* Dublin, 1895.

Elliot, Alexander. *Lochee: As It Was and as It Is; and a Series of Sketches Descriptive of Olden Time Vestiges in the Neighbourhood.* Dundee, 1911.

George, Henry, Jr. *The Life of Henry George.* London, 1900.

George, Henry. *The Irish Land Question: What It Involves, and How Alone It Can Be Settled. An Appeal to the Land Leagues.* London, 1881.

———. *Progress and Poverty: An Inquiry into the Cause of Industrial Depressions, and of Increase of Want with Increase of Wealth. The Remedy.* New York, [1879] 1881.

———. *Social Problems.* New York, 1883.

Holyoake, George Jacob. *Sixty Years of an Agitator's Life.* London, 1892.

The Irish Crisis of 1879–80: Proceedings of the Mansion House Relief Committee. Dublin, 1881.

Hyndman, H. M. *The Nationalization of the Land in 1775 and 1882.* London, 1882.

James, Henry. *The Work of the Irish Leagues: The Speech of Sir Henry James, Replying in the Parnell Commission Inquiry.* London, 1890.

Joynes, J. L. *Adventures of a Tourist in Ireland.* London, 1882.

Kelvin, Norman, ed. *The Collected Letters of William Morris.* 4 vols. Princeton, NJ, 1984–2014.

Marx, Karl, and Friedrich Engels. *Ireland and the Irish Question.* Moscow, 1971.

Mulhall, M. G., and E. T. Mulhall. *Handbook of the River Plate Republics, Comprising Buenos Ayres and the Provinces of the Argentine Republic and the Republics of Uruguay and Paraguay.* London, 1875.

Murray, Thomas. *The Story of the Irish in Argentina.* New York, 1919.

"Native of P. E. Island." *Fenianism, Irish Land Leagueism, and Communism.* n.p., 1881.

O'Brien, Richard Barry. *The Life of Charles Stewart Parnell, 1845–91.* New York, 1898.

O'Brien, William, and Desmond Ryan, eds. *Devoy's Post Bag, 1871–1928, 2 Vols, 1880–1928.* Dublin, 1948–53.

O'Brien, William. *The Great Famine in Ireland and a Retrospect of the Fifty Years 1845–95.* London, 1896.

———. *Recollections.* London, 1905.

O'Connor, T. P. *Gladstone-Parnell, and the Great Irish Struggle.* Philadelphia, 1886.

———. *Memoirs of an Old Parliamentarian.* 2 vols. London, 1929.

O'Grady, Standish. *The Story of Ireland.* London, 1894.

O'Leary, Peter. *Travels and Experiences in Canada, the Red River Territory, and the United States.* London, 1877.

Ryan, W. P. *The Irish Labour Movement: From the Twenties to Our Own Day.* Dublin, 1919.

———. *The Irish Literary Revival: Its History, Pioneers, and Possibilities.* London, 1894.

Pageitt Greene, Arthur. *Recollections of an Irish Born Doctor in Nineteenth-Century Argentina.* Edited by Susan Wilkinson. Washington, Tyne & Wear, 2015.

Parnell, Anna. *Tale of a Great Sham.* Dublin, 1986.

Parnell, John H. *Charles Stewart Parnell: A Memoir.* London, 1916.

Powderly, Terence V. *The Path I Trod.* New York, 1940.

Report of the International Council of Women, Assembled by the National Woman Suffrage Association, Washington, D.C., U. S. of America, March 25 to April 1, 1888. Washington, DC, 1888.

Sheehy Skeffington, Francis. *Michael Davitt: Revolutionary, Agitator, and Labour Leader.* Boston, 1909.

Sixteenth Detailed Annual Report of the Registrar-General of Marriages, Births, and Deaths in Ireland, 1879. Dublin, 1880.

Stiles, Henry Reed. *Kings County: A History of the City of Brooklyn.* Brooklyn, 1870.

Sullivan, Margaret. *The Ireland of To-Day: The Causes and Aims of Irish Agitation.* Philadelphia, 1881.

Taylor, Helen. *Nationalisation of the Land.* London, [ca. 1890].

Tynan, Katherine. *Twenty-five Years: Reminiscences.* London, 1913.

Upton, William C. *Uncle Pat's Cabin, or, Life among the Agricultural Labourers.* Dublin, 1882.

Willard, Francis E., and Mary A. Livermore, eds. *Great American Women of the Nineteenth Century.* New York, [1897] 2005.

SELECT SECONDARY SOURCES

Aiken, Síobhra, "'Sinn Féin permits . . . in the heels of their shoes': Cumann na mBan Emigrants and Transatlantic Revolutionary Exchange." *Irish Historical Studies* 44, no. 165 (2020): 106–30.

Akenson, D. H. *The Irish Diaspora: A Primer.* Toronto, 1996.

Allen, Joan. *Joseph Cowen and Popular Radicalism on Tyneside, 1829–1900*. London, 2007.

Barr, Colin. *Ireland's Empire: The Roman Catholic Church in the English-Speaking World, 1829–1914*. Cambridge, 2020.

Bartlett, Thomas, ed. *The Cambridge History of Ireland, Volume IV: 1880 to the Present*. Cambridge, 2018.

Bell, Stephen. *Rebel, Priest, and Prophet: A Biography of Dr. Edward McGlynn*. New York, 1937.

Berger, Stefan, and Sean Scalmer, eds. *The Transnational Activist: Transformations and Comparisons from the Anglo-World since the Nineteenth Century*. New York, 2018.

Bew, Paul. *Land and the National Question in Ireland, 1858–82*. Dublin, 1978.

Biagini, Eugenio. *British Democracy and Irish Nationalism, 1876–1906*. Cambridge, 2007.

Binckes, Faith, and Kathryn Laing. *Hannah Lynch, 1859–1904: Irish Writer, Cosmopolitan, New Woman*. Cork, 2019.

Boyle, John W. *The Irish Labour Movement in the Nineteenth Century*. Washington, DC, 1988.

———. "A Marginal Figure: The Irish Rural Laborer." In *Irish Peasants: Violence and Political Unrest, 1780–1914*, edited by Samuel Clark and James S. Donnelly Jr., 311–38. Madison, WI, 1983.

Briones, Claudia, and Walter Delrio. "La 'Conquista del Desierto' desde perspectivas hegemónicas y subalternas." *Runa* 27 (2007): 23–48.

Bronstein, Jamie L. *Land Reform and Working-Class Experience in Britain and the United States*. Stanford, CA, 1999.

Brown, Michael. *The Irish Enlightenment*. Cambridge, MA, 2016.

Brubaker, Rogers. *Ethnicity without Groups*. Cambridge, MA, 2004.

———. "The 'Diaspora' Diaspora." *Ethnic and Racial Studies* 28, no. 1 (2005): 1–19.

Brundage, David. *Irish Nationalists in America: The Politics of Exile, 1798–1998*. New York, 2016.

Bulik, Mark. *The Sons of Molly Maguire: The Irish Roots of America's First Labor War*. New York, 2015.

Bull, Philip. *Land, Politics, and Nationalism: A Study of the Irish Land Question*. Dublin, 1996.

Cameron, Ewen. "Communication or Separation? Reactions to Irish Land Agitation and Legislation in the Highlands of Scotland, c. 1870–1910." *English Historical Review* 120, no. 487 (2005): 633–66.

Campbell, Fergus, and Tony Varley, eds. *Land Questions in Modern Ireland*. Manchester, 2013.

Campbell, Judith E. "The Bold Fenian Wife: Mary Jane O'Donovan Rossa." In *Ireland's Allies: America and the 1916 Easter Rising*, edited by Miriam Nyhan Grey, 61–72. New York, 2016.

Carter, J. W. H. *The Land War and Its Leaders in Queen's County, 1879–82*. Portlaoise, 1994.

Casey, Brian. *Class and Community in Provincial Ireland, 1851–1914*. Basingstoke, 2018.

Casey, Brian, ed. *Defying the Law of the Land: Agrarian Radicals in Irish History*. Dublin, 2013.

Chase, Malcolm. *Chartism: A New History*. Manchester, 2007.

Clark, Samuel. *The Social Origins of the Irish Land War*. Princeton, NJ, 1979.

Coghlan, Eduardo. *El Aporte de los Irlandeses a la Formación de la Nación Argentina*. Buenos Aires, 1982.

———. *Los Irlandeses en la Argentina: Su Actuación y Descendencia*. Buenos Aires, 1987.

Cohen, Deborah. "Love And Money in the Informal Empire: The British In Argentina, 1830–1930." *Past and Present* 245, no. 1 (2019): 79–115.

Comerford, R. V. *The Fenians in Context: Irish Politics and Society, 1848–82*. Dublin, 1985.

———. "The Land War and the Politics of Distress, 1877–82." In *A New History of Ireland, Vol. IV: Ireland under the Union, II 1870–1921*, edited by W. E. Vaughan, 26–52. Oxford, 1996.

Collins, Brenda. "The Origins of Irish Immigration to Scotland in the Nineteenth and Twentieth Centuries." In *Irish Immigrants and Scottish Society in the Nineteenth and Twentieth Centuries*, edited by T. M. Devine, 1–18. Edinburgh, 1991.

———. "Proto-Industrialization and Pre-Famine Emigration." *Social History* 7, no. 2 (1982): 127–46.

Conley, Carolyn. *Melancholy Accidents: The Meaning of Violence in Post-Famine Ireland*. Lanham, MD, 1999.

Conrad, Sebastian, and Dominic Sachsenmaier, eds. *Competing Visions of World Order: Global Moments and Movements, 1880s–1930s*. New York, 2007.

Cooper, Sophie E. "Irish Migrant Identities and Community Life in Melbourne and Chicago, 1840–1890." PhD diss., University of Edinburgh, 2017.

Cooter, Roger. *When Paddy Met Geordie: The Irish in County Durham and Newcastle, 1840–1880*. Sunderland, 2005.

Côté, Jane McL. *Fanny and Anna Parnell: Ireland's Patriot Sisters*. Basingstoke, 1991.

Crawford, Elizabeth. *The Women's Suffrage Movement in Britain and Ireland: A Regional Survey*. New York, 2006.

Curtis, L. Perry, Jr. *The Depiction of Eviction in Ireland, 1845–1910*. Dublin, 2011.

———. "Landlord Responses to the Irish Land War, 1879–87." *Éire-Ireland* 38, no. 3 (2003): 134–88.

Deacon, Desley, Penny Russell, and Angela Woollacott, eds. *Transnational Lives: Biographies of Global Modernity, 1700–Present*. Basingstoke, 2010.

Delaney, Enda. "Our Island Story? Towards a Transnational History of Late Modern Ireland." *Irish Historical Studies* 37 no. 148 (2011): 83–105.

Delaney, Enda, and Donald M. MacRaild, eds. *Irish Migration, Networks, and Ethnic Identities since 1750*. London, 2007.

Delrio, Walter, Diana Lenton, Marcelo Musante, Mariano Nagy, Alexis Papazian, and Pilar Pérez. "Discussing Indigenous Genocide in Argentina: Past, Present, and Consequences of Argentinean State Policies toward Native Peoples." *Genocide Studies and Prevention* 5, no. 2 (2010): 138–59.

Devoto, Fernando. *Historia de la Inmigración en la Argentina*. Buenos Aires, 2009.

Diner, Hasia. *Erin's Daughters in America: Irish Immigrant Women in the Nineteenth Century*. Baltimore, MD, 1983.

Donlan, Regina. *German and Irish Immigrants in the Midwestern United States, 1850–1900.* Cham, 2018.

Donnelly, James S., Jr. *The Land and the People of Nineteenth-Century Cork: The Rural Economy and the Land Question.* London, 1975.

Dorronzoro, Martín. *Pago, villa y ciudad de Luján.* Buenos Aires, 1950.

Douglas, Roy. *Land, People, and Politics: A History of the Land Question in the United Kingdom, 1878–1952.* London, 1976.

Doyle, Joe. "Striking for Ireland on the New York Docks." In *The New York Irish*, edited by Ronald H. Bayor and Timothy J. Meagher, 357–573. Baltimore, 1996.

Fitzpatrick, David. *The Americanisation of Ireland: Migration and Settlement, 1841–1925.* Cambridge, 2020.

———. "The Disappearance of the Irish Agricultural Labourer, 1841–1912." *Irish Economic and Social History* 7 (1980): 66–92.

———. "'A Peculiar Tramping People': The Irish in Britain, 1801–70." In *A New History of Ireland, Volume V: Ireland under the Union, I, 1801–70*, edited by W. E. Vaughan, 623–60. Oxford, 1989.

Foner, Eric. *Politics and Ideology in the Age of the Civil War.* New York, 1980.

Foster, R. F. *Charles Stewart Parnell: The Man and His Family.* Hassocks, 1976.

———. "'An Irish Power in London': Making It in the Victorian Metropolis." In *"Conquering England": Ireland in Victorian London*, edited by Fintan Cullen and R. F. Foster, 12–25. London, 2005.

———. *Vivid Faces: The Revolutionary Generation in Ireland, 1890–1923.* London, 2014.

Gamble, John. *Society and Manners in Early Nineteenth-Century Ireland.* Edited by Breandán Mac Suibhne. Dublin, 2011.

George de Mille, Anna. *Henry George: Citizen of the World.* Chapel Hill, NC, 1950.

Gleeson, David T. "Failing to 'Unite with the Abolitionists': The Irish Nationalist Press and U.S. Emancipation." *Slavery & Abolition* 37, no. 3 (2016): 622–37.

Godine, Amy. "The Abolitionist and the Land Reformer: Gerrit Smith and Tom Devyr." *Hudson River Valley Review* 30, no. 2 (2014): 17–39.

Gordon, Eleanor. *Women and the Labour Movement in Scotland, 1850–1914.* Oxford, 1991.

Gould, Frederick J. *Hyndman: Prophet of Socialism.* London, 1928.

Gutiérrez, Jose Antonio, and Federico Ferretti. "The Nation against the State: The Irish Question and Britain-Based Anarchists in the Age of Empire." *Nations and Nationalism* 26, no. 3 (2020): 611–27.

Harper, Marjory. "Enticing the Emigrant: Canadian Agents in Ireland and Scotland, c. 1870—c. 1920." *Scottish Historical Review* 83 (2004): 41–58.

Healy, Claire. "Migration from Ireland to Buenos Aires, 1776–1890." PhD diss., National University of Ireland, Galway, 2005.

Hodges, Elizabeth Lee. "A Transatlantic Profile of Marguerite Moore." *New York Irish History* 32 (2018): 38–53.

Holton, Sandra Stanley. "Silk Dresses and Lavender Kid Gloves: The Wayward Career of Jessie Craigen, Working Suffragist." *Women's History Review* 5, no. 1 (1996): 129–50.

Hoppen, K. Theodore. *Governing Hibernia: British Politicians and Ireland, 1800–1921*. Oxford, 2016.

Horn, Pamela L. R. "The National Agricultural Labourers' Union in Ireland, 1873–79." *Irish Historical Studies* 17, no. 67 (1971): 340–52.

Hughes, Kyle, and Donald M. MacRaild. *Ribbon Societies in Nineteenth-Century Ireland and Its Diaspora*. Liverpool, 2018.

Huston, Reeve. *Land and Freedom: Rural Society, Popular Protest, and Party Politics in Antebellum New York*. New York, 2000

———. "Thomas Ainge Devyr and Transatlantic Land Reform." In *Transatlantic Rebels*, edited by Thomas Summerhill and James C. Scott, 137–66. East Lansing, MI, 2004.

International Council of Women. *Women in a Changing World: The Dynamic Story of the International Council of Women since 1888*. London, 1966.

Irwin, Julia F. *Making the World Safe: The American Red Cross and a Nation's Humanitarian Awakening*. New York, 2013.

Jackson, Alvin. *Home Rule: An Irish History, 1800–2000*. London, 2003.

Janis, Ely M. *A Greater Ireland: The Land League and Transatlantic Nationalism in Gilded-Age America*. Madison, WI, 2015.

Jenkins, William. *Between Raid and Rebellion: The Irish in Buffalo and Toronto, 1867–1916*. Ithaca, NY, 2013.

Jordan, Donald E. *Land and Popular Politics in Ireland: County Mayo from the Plantation to the Land War*. Cambridge, 1994.

———. "The Irish National League and the 'Unwritten Law': Rural Protest and Nation-Building in Ireland, 1882–1890." *Past & Present*, 158, no.1 (1998): 146–171.

Kehoe, S. Karly. *Creating a Scottish Church: Catholicism, Gender, and Ethnicity in Nineteenth-Century Scotland*. Manchester, 2013.

Kelly, Helen. *Irish "Ingleses": The Irish Immigrant Experience in Argentina, 1840–1920*. Dublin, 2009.

Kelly, Matthew. "Radical Nationalisms." In *The Cambridge History of Ireland, Volume IV: 1880 to the Present*, edited by Thomas Bartlett, 33–61. Cambridge, 2018.

Kenny, Kevin. "Diaspora and Comparison: The Global Irish as a Case Study." *Journal of American History* 90, no. 1 (2003): 134–62.

———. *Diaspora: A Very Short Introduction*. New York, 2013.

———. *Making Sense of the Molly Maguires*. Oxford, 1998.

Keogh, Dermot. *La Independencia de Irlanda: La Conexión Argentina*. Buenos Aires, 2016.

Keyes, Michael. *Funding the Nation: Money and Nationalist Politics in Nineteenth-Century Ireland*. Dublin, 2011.

Khuri-Makdisi, Ilham. *The Eastern Mediterranean and the Making of Global Radicalism, 1860–1914*. Berkeley, CA, 2010.

King, Carla. *Michael Davitt: After the Land League, 1881–1906*. Dublin, 2016.

Korol, Juan Carlos, and Hilda Sabato. *Cómo Fue la Immigración Irlandesa en Argentina*. Buenos Aires, 1981.

Laird, Heather. "Decentering the Irish Land War: Women, Politics, and the Private Sphere." In Campbell, Fergus, and Tony Varley, eds. *Land Questions in Modern Ireland*, edited by Fergus Campbell and Tony Varley, 175–93. Manchester, 2013.

———. *Subversive Law in Ireland: From "Unwritten Law" to the Dail Courts, 1879–1920*. Dublin, 2005.

Lane, Fintan, and Andrew Newby. *Davitt: New Perspectives*. Dublin, 2009.

Lane, Fintan. *The Origins of Modern Irish Socialism, 1881–1896*. Cork, 1997.

———. "P. F. Johnson, Nationalism, and Irish Rural Labourers, 1869–82." *Irish Historical Studies*, 33 (2002): 191–208.

———. "'Practical Anarchists, We': Social Revolutionaries in Dublin, 1885–87." *History Ireland* 16, no. 2, (2008): n.p.

Lane, Fintan, and Donal Ó Drisceoil, eds. *Politics and the Irish Working Class, 1830–1945*. Basingstoke, 2005.

Laqua, Daniel. *The Age of Internationalism and Belgium, 1880–1930: Peace, Progress, and Prestige*. Manchester, 2013.

Lause, Mark A. *Young America: Land, Labor, and the Republican Community*. Urbana, IL, 2005.

Lee, Joe. "The Irish Diaspora in the Nineteenth Century." In *Nineteenth-Century Ireland: A Guide to Recent Research*, edited by Laurence M. Geary and Margaret Kelleher, 182–222. Dublin, 2005.

———. "The Land War." In *Milestones in Irish History*, edited by Liam De Paor, 106–16. Cork, 1986.

———. *The Modernisation of Irish Society, 1848–1918*. Dublin, 2008.

Leerssen, Joep, ed. *Parnell and His Times*. Cambridge, 2020.

Lucey, Donnacha Sean. *Land, Popular Politics, and Agrarian Violence in Ireland: The Case of County Kerry, 1872–86*. Dublin, 2011.

Luddy, Maria. *Women and Philanthropy in Nineteenth-Century Ireland*. Cambridge, 1995.

———. *Women in Ireland, 1800–1918: A Documentary History*. Cork, 1995.

Lyons, F. S. L., and R. A. J. Hawkins, eds. *Ireland under the Union: Varieties of Tension— Essays in Honour of T. W. Moody*. Oxford, 1980.

Mac Suibhne, Breandán. *The End of Outrage: Post-Famine Adjustment in Rural Ireland*. Oxford, 2017.

MacPherson, D. A. J. "Domesticity and Irishness Abroad: Irish Women's Associational Life in the North East, 1880–1914." In *What Rough Beasts? Irish and Scottish Studies in the New Millennium*, edited by Shane Alcobia-Murphy, 102–20. Newcastle, 2008.

MacPherson, D. A. J., and M. J. Hickman, eds. *Women and Irish Diaspora Identities: Theories, Concepts, and New Perspectives*. Manchester, 2014.

MacRaild, Donald M. *The Irish Diaspora in Britain, 1750–1939*. Basingstoke, 2011.

Mannion, Patrick. *A Land of Dreams: Ethnicity, Nationalism, and the Irish in Newfoundland, Nova Scotia, and Maine, 1880–1923*. Montreal, 2018.

Marley, Laurence. "The Georgeite Social Gospel and Radical Intersections in Late Nineteenth-Century Belfast." In *Culture and Society in Ireland since 1750: Essays in Honour of Gearóid Ó Tuathaigh*, edited by John Cunningham and Niall Ó Ciosáin, 303–31. Dublin, 2015.

———. *Michael Davitt: Freelance Radical and Frondeur*. Dublin, 2007.

McBride, Terence. "John Ferguson, Michael Davitt, and Henry George—Land for the People." *Irish Studies Review* 14, no. 4 (2006): 421–30.

McCarthy, Tara M. *Respectability and Reform: Irish American Women's Activism, 1880–1920*. Syracuse, NY, 2018.

McCready, Richard B. "The Social and Political Impact of the Irish in Dundee, ca. 1845–1922." PhD diss., University of Dundee, 2002.

McGuire, James, and James Quinn, eds. *Dictionary of Irish Biography*. Cambridge, 2009.

McKenna, Patrick. "Irish Migration to Argentina." In *The Irish World Wide: History, Heritage, Identity, Vol. 1: Patterns of Migration*, edited by Patrick Sullivan, 63–83. Leicester, 1992.

McKivigan, John R. *Forgotten Firebrand: James Redpath and the Making of Nineteenth-Century America*. Ithaca, NY, 2008.

McLaughlin, Eoin. "Competing Forms of Cooperation? Land League, Land War, and Cooperation in Ireland, 1879–1914." *Agricultural History Review* 63, no. 1 (2015): 81–112.

McMahon, Cian. *The Global Dimensions of Irish Identity: Race, Nation, and Popular Press, 1840–1880*. Chapel Hill, NC, 2015.

Meagher, Timothy J. *Inventing Irish America: Generation, Class, and Ethnic Identity in a New England City, 1880–1928*. Southbend, IL, 2001.

Meaney, Geraldine, Mary O'Dowd, and Bernadette Whelan. *Reading the Irish Woman: Studies in Cultural Encounter and Exchange, 1714–1960*. Liverpool, 2013.

Miller, Kerby A. *Emigrants and Exiles: Ireland and the Irish Exodus to North America*. Oxford, 1985.

———. *Ireland and Irish America: Culture, Class, and Transatlantic Migration*. Dublin, 2008.

———. "'Revenge for Skibbereen': Irish Emigration and the Meaning of the Great Famine." In *The Great Famine and the Irish Diaspora in America*, edited by Arthur Gribben, 180–95. Amherst, MA, 1999.

Mitchell, Martin J. "Irish Catholics in the West of Scotland in the Nineteenth Century: Despised by Scottish Workers and Controlled by the Church?" In *New Perspectives on the Irish in Scotland*, edited by Martin J. Mitchell, 1–19. Edinburgh, 2008.

Moloney, Deirdre M. *American Catholic Lay Groups and Transatlantic Social Reform in the Progressive Era*. Chapel Hill, NC, 2002.

Moody, T. W., *Davitt and the Irish Revolution*. Oxford, 1984.

Moran, Gerard. "'Giving a Helping Hand': International Charity during the Forgotten Famine of 1879–81." *New Hibernia Review* 24, no. 2 (2020): 132–49.

———. *A Radical Priest in Mayo: Father Patrick Lavelle—The Rise and Fall of an Irish Nationalist, 1825–86*. Dublin, 1994.

———. *Sending Out Ireland's Poor: Assisted Emigration to North America in the Nineteenth Century*. Dublin, 2004.

Mulholland, Marc. "Land War Homicides." In *Uncertain Futures: Essays about the Irish Past for Roy Foster*, edited by Senia Pašeta, 81–96. Oxford, 2016.

Murray, Edmundo. *Devenir Irlandes: Narrativas Intimas de La Emigracion Irlandesa a la Argentina, 1844–1912*. Buenos Aires, 2004.

———. "Ireland and Latin America: A Cultural History." PhD diss., University of Zurich, 2010.

Newby, Andrew. *Ireland, Radicalism, and the Scottish Highlands, ca. 1870–1912*. Edinburgh, 2007.

———. *The Life and Times of Edward McHugh*. Lewiston, 2005.

Nolan, Janet. *Servants of the Poor: Teachers and Mobility in Ireland and Irish America*. Notre Dame, IN, 2004.

Nyhan Grey, Miriam. "Dr. Gertrude B. Kelly and the Founding of New York's Cumann na mBan." In *Ireland's Allies: America and the 1916 Easter Rising*, edited by Miriam Nyhan Grey, 75–89. Dublin, 2016.

Ó Catháin, Máirtín. *Irish Republicanism in Scotland, 1858–1916: Fenians in Exile*. Dublin, 2007.

———. "Michael Davitt and Scotland." *Saothar*, 25 (2000): 19–26.

O'Connor, Emmet. *A Labour History of Ireland, 1824–2000*. Dublin, 2011.

O'Day, Alan. "Imagined Irish Communities: Networks of Social Communication of the Irish Diaspora in the United States and Britain in the Late Nineteenth and Early Twentieth Centuries." *Immigrants & Minorities*, 23, no. 2–3, (2005): 399–424.

O'Donnell, Edward T. *Henry George and the Crisis of Inequality: Progress and Poverty in the Gilded Age*. New York, 2015.

Ó Gráda, Cormac. "Fenianism and Socialism: The Career of J. P. McDonnell." *Saothar* 1 (1975): 31–41.

———. *Ireland: A New Economic History, 1780–1939*. Oxford, 1994.

O'Sullivan, Patrick, ed. *The Irish World Wide*. 6 vols. Leicester, 1992–97.

O'Toole, Alan. *With the Poor People of the Earth: A Biography of Doctor John Creaghe of Sheffield and Buenos Aires*. London, 1982.

Ó Tuathaigh, Gearóid. "The Irish in Nineteenth-Century Britain: Problems of Integration." *Transactions of the Royal Historical Society* 31 (1981): 149–73.

———. "Irish Land Questions in the State of the Union." In *Land Questions in Modern Ireland*, edited by Fergus Campbell and Tony Varley, 3–24. Manchester, 2013.

Offen, Karen. *European Feminisms, 1700–1950: A Political History*. Stanford, CA, 2000.

Osterhammel, Jürgen. *The Transformation of the World: A Global History of the Nineteenth Century*. Translated by Patrick Camiller. Princeton, NJ, 2014.

Parfitt, Stephen. *Knights across the Atlantic: The Knights of Labor in Britain and Ireland*. Liverpool, 2016.

Pašeta, Senia. "Feminist Political Thought and Activism in Revolutionary Ireland, ca. 1880–1918." *Transactions of the RHS* 27 (2017): 193–209.

———. *Irish Nationalist Women, 1900–1918*. Cambridge, 2013.

Peard, Julyan G. *An American Teacher in Argentina: Mary Gorman's Nineteenth-Century Odyssey from New Mexico to the Pampas*. Lewisburg, PA, 2016.

Phemister, Andrew. "'The Grandest Battle Ever Fought for the Rights of Human Beings': Radical Republicanism and the Universalization of the Land War." *Éire-Ireland* 51, nos. 1–2 (2016): 192–217.

———. "'Our American Aristotle': Henry George and the Republican Tradition during the Transatlantic Irish Land War, 1877–1887." PhD diss., University of Edinburgh, 2016.

Putnam, Lara. "The Transnational and the Text-Searchable: Digitized Sources and the Shadows They Cast." *American Historical Review* 121, no. 2 (2016): 377–402.

Quail, John. *The Slow Burning Fuse: The Lost History of the British Anarchists.* London, 1978.

Quesada, María Sáenz. "Eduardo Casey." In *Argentina del Ochenta al Centenario,* edited by Gustavo Ferrari and Ezequiel Gallo, 541–53. Buenos Aires, 1980.

Qureshi, Sadiah. "Dying Americans: Race, Extinction, and Conservation in the New World." In *From Plunder to Preservation: Britain and the Heritage of Empire, 1800–1950,* edited by Astrid Swenson and Peter Mandler, 269–88. Oxford, 2013.

Rama, Carlos M. "La Revolución Mexicana en el Uruguay." *Historia Mexicana* 7 (1957): 161–86.

Rock, David. *Argentina, 1516–1987.* Berkeley, CA, 1985.

———. *The British in Argentina: Commerce, Settlers, and Power, 1800–2000.* Basingstoke, 2019.

Roddy, Sarah, Julie-Marie Strange, and Bertrand Taithe. *The Charity Market and Humanitarianism in Britain, 1870–1912.* London, 2019.

Rodechko, James Paul. *Patrick Ford and His Search for America: A Case Study of Irish-American Journalism, 1870–1913.* New York, 1976.

Rodgers, Daniel T. *Atlantic Crossings: Social Politics in a Progressive Age.* Cambridge, MA, 1998.

Roger, María José. "The Children of the Diaspora Irish Schools and Educators in Argentina, 1850–1950." *Irish Migration Studies in Latin America* 1, no. 1 (2003): 5–25.

Rowbotham, Sheila. *Edward Carpenter: A Life of Liberty and Love.* London, 2008.

Sabato, Hilda. *Agrarian Capitalism and the World Market: Buenos Aires in the Pastoral Age, 1840–1890.* Albuquerque, NM, 1990.

Schneller, Beverly E. *Anna Parnell's Political Journalism: Contexts and Texts.* Dublin, 2005.

Scott, Caroline L. "A Comparative Re-examination of Anglo-Irish Relations in Nineteenth-Century Manchester, Liverpool, and Newcastle-upon-Tyne." PhD diss., Durham University, 1998.

Shiels, Damian. *The Irish in the American Civil War.* Dublin, 2013.

Shumway, Nicolas. *The Invention of Argentina.* Berkeley, 1991.

Sim, David. *A Union Forever: The Irish Question and U.S. Foreign Relations in the Victorian Age.* Ithaca, NY, 2013.

Sluga, Glenda. *Internationalism in the Age of Nationalism.* Philadelphia, 2013.

Sluga, Glenda, and Patricia Clavin, eds. *Internationalisms: A Twentieth Century.* Cambridge, 2018.

Smith, Cathal. *American Planters and Irish Landlords in Comparative and Transnational Perspective: Lords of Land and Labor.* New York, 2021.

Smith, Janet. "Helen Taylor's Work for Land Nationalisation in Great Britain and Ireland 1879–1907: Women's Political Agency in the British Victorian Land Movement." *Women's History Review* 27, no. 5 (2018): 778–98.

Solow, Barbara L. *The Land Question and the Irish Economy, 1870–1903*. Cambridge, MA, 1971.

Speight, Patrick. *Irish-Argentine Identity in an Age of Political Challenge and Change, 1875–1983*. New York, 2019.

Summers, Anne. "British Women and Cultures of Internationalism, ca. 1815–1914." In *Structures and Transformations in Modern British History*, edited by David Feldman and Jon Lawrence, 187–209. Cambridge, 2011.

Suriano, Juan. *Anarquistas: Cultura y política libertaria en Buenos Aires, 1890–1910*. Buenos Aires, 2001.

Swift, Roger. "Identifying the Irish in Victorian Britain: Recent Trends in Historiography." *Immigrants & Minorities* 27, nos. 2–3 (2009): 134–51.

Swift, Roger, and Sheridan Gilley, eds. *The Irish in Victorian Britain: The Local Dimension*. Dublin, 1999.

TeBrake, Janet K. "Irish Peasant Women in Revolt: The Land League Years." *Irish Historical Studies*, 28 (1992): 63–80.

Thompson, Dorothy. "Ireland and the Irish in English Radicalism before 1850." In *The Chartist Experience: Studies in Working-Class Radicalism and Culture, 1830–60*, edited by J. Epstein and Dorothy Thompson, 120–51. London, 1982.

Thompson, E. P. *William Morris: Romantic to Revolutionary*. London, 1955.

Thompson, Frank. *The End of Liberal Ulster: Land Agitation and Land Reform, 1868–1886*. Belfast, 2001.

Tindley, Annie. *Lord Dufferin, Ireland and the British Empire, c. 1820–1900: Rule by the Best?* Abingdon, 2021.

Tomlinson, Jim. *Dundee and the Empire: "Juteopolis," 1850–1939*. Edinburgh, 2014.

Townend, Paul A. *Road to Home Rule: Anti-Imperialism and the Irish National Movement*. Madison, WI, 2016.

Tyrrell, Ian. *Reforming the World: The Creation of America's Moral Empire*. Princeton, NJ, 2010.

Vaughan, William E. *Landlords and Tenants in Mid-Victorian Ireland*. Oxford, 1994.

Viaene, Vincent. "Nineteenth-Century Catholic Internationalism and Its Predecessors." In *Religious International in the Modern World: Globalization and Faith Communities Since 1750*, edited by Abigail Green and Vincent Viaene, 82–110. Basingstoke, 2012.

Walker, William M. "Irish Immigrants in Scotland: Their Priests, Politics, and Parochial Life." *Historical Journal* 15, no. 4 (1972): 649–67.

———. *Juteopolis: Dundee and Its Textile Workers, 1885–1923*. Edinburgh, 1979.

Wallace, José Bernardo. "Casey, Eduardo (1847–1906)." In *Irish Migration Studies in Latin America* (November-December 2005): www.irlandeses.org.

Ward, Margaret. "Gendering the Union: Imperial Feminism and the Ladies' Land League." *Women's History Review*, 10 (2001): 71–92.

———. *Unmanageable Revolutionaries: Women and Irish Nationalism*. Dublin, 1983.

Wenzer, Kenneth C., ed. *Henry George, the Transatlantic Irish, and Their Times.* Bingley, 2009.

Whelan, Bernadette. "The Transatlantic World of Charles Stewart Parnell, 1846–91." *Journal of Transatlantic Studies* 14, no. 3 (2016): 276–303.

———. "Women on the Move: A Review of the Historiography of Irish Emigration to the USA, 1750–1900." *Women's History Review*, 24 (2015): 900–916.

Whelehan, Niall. *The Dynamiters: Irish Nationalism and Political Violence in the Wider World, 1867–1900.* Cambridge, 2012.

———. "Youth, Generations, and Collective Action in Nineteenth-Century Ireland and Italy." *Comparative Studies in Society and History*, 56, no. 4 (2014): 934–66.

Wilentz, Sean. *Chants Democratic: New York City and the Rise of the American Working Class, 1788–1850.* New York, [1984] 2004.

Wilkie, Jim. *Across the Great Divide: A History of Professional Football in Dundee.* Edinburgh, 2000.

Zaragoza, Gonzalo. *Anarquismo Argentino, 1876–1902.* Madrid, 1996.

INDEX

abolitionist movement, 135–36, 137–39

abstinence, alcohol, 23

"Address to the Middle Classes of the North of England" (Devyr), 128

agrarian capitalism, 95

agricultural depression, 11

Agricultural Labourers Union, 17, 29

All Hallow's College, Dublin, 100

American Civil War, 59, 96, 135, 137, 138, 145

American Homestead Act, 112

American Midwest, 18

American Woman Suffrage Association, 45

anarchism, 34, 112; in Argentina, 94, 96, 117, 119; Creaghe and, 118–20; militancy and, 118

Anderson, Benedict, 5

Anthony, Susan B., 66

anti-Asian sentiment, 19

Anti-Poverty Society (New York), 64

anti-rent movement (New York 1840s), 129–31

Argentina, 18; anarchism in, 94, 96, 117, 119; Conquest of the Desert, 105–9; emigrant activism in, 96–97, 99; end of migration to, 104; free passage to, 102; fundraising from, 98; genocidal campaigns in, 107–8; immigration in, 100–101, 105, 171n12; inequality in, 112; Irish Catholics in, 94; Land League in, 109, 111, 119; land monopoly in, 105–6; land question in, 109–20

Argentinians, Irish, 97–98, 100

arrests, 33, 51; of Devyr, 134; of Moore, M., 52; of women, 55

assisted emigration, 17–18, 172n45; Dillon, P., and, 99–105; promotion of, 17, 23–24; propaganda for, 101–2

Barings Bank crisis (1890), 117

Barton, Clara, 59, 66

Beaumont, Augustus Hardin, 127, 176n19

Becker, Lydia, 31

Bennett, James Gordon, 21–22

Bernard, Agnes Morrogh, 59

Blaine, James, 143

Blake, Lillie Devereux, 65–66

Blakey, Robert, 127

Bligh, Mary Agnes, 53

boycotting, 49–50, 55, 90, 129, 135, 149; of British shipping in New York, 68; Charles Boycott, 32; Creaghe on, 118

Bradlaugh, Charles, 36, 134–35

Brennan, Thomas, 29, 153n5

British labor, Land War and, 28–35, 39–40

Bronterre O'Brien, James, 127, 133

Brown, John, 137

Bryan, William Jennings, 67

Bryson, John, 11, 36–38, 39, 54

Buenos Aires, 95, 97–98, 100, 104, 106, 114, 170n2

Bulfin, William, 109

Burt, Thomas, 37

Butt, Isaac, 17

Butti, Peter, 88–89, 90

Byrne, Frank, 27

Callan, Philip, 103–4

Camperdown Works, Dundee, 72

ABOUT THE AUTHOR

Niall Whelehan is an Irish historian based at the University of Strathclyde, Glasgow. He is the author of *The Dynamiters: Irish Nationalism and Political Violence in the Wider World, 1867–1900.*